Marketing and Property People

Macmillan Building and Surveying Series

Series Editor: Ivor H. Seeley
    Emeritus Professor, Nottingham Polytechnic

Series Standing Order

If you would like to receive future titles in this series as they are published, you can make use of our standing order facility. To place a standing order please contact your bookseller or, in case of difficulty, write to us at the address below with your name and address and the name of the series. Please state with which title you wish to begin your standing order. (If you live outside the United Kingdom we may not have the rights for your area, in which case we will forward your order to the publisher concerned.)

Customer Services Department, Macmillan Distribution Ltd
Houndmills, Basingstoke, Hampshire, RG21 2XS, England.

Marketing and Property People

Owen A. Bevan

ARICS, MBCS, ACIS
The College of Estate Management, Reading

MACMILLAN

First published 1991

Published by
MACMILLAN EDUCATION LTD
Houndmills, Basingstoke, Hampshire RG21 2XS
and London
Companies and representatives
throughout the world

Typeset by
Ponting–Green Publishing Services, London

Printed in Hong Kong

British Library Cataloguing in Publication Data
Bevan, Owen
    Marketing and property people. – (Building and surveying series)
    1.
    I. Title   II. Series
    658.8
    ISBN 0–333–55502–3
    ISBN 0–333–55503–1 pbk

Contents

Foreword

The timing of the publication of this book could not have been better. The first year of the last decade of the twentieth century saw the collapse of the property market in the United Kingdom and in many parts of the Western World. It also witnessed the opening up of new markets; the destruction of the Berlin Wall, the gradual drawing back of the Iron Curtain and the rapid progress towards the formal creation of the EEC produced both new opportunities and new competition.

Political and economic forces have now produced a truly global property market. Large investing institutions are seeking prestige property investments throughout the world. In doing so they are looking for property professionals who can operate at the highest level in all aspects of property investment, development appraisal and management.

There is increasing recognition that the skills possessed by the chartered surveyor are better suited to the needs of the international investor than those posssessed by other professions.

What is now desperately needed is the confidence and the ability to market these skills to the ever-growing number of international investors. The theory and practice of marketing go far beyond the normal agency activities.

This book, although using examples of residential and commercial property marketing, goes deeply into the whole process of marketing and directs readers into a rewarding examination of the techniques available to them in the marketing of their firms and their services.

The remainder of this final decade of the twentieth century will present enormous challenges to the property profession, skilful marketing will be the difference between those who succeed and those who fail.

I commend this book to both students and practitioners; the lessons to be learnt from it will ensure their success in a highly competitive property market.

Peter W. Huntsman FRICS
Principal, The College of
Estate Management

Preface

The vast majority of property professionals in the UK run small businesses in an environment where there has traditionally been more than enough work to go around and where the possession of a professional qualification was virtually a meal ticket for life. As such they had little need for formal marketing or management training; after all why do you need to know how to compete if you don't need to compete?

The 1980s have seen swingeing changes in this – and other – professions and professional markets. Banks and building societies have moved into residential estate agency in force. Many commercial surveyors have been caught up as their firms took the residential golden penny and their commercial arms were amalgamated into what were planned to be nation-wide commercial chains.

At the same time fundamental changes in the mainstream commercial arena became noticeable as trends moved into growth strategies. The commercial market is increasingly polarising into a relatively small number of international megafirms, well established and well positioned in major UK cities to attract prestige instructions, closely followed by a small number of large UK firms, well presented in the provinces. In addition to these is a diminishing number of established regional firms and the main mass of the professions practising in groups of up to five partners.

At a recent seminar in Reading, Professor John Magee of Templeton College, Oxford, the author of the Management Analysis Centre report which highlighted the lack of management skills within the profession, predicted an increasing polarisation of such firms towards the very big and the very small – the small players concentrating on niche markets. His view of the middle players? 'They will be squeezed – from both sides'.

The landed professions are not under attack solely from within their established professional ranks. Overlapping professional skills and spheres of activity have made it almost inevitable that opportunities to advise on matters of a professional nature would attract interest from other professions. Cost accountants have much in common with quantity surveyors; financial accountants are well equipped to advise upon investment matters; architects and structural engineers have been in regular demand as advisors upon matters structural; merchant bankers are realising that their financial expertise positions them well for the disposal of property portfolios.

Perhaps most alarming of all for property advisors is the growing realisation that the importance of property holdings as strategic assets brings property advice firmly into the court of the large mixed discipline management consultancy organisations which are able to use their established high level contact networks to develop new areas of perceived expertise.

The professional property advisor in the nineties, therefore, is faced with challenges unlike those which he has ever had to face before. Not only does he have to face competition from his direct contemporaries, he also has to face challenge from increasingly sophisticated 'outside' competitors.

At the level of the sole practitioner the problems are, perhaps, slightly different in that he can still rely to a large extent upon his individual flair in cultivating local market influences and in building contact networks from which his business can flourish. Even here, however, clients are becoming more sophisticated and are demanding an even higher level of professional skill and sophistication to match their own expertise. The days when a 'Marketing Plan' could comprise a list of proposed advertisements are numbered, if not long gone.

The large firms and their major competitors are marketing-literate. They have to be if they are to retain their competitive edge. Yet even here 1990 brought a spate of redundancies as firms, responding to the market turndown, sought to find economies where they could – and where better than in the 'non-core' service areas which appear not to contribute directly to short term profits. The 'British Disease' strikes again – with a vengeance.

Given the fundamental importance of marketing as a management discipline – and this is the standpoint of this book – it is worth wondering whether the sacrifice, by these leading firms, of expertise in this discipline relates to a lingering misunderstanding amongst senior members of our profession of the role that marketing can, and should, play in the development and management of their businesses. Perhaps the marketing specialists, recognising the inherent limitations to understanding of their potential contribution, have contributed to their own downfall by producing what was expected – rather than by marketing their own potential adequately.

Why 'another' book on marketing?

When I was interviewed for the position of tutor in marketing I was asked if I could teach marketing. Having run my own practice for several years with responsibility for marketing property and developing working practices I was able confidently to reply 'Yes' – as would most chartered surveyors.

I was somewhat taken aback upon taking up my post to discover that marketing, far from being an extension of advertising and selling, was actually a broad-based discipline with an extensive literature, vocabulary and mythology of its own, and that few attempts had been made to link this body of knowledge to the specialist needs of the property professional. There was one honourable exception; Ted Cleavely's book (1984), *The Marketing of Industrial and Commercial Property*, is a worthy attempt by a marketing professional to weld the two disciplines together and to provide a bridge of understanding.

This book is a second attempt to bridge the gap – written from the viewpoint of a property professional who has come to marketing late in life – and found within it a wealth of ideas, knowledge and information that would have been invaluable in his earlier career. If, therefore, the reader detects an element of evangelism in some of the literary style and choice of examples, I am delighted as this reflects both the excitement of discovery in my own research and probably my Celtic heritage in wishing to pass on these 'discoveries' and 'insights' to others.

The book, as it stands, is a synthesis of considerable delving into some of the literature currently available covering marketing in general and some of its more arcane aspects in particular. This research has been a necessary basis for the development of teaching and course material at The College of Estate Management and the book aims both to make the bones of the material accessible, with expansions, to students preparing for property-oriented examinations and to stimulate the thinking and imagination of the mature property professional who has had neither the time nor the motivation in the past to undertake such research.

The form of the book

The book is written upon the premise that marketing is much more than a collection of techniques and ideas. Marketing is the whole basis upon which a business is run; it is a way of thinking; to some a way of life. Tom Peters says 'Business is easy; it's about making things and selling things'. Add 'profitably' to this and you virtually have a working definition of marketing as it is perceived within this book.

The word 'perceived' rears its head this early! Tom Peters (again) in *A Passion for Excellence* debates the statement 'mere perception' and makes the point that 'Perception is all there is'.

I commend this statement to marketers. The only reality is what you think things to be. Marketing is about the creation and manipulation of reality in the minds of buyers.

Some readers may be disappointed in the book. It does not contain any 'marketing techniques'. This was not deliberate. It simply reflects the fact that in two years' research I have not found any! I found plenty of sales techniques, advertising techniques, research techniques, planning techniques, product design and packaging techniques and so on – but no marketing techniques. This is because there aren't any. Marketing is a way of thinking and a way of relating specific techniques into a cohesive strategic approach. It's a way of thinking about running a business.

The book reflects this approach to marketing. Nowhere will the reader find a 'how to do it'. There are, rather, principles which underlie approaches to problem solving in the marketing arena and it is towards the expansion of these principles that the book's thrust is directed. Each chapter should stand in its own right as providing ideas on how problem solving in particular areas can be approached. Most property people are already highly skilled in solving marketing problems. The book attempts to add a framework which can help to identify the problems and to provide some avenues down which root problems rather than symptoms can be identified.

We look at a number of areas. First products – what is a product in a property context? The answer to a question like this is not as obvious as it may seem and its exploration can point the way to changes of emphasis in product identification which can make a significant difference to the development of competitive advantage.

Given a product, how and why do people buy it? The exploration of process and motivation, both within the consumer environment and organisational environments provides significant pointers to potential changes in product design, packaging and delivery systems and leads to one of the most fundamental concepts in marketing – segmentation and targeting.

How does this translate into advantage? We consider the basics of product strategy from the viewpoint of the search for and development of competitive advantage. But strategies have to be implemented and this leads us into a consideration of the tactical weapons available to the marketer. In their book *Marketing Warfare* Al Ries and Jack Trent identify strategy with the successful implementation of tactical advantage. This theme is explored and the nature of tactical weapons available to property people examined.

Marketing is a management function and management implies planning and control. The book's final theme is the development of a marketing plan as the basis for a coherent implementation of advantage.

Objectives of the book

The principal objectives of the book can be summarised readily.

(i) To the student it should provide an overview of marketing as a subject for study together with sufficient property-related detail to allow the student to prepare for professional examinations with confidence. In this context the book's level of complexity increases as it progresses. For the RICS Diploma finalist the whole book should be relevant; for other, less advanced students, the earlier chapters may be more important.

(ii) To the mature surveyor it should provide a broad introduction to marketing as a discipline and should repay its reading through a contribution to the reader's ability to identify competitive advantage both in his own products and in those of his clients. In doing this the book should help to demystify the discipline and remove uncertainties inherent in the use of 'professional jargon'.

In writing the book I have been acutely conscious that the body of marketing and related literature available to the student or seeker after knowledge is very large. I am also acutely aware that most of the best thinking within this field has already been done.

I have, therefore, drawn heavily on other sources in preparing the book, following conventions already well established and have tried, rather than reinventing the wheel, to express their ideas, where I found them appropriate, in terms which could be easily accessible to the property professional and property student.

The guiding light, throughout, has been to pass on the information that I would have found invaluable 10 years ago.

This means, inevitably, that I must acknowledge the great debt which this book owes to a number of authors, in particular:

Philip Kotler and Gary Armstrong, *Principles of Marketing* (1989) which is an invaluable and exhaustive introductory text dealing with marketing as a discipline;

Richard Normann, *Service Management* (1988) whose ideas and research into the fundamental principles of managing the delivery of services as a product form the basic structure to Chapter 5;

Michael E. Porter, *Competitive Advantage* (1985) from whom the concepts of the value chains and a rigorous approach to the identification and development of competitive advantage is derived;

J. F. Engel, R. D. Blackwell and P. W. Miniard, *Consumer Behaviour* (1990) whose scholarly work has provided a wealth of relevant and difficult-to-find research findings.

I am also acutely aware that the writing of this book has involved a triumph of application over my innate indolence and that it would have never happened at all without massive amounts of encouragement and help from many sources.

Foremost amongst these has been my colleague Karl Wiggins at The College of Estate Management who has borne the brunt of my natural Celtic tendencies towards manic depression and whose gentle prodding has helped immeasurably to restore equanimity and optimism when it was needed. In addition he has been, almost invariably, the uncomplaining sounding-board to whom each chapter has been committed for 'reading and opinion' hot off the press. His comments and suggestions have been gratefully received, as have those of others similarly 'pressed': Peter Blake of The College of Estate Management, Richard Field, Peter Noblett (of Noblett Cuddy & Co. Preston), Dr Ken Hastings of TSB Property Services, being notable amongst them. I should also thank Professor Ivor Seeley, the Series Editor, for his helpful and encouraging comments.

Most importantly I must thank Carole Moody and Gail Martin of The College of Estate Management who have uncomplainingly battled with both my moods and my almost illegible handwriting in translating the text into readable matter.

I must also thank Peter Huntsman and Peter Goodacre of The College for their encouragement and forbearance during the preparation of the book, without which the research and writing time needed would have been impossible to find.

Finally, to my family, who have had to listen to my moans, groans and developing ideas – not without complaint but certainly with an excess of tolerance – my grateful thanks.

I should also stress, in acknowledging the unstinting input of others, that responsibility for the attitudes expressed and the final content of the book remains firmly where it belongs – with me!

1 Marketing Principles

Introduction

There are many misconceptions within the community at large, not just within the property profession, as to the nature and scope of the discipline of marketing. This chapter sets out to introduce the fundamental nature of the marketing discipline as being central to the well being and continued existence of an enterprise. It then considers some of the basic concepts within the discipline and relates them to practice with the property profession.

In order to do this it addresses the question 'what is marketing?' This is followed by discussion of the 'marketing mix – Product, Price, Place and Promotion' – terms which crop up continually throughout the book.

What is marketing?

A survey of three hundred American college administrators were asked this question in 1978. Their answers were illuminating and would probably be mirrored in a similar survey of property professionals: 90 per cent said 'selling, advertising or public relations'; 9 per cent included 'needs assessment, market research, product development, pricing, distribution'.

This was mirrored by a selection of delegates at the Reading CPD Summer School in 1990 whose responses are shown below.

Most people think that marketing = promotion (advertising, PR etc). It does not. Some commonly used definitions are worth examining. Peter Drucker (1973) (one of the leading management writers) said, 'the aim of marketing is to make selling superfluous' – give the customer what he wants and needs at a price he is prepared to pay and the product sells itself. As far as it goes, this sums up the marketing philosophy fairly well. It does not actually tell us much about how to do things. Some other definitions may help to illuminate the subject.

'All activities having to do with effecting changes in ownership and possession of goods and services.'

1

Headings	Percentage
Promotion (promotions, advertisements, selling, PR)	100
Research	53
Targeting	29
Product	23
Management	12
Profits	12
Strategy	12
Pricing/costs	12
Needs	6
Service delivery	6

'Marketing is that part of economics which deals with the creation of time, place and possession utilities.'

'Marketing is the delivery of a standard of living.'

'The primary business of every business is to stay in business and to do that you have to get and keep customers.'

These 'definitions' are interesting and help to suggest some of the ideas that marketing embraces but they still don't tell the whole story. What they do show is the difficulty of defining a topic that is seen to have different objectives from differing perspectives. No wonder the university administrators were in trouble!

For the purpose of this book we prefer the definition proposed by the Institute of Marketing.

Definition

Marketing is:

The management process responsible for

Identifying
Anticipating }   Customer requirements
Satisfying }

Profitably

This definition is particularly helpful because it clearly highlights the principal activities and areas of responsibility which marketing embraces. It is worth considering these further.

Management process

Marketing is not something which just happens. It is identifiable as a key management function which must be planned, implemented and monitored. Planning implies strategy and strategic thinking is a key element of the marketing philosophy.

Identifying and anticipating

In order to identify and anticipate anything research and analysis is required. Marketing research includes consideration of customer attitudes – their needs and wants, perceptions of current and proposed product offerings, consideration of environmental change – geographic, demographic or psychographic – in terms of its effect upon needs and wants. Market research focuses on the size and nature of markets, size and frequency of transaction, transaction circumstances and so on.

Satisfying

In addition to the research function above the notion of satisfying customers' wants and needs implies product/service design to ensure that these needs are fully met – when they are needed and where they are needed.

Customer requirements

It is easy (and misleading) to think that customer requirements are simple. For example there is a strong temptation for mousetrap designers and providers to think that a customer wants mousetraps to catch mice. He does not – he wants to be rid of the mice. He might even be happy to put up with the mice if he can be certain that they won't be any kind of a nuisance!

Profitability

Businesses require profit in order to remain in business. It is all very well identifying customer needs and wants, even developing products to meet them – but if that product cannot be supplied at a profit to the business then the business will quickly cease to exist. Marketing is concerned with the continuation of the business and must, therefore, express its attempts in terms of profit potential.

The marketing mix

Definition

The marketing mix has been defined by Kotler as 'the set of CONTROLLABLE MARKET VARIABLES that the FIRM BLENDS to PRODUCE the RESPONSE it WANTS in the TARGET MARKET'.

This is a fundamental pillar of the marketing discipline and introduces many of the concepts to be tackled within the book. It also limits the scope of discussion to a manageable level. Let us consider the principal ideas in more detail.

Controllable market variables

An enormous number of variables affect the activities of any market; some of these will be external to the company – e.g. demographic changes, political environment, geographic factors; others will be internal to a greater or lesser extent. For example, advertising and product design are clearly internally controllable variables.

These 'controllable' variables are grouped (and discussed below) under four headings:

PRODUCT
PRICE
PLACE
PROMOTION

Management

Marketing management is a deliberate process designed to mix resources applied to the controllable variables in such a way that a desired response from chosen markets is produced. In the typical estate agency office the majority of resources might appear to be channelled into promotion – of the office, particular properties, personalities etc., but a moment's thought will reveal that significant sums are already invested in other parts of the mix – the office location (phone), office decor (promotion), choice of preferred market (product), sole agency/multiple agency structure (price). The task of marketing management is to ensure that the best use of resources in all these areas is mixed to produce maximum on-going profitability.

Target market

Two major marketing concepts appear here. First of all the market. A market is defined as 'the set of actual and potential buyers of a product'. This is a finite concept and is of course related to the definition of a product. In estate agency terms the products offered are:

a) the agency service;
b) individual properties.

Quite clearly the markets for these two different types of product, whilst probably overlapping, differ considerably at any point in time.

'Target' is probably the principal key word in any consideration of marketing at a practical level. It simply means the identification as a subject of an overall product/market which can be defined as potentially profitable in its own right and which will respond to specifically directed stimuli.

The market for agency services in respect of property, for example, is very wide. It includes:

Residential

Small terraced houses
Large terraced houses
Small semis
Large semis
Small detached
Large detached
etc.

Commercial

Old factory units
Modern factory units (small/medium/large)
New build factory units
Hi-tech
Offices
Retail
etc.

The needs and wants of consumers in these markets vary enormously and it is unlikely that an agency would find it profitable to attempt to provide a specialised service to each. An element of targeting therefore comes into play and the firm, consciously or unconsciously, tends towards specialising in, and targeting, particular areas of the market to which its talents are best suited. It concentrates on specific market segments – or target markets.

Product, price, place, promotion

Estate agents, commercial, residential or agricultural, operate in two completely different modes. In the first place they sell their own services – agency, surveying, auctioneering, valuation etc.; in the second they act as marketing consultants advising clients on the appropriate marketing mix to be applied to their properties. Having secured instructions they may also act for clients as marketing managers and property managers. Their duties in this respect will emerge in later chapters. At this stage the marketing mix will be considered in principle – application to specific aspects of agency will be mentioned as illustration but more detailed consideration left until later.

Product

This is the goods/service offered to a target market. The estate agent offers:

> marketing advice
> estate brokerage
> property management

packaged as a service to the client and called 'estate agency'.

In providing marketing advice to a client the agent must identify the qualities of the product on offer. For example – a 4 bedroomed house with a large garden might be identified solely as that. In many cases, however, the agent may, on behalf of his client, identify two products – a 4 bedroomed house – plus a potential building plot.

In specific cases he may identify the product in quite different terms. For example, the above house within walking distance of a very desirable school might be better identified as 'a place to live close to XYZ school, which just happens to have four bedrooms and a large garden' – with a considerable effect on the way that

(a) potential purchasers might perceive the benefits of the property, and
(b) the agent will advise promotion of the property to find that potential purchaser.

A good aide-memoire to this approach to identifying products is the statement by Charles Revson, founder of Revlon, 'In the factory we make cosmetics – in the shop we sell hope'.

The concept of the product includes not only identification as discussed but also packaging and product support. For example IBM in the early days of selling computers realised that customers wanted not just machines but problem solving business packages. It therefore sold its machines 'complete with' bundled software – payroll systems, programming languages and in some cases inclusive engineering support. Just to complete the picture it painted its machines electric blue as an aid to instant recognition and to build a corporate identity. (So successful was it that IBM to this day is known in the computer world as 'Big Blue'.)

Estate agents bundle their offering in a similar way. Up to 1960 it was normal for valuation advice prior to sale to be charged for separately.

Today few estate agents would offer a package which did not include 'free valuation for sale'. A recent development in packaging which mirrors IBM is the yellow jackets of the Century 21 franchise – immediately identifying its members as part of a national marketing organisation.

Price

The amount of money that customers have to pay for the product. A detailed analysis of pricing methods and structures is outside the scope of this chapter but price – whilst it must reflect cost in order to achieve the override (profit) – must be perceived more positively as reflecting value to the consumer. If the consumer does not see the product as value for money at the price he will be tempted to seek alternatives that do.

Some of the questions which a marketer should ask about price are:

'How much can we charge?'

which implies the question

'How does the customer perceive value?'

or

'What is the customer prepared to pay for this product/service?'.
'Should we give discounts?'

An estate agent will often give a discount on fees in exchange for a sole agency instruction. Similarly he will probably give a volume discount to a builder who is a regular customer. A property vendor, in exchange for a quick contract and completion may be quite willing to give a price discount. (Note that this is different in nature from a 'discount' given in negotiation where a potential purchaser, in discovering defects in the property effectively redefines the property being offered in terms of his perception of value for money.)

Place

'Where is/where should be/the product available?' For the property professional, this encompasses a wide range of activities. In his function of selling his agency service he needs to consider where, exactly, his office or offices should be located. Should the client come to the office or should he go to the client? Should there be a new office serving a very local community, or does the high powered town centre office offer an adequate vehicle? Should he have London (or any other big city) representation to reach the high spending specialist purchaser?

In the commercial world, can he work from home (with low overheads) or should he locate himself close to other professionals in the commercial centre? Does he need a distributed office network or is a London head office sufficient? In dealing with the client's property (which obviously cannot be moved – or can it? What about mobile homes?), in which offices should it be displayed? Should he recommend and arrange sub-agencies or multi-listing to ensure maximum purchaser saturation or would the property be better offered to a restricted (but highly qualified) target list?

The builder/developer faces similar problems. Should he sell through a site office/local agent/national agent or open his own high street marketing organisation?

In addition he faces further questions. Should he 'make to order' only or should he build, speculatively, 'stock' properties for sale in advance of enquiries? A little thought will open up other avenues to explore.

Promotion

In many ways this is the easiest part of the mix as most people already equate it with marketing. On closer examination, however, it covers a wide area – advertising, personal selling, telesales, sales promotion, public relations, publicity and media relations – and each of these demands detailed knowledge, not just of the chosen media or discipline, but also of the ways that users of these media interact with potential purchasers. In simple terms the question 'How do we tell the customer?' suggests the scope of the term.

Marketing strategies

It has been suggested that all marketing strategies are by their nature based on a 'preferred mix' of the following three 'generic variables'. These are:

Cost
Differentiation
Focus

It is worth examining these in a little more detail as they introduce a fundamental marketing concept which has a wide ranging impact on property professionals. This is market segmentation.

Cost

In this context it is most important that cost is clearly distinguished from price. Whilst price manipulation can be an effective tactical weapon – for example, cutting prices to 'buy' market share in the short term – a price advantage over competitors can only be maintained if it is based on a cost advantage. A high-cost operator can only cut prices short term – any attempt to prolong tends to lead rapidly to Carey Street. A low cost operator trading at market price levels has higher profitability. Surplus profits are available for research and development which tend to maintain the cost advantage thus safeguarding the firms against tactical price cutting from higher cost operators.

Differentiation

In this strategy area the product is identified as being in some way different from its competitors. For example, a 'hot hatch' is differentiated from a family hatchback by better seats, better engine, fuel injection, aluminium wheels, spoiler and 'go-faster' stripes. Although made on the same assembly line using the same basic technology it is perceived as a different product. The question, of course, to be asked is 'why'?

The 'new' product is aimed at a specific and clearly definable consumer market whose aspirations (wants and needs) will be met more closely by the 'hot' version than say the 'basic' popular version. The product is 'differentiated' to meet the needs of a specific market segment. Similar product differentiation can be readily seen in the offerings of a Kensington showroom full of Ferraris, Porches and Rolls-Royces compared with those of 'Ken the Car' where displays like 'Pick of the Week' – a pickaxe – and 'no reasonable offer refused' – from a caricatured scantily clad blonde with a 'come-hither' smile – tell their own tale of 5 to 10-year-old second hand cars.

Focus

Hand in hand with differentiation is the concept of focus. There is no point in differentiating a product if there is no clearly discernible market for it. The strategy of focus implies the identification of a definable, specific market for a product and then tailoring the product to meet the specific wants and needs of that product/market.

Some examples of products are:

The 'Seekers' property shop chain which focuses in two ways. First it focuses on the (not inconsiderable) market amongst house sellers for a low cost service. That they are prepared to pay 'up front' is a measure of the desire within that market grouping for low cost, but apparently effective, service.

Secondly it focuses on the demand amongst entrepreneurial people for a high profile, low cost business which can quickly generate income with minimum training (provided) and corporate back-up if required (franchising).

The Citroen, Renault, Volkswagen, Vauxhall, Ford and other 'hot hatches' which are targeted specifically at the 'young entrepreneur' who wishes to provide a self-confident, aggressive, 'man about town', 'going places quickly' type of image. The success of these ranges and the degree of competition is some measure of the spread of such perceptions in the UK in 1989–91.

Stern Studios – London agents who specialise solely in small studio flats to the ever-changing London population of 'young singles'.

It will be readily seen that, if we aim our offering at a particular market of subject consumers, and we design the features of our offering to fit as closely as possible the pattern of wants and needs within that particular market, then we must be able to identify that specific market in some way. The process of identifying market subjects is the market segmentation referred to earlier.

To conclude our discussion on strategy it should not be thought that the elements are in any way mutually exclusive. To the contrary, focus and differentiation are often inextricably linked and the concept of cost leadership applies across arbitrary boundaries. Strategies for survival, product development, market penetration or whatever are developed using any or a combination of these factors. When you next pick up a newspaper or watch television consider some of the products being offered – in advertising or through PR releases – and think around the marketing strategies being used, in particular, the idea of segmented markets, focus and differentiation.

Market segmentation

The principles

As we have seen, at the heart of any discussion of marketing strategies based on differentiation or focus is the concept of market segmentation. Market segmentation is defined by Kotler as 'dividing a market into distinct groups of buyers who might merit separate products or marketing mixes'.

The first task therefore is to identify possible factors which might allow a market to be segmented. The second task is to evaluate the segment to ensure that it has the potential to produce profitable results.

It is important again to remember that variables used for segmenting a market are unlikely to be used in isolation. It is far more likely that combinations of variables will apply to a market – and in fact the most productive focusing of resources will tend to be at tightly segmented markets.

What sort of variables might be used? An obvious variable in the residential market might be timber frame or non-timber frame. Some buyers (already converted to the high insulation standards normally implied in modern timber frame) would not consider buying a property constructed in any other way. A large number of buyers, however, (no doubt influenced by TV horror stories and simple, old fashioned inertia) will have grave reservations about timber frame. Some indeed would not have such a property as a gift.

Some other specific variable might be

walking distance to a school – this may be a prerequisite for single car families
easy access to motorway – for the rep who has everything
minimum three bedrooms – for the growing family
east side of town
anywhere except the east side.

Clearly such variables can be produced in a random list almost ad finitum but it is productive in both a learning and an analytical, practical situation to consider them in a more structured way.

Segmentation variables – consumer markets

- Geographic
- Demographic
- Psychographic
- Behaviouristic

These principal headings have been applied to segmentation variables and it is worth examining them in a little more detail.

Geographic

Region

- North, South, East, West
- London area, London East, Golden Triangle
- M4 Corridor
- 12 miles (approx 20 km) radius Hyde Park Corner

Timescale

- 1 hour from Hyde Park Corner
- 2 hours from Paris/Frankfurt
- 10 minutes walk to the Stock Exchange

Town/City Size

- Pop 150–200 000
- Catchment 400 000 shoppers
- Village maximum 200 people

Density

- Urban

– Suburban
– Rural
– 15 to the acre (6/ha)
– 40/acre (16/ha)

Climate

– Close to seaside
– Above 500′ (150 m) South
– Above 500′ (150 m) North
– East facing
– South facing

Demographic

These variables refer to population descriptions:

Age	– normally expressed in age bands e.g., 12–19, 65+
Sex	
Family size	
Family life cycle	– e.g., bachelor stage – ′ young single person not living at home' 'Empty Nest' – older married couples with no dependent children but full income from labour market
Income band	
Occupations	– professional, managers, artisan, unemployed, etc.
Education	– 'O' Levels 'A' Levels Degree Professional qualifications Public school/comprehensive Oxbridge/Redbrick
Religion	
Race	
Nationality	

(Note here that 'demographic acronyms' creep into everyday language, e.g. WASP = White Anglo Saxon Protestant in US Society, 'DINKIE' = Double Income No Kids in 1988 London.)

Psychographic

Social class

  A Upper
  B Upper Middle
  C^1 Lower Middle
  C^2 Skilled Working
  D Working
  E Subsistence

Note – there are a number of classifications applied to social class but these are in fairly common UK usage.

Lifestyle

In 1983 Arnold Mitchell developed the VALS – Values and Life Styles Classification (The Nine American Lifestyles). These were a series of descriptions which were a shorthand method of conveying a profile of particular types of buyer.

These descriptions have been refined and redescribed by other authors, notably by William Meyers in *The Image Makers*.

A UK example of similar (but less sophisticated) imagery is found in the 'Yuppie' label which immediately conveys an image of the thrusting, achievement-oriented city trader of the 1980s seated at a black-stained oak desk, making calls on a personal telephone prompted by notes in his Filofax. Meanwhile his Porsche (or his XR3i if he hasn't quite made it yet) awaits the nightly trip to the fleshpots.

A visit to the 1980s showhouse quickly shows the importance attaching to such imagery. The 'executive' furniture in the lounge contrasts with chintzy curtains in the main bedroom (designed to appeal to the 'traditionalist') and the more strident artworks in the second bedroom (appealing to the more artistic intellectual). These are not chance images!

Personality – innovative, adaptive, gregarious, authoritarian...

Behaviouristic

  Purchase occasion – regular purchase, occasional, one-off
  Benefits sought – quality, service, economy, status, social
  User status – non-user, ex-user, potential user, first time, regular
  Usage rate – light, heavy, medium
  Loyalty status – none, medium, strong, absolute
  Readiness stage – unaware, aware, informed, interested, ready to buy
  Attitude to product – enthusiastic $\longleftrightarrow$ hostile

(Note – there is a wide body of literature covering these areas. See Kotler and Armstrong (1989), Packard (1957), Meyers (1985).

In later sections of the book we will return to some of the segmentation variables and examine them in more detail with specific reference to the property market.

It is, however, at this point worth reiterating that

a) segmentation will almost invariably involve construction of a number of segmentation variables;

b) the 'state of the art' of market segmentation research, particularly in the area of behavioural and psychological variables is still imprecise – although this impression does not and should not invalidate the principles or attempts to operate them in practice;

c) segmentation is only worth considering where the potential market is large enough to generate a profitable return.

The commercial world

The bases for segmentation discussed above are generic and apply to both consumer and corporate markets. There are, however, differences in the way that corporate buying decisions are made and also in the practical operation of the commercial market. It is reasonable, therefore, to consider some additional bases for segmentation which may be appropriate.

End user – Retail, offices, light industrial, hi-tech etc.;
Primary user – Direct end use as above;

> investment
> development
> customer size – Large, medium, small, mega-
> customer type – Professional advisor
> end user
> government office
> insurance company
> fund manager
> major account
> future/current user etc.

Kotler suggests four tests in assessing the suitability of a market segment. These are:

Measurability   – the degree to which the segment can be measured.
Accessibility   – can the segment be effectively reached and serviced?
Substantiality (size) – is it large enough to bother about?
Actionability   – has the firm the resources to develop the segment?

Further concepts

Two more fundamental concepts should be mentioned. These are:

- Differential advantage
- Positioning

Differential advantage

It is all very well identifying market segments in which a firm can see potential benefits. These benefits, however, remain potential until they are realised. They also remain attractive to other firms who, assuming that they go through a similar analysis process, are likely to be – or quickly become – similarly aware.

In order to achieve potential, therefore, the firm must develop an edge – or advantage – over its potential competitors in the chosen product/market. This edge is known as differential – or competitive – advantage.

It is interesting to note that, at the time of writing (1990), a number of the major new entrants to the residential estate agency field have identified that consumers perceive estate agency to be lacking in the area of customer service. They have, therefore, targeted improved service as being their key to competitive advantage. This they aim to achieve, in broad terms, through better training, better use of customer relationships.

Assuming that no one of them has a markedly better approach than any of the others it is reasonable to suppose that all of them will, therefore, achieve a similarly improved quality of service. Where, then, is the competitive advantage – and over whom?

Positioning

Within a product/market there will be a range of potential customers each of whom will react differently to different aspects of a product's benefits to them. For example, in the decision 'which house agent should I use?' there are a variety of key factors which will influence customers. These could range through

- low price of service
- perceived low price to be achieved, but quick sale
- perceived high price to be achieved, but slow sale
- high quality service
- 'appeals to up-market customers'
- the smell of success
- imagined relationship with high-achieving principal
- supermarket high street presence
- 'closed' high sales content secondary office

and many more.

With or without assistance from the agent consumers will gain a perception of the kind of service that the agent offers – and this perception will relate to one or more of the factors listed. The perception gained is that of the agent's positioning within the product market.

The marketing orientated supplier will not let this positioning develop by chance but will package his offering to make the most of the features that define his chosen positioning within the product market.

Refer back to the examples of motor traders and consider how their corporate packaging positions them within the used car market place.

Conclusion

This brief introduction to marketing concepts should be treated as no more than a taster for further studies. Each of the main concepts identified is explored in greater detail within the book. The objective of this introduction is to provide an overview so that later reading forms part of an identifiable whole.

References and further reading

P.F. Drucker (1973), *Management: Tasks and Responsibilities*, Harper & Row, New York, pp. 64–65

Institute of Marketing

P. Kotler (1986), *Principles of Marketing*, Prentice-Hall International, pp. 26, 43, 296

W. Meyers (1985), *The Image Makers*, Orbis Publishing, London, pp. 13, 14, 15

A. Mitchell (1983), *The Nine American Lifestyles*, Macmillan, New York

Patrick A. Murphy and Richard A. Megarrity (1978), 'Marketing Universities: A Survey of Student Recruiting Activities', *College & University*, Spring, pp. 249–61.

V. Packard (1970), *The Hidden Persuaders*, Penguin

M.E. Porter (1980), *Competitive Strategy*, The Free Press, Macmillan Inc.

2 The Product

Case study – What do estate agents sell?

One of my favourite activities is asking residential estate agents what they sell. This is a typical question/response sequence which could have come from any of 20 to 30 different lecture sessions where the audiences have comprised property people ranging from the most raw recruit to highly experienced property professionals.

Lecturer 'What do estate agents sell?'
Response 'Houses and other property'.
L   Ok, they sell those for other people but what do they, themselves, sell?'
R   'Service.'
R   'The company.'
R   'Ourselves.'
L   'Ok – service; I'll bring the car round in the morning.'
R   'No, we didn't mean that.'
L   'Ok – the company – that's fairly relevant in 1990 where we've seen losses being reported and a number of companies have changed hands (or tried to).₁
R   'No, we didn't mean that either'.
L   'Ok – yourselves – how much do you charge?'
R   'We certainly didn't mean that!'
L   'No, I'm sure you didn't, but it does start to illustrate the problem!' 'Let's make it a bit easier. If I wished to use your services what would I be wanting to buy from you? Put yourself in the buyer's position and ask the question.'
R   'Our service/experience of the market/advice...'
L   'Ok so your client's ask your advice then pay you for it do they?'
R   'Actually, no.'
L   'What do you have to do before they pay you anything?'
R   'Sell their house.'

17

L   'And what do you have to provide in order to sell their house?'
R   'A buyer.'
L   'So why didn't you say so? Why have you just spent 10 minutes selling me anything except the one thing that I wanted to buy?'

I stress that this is not an isolated incident; the conversation reported above takes place time and time again in all sorts of gatherings.

We are so used to our business that we forget the simple things.

Introduction

It often comes as a shock to service providers to hear their professional services described as a product. Products are 'things' – like fountain pens, biros, washing powder, motor cars – aren't they? In recent years, however, there has been a considerable body of thought and research directed at the area of service products and it is in this area that both the provision of professional services and the 'tangible' products with which we deal – land, buildings, interests in land – tend to fit readily.

This chapter introduces the concepts of product structure – core product, tangible product and augmented product – and relates this structure to the services and facilities covered by residential estate agents, as an example. We return to this analysis in Chapter 5 where we consider the nature of commercial property and property advice, building upon the content of this chapter.

The term 'product', in marketing terms, includes the concepts of packaging, branding and positioning. These terms are introduced and explained with reference to the property industry.

The product – What are we talking about

'A product' has been defined by Kotler (1986) as:

> 'anything that can be offered to a market for attention, acquisition, use or consumption that might satisfy a want or need. It includes physical objects, services, persons, places, organisations and ideas.'

As is usual in any definition or discussions culled from the world of marketing this definition is pretty all-embracing. It is, however, quite clear that services, places, organisations and ideas or concepts are specifically included.

It is reasonable then to conclude that marketing for property professionals includes the services provided – agency, valuation, management, auctioneering, negotiation, surveys, dilapidations – physical objects – plots of land, buildings, chattels, plant and machinery and ideas or concepts –

interests in land, new products – e.g. 'waterside working', 'Hitec sheds' and so on.

It should also be noted from the definition that it introduces a clear distinction into what the customer is actually buying. This is the distinction between 'wants' and 'needs'. Reference is made to this distinction within this chapter but the concepts are expanded in Chapter 3 – 'why and how people buy' – and it is recommended that both of these Chapters be read in conjunction so that a better understanding of the overall topic can be developed.

The nature of a product

A cursory glance at any product leads you quickly to the conclusion that its definition is simple. It is something that someone might want to buy. Consider that a little further. What exactly is it that someone might want to buy. Take a fountain pen. What is being offered? The ability to make marks on paper which can be construed as writing. Fine – the same facility can be provided by a pencil, a biro, a felt tip, a piece of chalk, a typewriter , a word processor, a multi-pin printer, a fax machine – the list is endless. There must, therefore, be something else which distinguishes the fountain pen. What might this be?

- The ability to use a rechargeable ink source?
- The crackled finish of the package?
- The gold nib?
- The ability to write in a 'classical' style?

Once again, the potential list of features is endless. But still there may be other areas to consider. Why, for instance, use a Parker rather than a Waterman's or a Schaeffer? Why use a fine rather than a medium or an italic nib? Why use the traditional lever action filler rather than cartridges? Some of the other features to consider are:

- after sales service;
- warranty period;
- style;
- appeal to status;
- the psychological difference between one method of writing and another or between one manufacturer's offering and another.

Marketing theory recognises these differences and attempts to classify them so that they can be given their proper weight in analysis.

Kotler identifies three levels of product:

Core product
Tangible product

Augmented product

Let us look at each of these in more detail, still taking our fountain pen as an example.

Core product

As we saw above the primary purpose of a fountain pen is to make marks on paper – which can hopefully (but not necessarily) be understood by other people. This is quite distinct from the 'instant perception' of a fountain pen as being a specific form of writing instrument. It immediately introduces the range of competitors for the ability to make such marks and focuses the mind on what is really being sold. At the heart of every product is a solution to a problem, in this case a method of making marks on paper with little effort.

A good example of this problem solving service is the distinction made by Revlon 'in the factory we make cosmetics – in the store we sell hope'. The core product then is the essence of the service being provided and if this is not recognised clearly then the potential competition is equally unclear.

The builders of the railways in the nineteenth century clearly recognised that their core product was the movement of goods from place to place. Using their recognition of this they also recognised that the canal system – moving goods far more cheaply – albeit more slowly – represented unwanted competition. What did they do? They bought out the canal companies thus giving themselves the ability to force traffic onto their railways and achieve the economies of scale needed to

a) make the railways profitable and
b) justify building even more railways till they reached the point that their operational speed eliminated the canal system's cost advantage for ever.

With careful attention to detail they also ensured that they would retain their competitive advantage by allowing the canal facilities to lapse into dereliction.

Tangible product

This means, quite literally, that part of the product offering which can be touched – or consciously experienced in the case of services. In the case of the fountain pen it refers to the obvious – the shape of the barrel, colour, type of clip, method of filling, gold nib, type of nib, brand name, plus the not so obvious implied features – styling, quality level, packaging.

Conventionally, the characteristics of the tangible product are grouped under five headings:

Quality Level
Features
Styling
Brand name
Packaging

It should be noted that, in the area of services marketing, the nature of the product is, essentially, intangible – you cannot touch a doctor's examination, a valuer's visit, the waiter's attitude and approach in a restaurant – but you can experience them consciously and, viewed in this light, they can be seen to exhibit the same basic tangible product characteristics. A good example of packaging and features attaching to a product lies in the early development of IBM.

By the mid 1940s IBM, at that time concentrating its efforts on punched card accounting systems, had developed a simple computer – partly because of its founder's interest in astronomy. This was displayed in their shop window in New York, attracting huge crowds as it demonstrated its ability to calculate past, present and future phases of the moon. At the same time a competitor had developed a far more advanced computer much more suitable for business use.

Following IBM's demonstration a number of businesses saw the potential of this marvellous machine for simple accounting uses – particularly payrolls which were an enormously time consuming and complex process in large companies. (For example, in 1965 the payroll for 5,000 men at a Cardiff steelworks took two days plus data preparation time to run on the early IBM 360 machine then installed!)

The competitor – still perceiving their advanced machine as a scientific tool – and perhaps thinking that they might 'let the side down a bit' by venturing into the rather mundane business world – after all a payroll is hardly in the same plane as the computation of prime numbers or the development of a chess playing facility – chose to ignore (virtually) this potential market place.

IBM, however, being primarily involved in this area already, saw the potential at once and also recognised that development of the market was dependent on providing systems that would allow users to 'get the job done'. They therefore concentrated on the development of computer based solutions to business products – including their computer almost as an afterthought. So successful was this strategy that, with a fundamentally inferior basic product (their relatively simple and unspecialised computer) they rapidly assumed market leadership and have held it to the present day.

Of course, the preceding anecdote illustrates the importance of recognising the core product (business solutions) but it also illustrates the development of augmenting features which are presented to the customer in the form of a complete product offering (much as does the offering of the estate agent or surveyor as we shall see later).

It is also interesting to note at this point that IBM has been at the forefront of development in other areas associated with the tangible product. Today IBM is known throughout the computer world as 'Big Blue' – reflecting

a) its size, and
b) its colour packaging adopted in the 1960s with the 360 series and continued throughout its product range.

Augmented product

Identification of the core product and the tangible product whilst essential to both product analysis and product development, is by no means the end of the story. As we shall see in Chapter 3 buyers in both consumer and organisational markets seek satisfaction for wants and needs at many levels both practical and psychological. It is at these levels – in particular the psychological level – that the concept of product augmentation is applied. In other words we look at the total consumption system in which the product is to exist. 'The way in which a purchaser of a product performs the total task of whatever it is that he is trying to accomplish when using the product.'

In Figure 2.1 product augmentation is seen in installation, after sale service, warranty, delivery and credit. These, however, are simply a sample

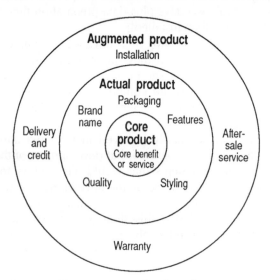

Figure 2.1 Levels of product

(Philip Kotler/Gary Armstrong, *Principals of Marketing*, 4e, 1989, p. 244.
Reprinted by permission of Prentice Hall, Englewood Cliffs, NJ.

of the areas in which a product can be augmented to meet consumer needs.

Refer back to the fountain pen. It has been established that, at its core is the ability to produce marks on paper. In tangible form it is a barrel with an ink reservoir, a nib, a means of refilling and a form of packaging which includes colour, style, brand name and quality level. Within the consumer's total package, however, the pen is much more than an instrument to write with. It is an expression of personality, of individuality, a statement both to self and to the world of the kind of person it is that is using it. Consequently the added value of the social positioning implied by brand name, packaging etc. may become more important than the simple quality implications which are evident at first sight.

In more complex products, particularly in the area of services, this implied added value may well be the most important features of a product. For example, ownership of a Rolls-Royce implies far more about a consumer than mere ownership of a quality car. This would probably be true even if the Rolls-Royce were to go through a period of poor reliability – that is, if its technical quality suffered – as long as its high price and social cachet could be maintained. A visit to a Harley Street surgeon implies much more than getting access to the 'best in the business'. In fact the surgeon may not be anywhere near the best in his field.

The overall product offering therefore, is a mix of factors which together form a package of benefits which aspire to meet customers' wants and needs. The extent to which a product will succeed in its chosen market is directly dependent upon the fit that can be achieved between the total product offered and the total package of wants and needs within the market.

Service products

The preceding discussion has explored principles which can be applied in the analysis and design of products in a generic sense. Current marketing thought, however, distinguishes a special category of products as service products. Kotler defines a service as

'any activity or benefit that one party can offer to another that is essentially intangible and does not result in the ownership of anything. Its production may or may not be tied to a physical product.'

There are many other definitions, as you might expect, but the one thing that most commentators stress is the principle that a service is basically intangible. Figure 2.2 shows a goods – service continuum which demonstrates the almost imperceptible merging of tangible goods with intangible services based on the relative dominance of tangible vs intangible product attributes.

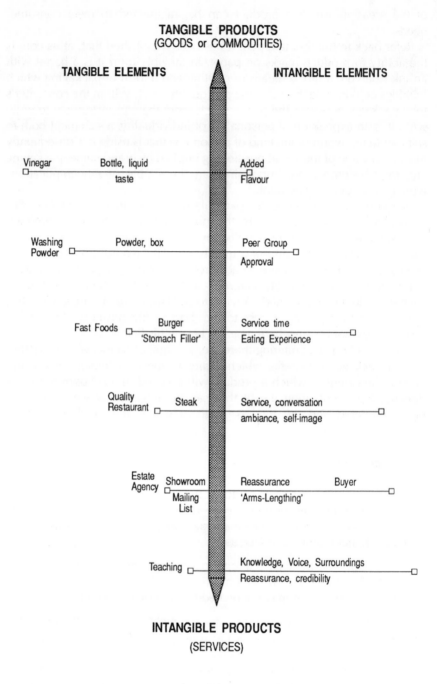

Figure 2.2 A goods service continuum

A number of quite specific attributes are visible in service products. These have been suggested under the following headings:

Intangibility
Inseparability
Heterogeneity
Perishability
Ownership

and it is worth looking at these in a little more detail.

Intangibility

A service is basically intangible. It can often not be handled, touched, smelt, seen, or heard before purchase. In particular it cannot be sampled as it only exists when it actually takes place. There is, therefore, a fundamental problem for the marketer in that the buyer has to exercise his buying judgement on the basis of faith in something still to be experienced rather than in tangible comparisons.

Inseparability

The service product differs from a tangible product in that it often cannot be separated from the person providing the service. Once a car has been made it exists and, barring accidents, remains in existence even though the person who made it may not. A barrister's appearance in court, however, is just that. Without the barrister there is no court appearance by him. There may be a different barrister but that then becomes a different service.

There is a further difference in that with a tangible product the functions of creating and consuming the product occur at different times – the car is made (finished), then someone drives it away. In the case of a service product the service is often consumed as it is created – the barrister creates his court appearance at exactly the same time as his client (the court) consumes it.

There is yet a further complication in that with a service product the client may actually become an integral part of the provision of the service – the performance of the client in the witness box may materially affect the performance of the barrister in delivering his service.

Heterogeneity

Because of the essentially transient nature of a service it is difficult, if not impossible, to ensure a standard level of performance of the service. As shown above the performance of the client interacting with the performance of the barrister affects the service performed in an unpredictable way – even if the barrister were able to apply the most rigorous standards to his own performance, the eventual service provided would differ in each unique occurrence. This creates problems both for the client – in judging the quality of the service, even after the event – and for the marketer in conveying the essence of the service to his target market.

Perishability

Services cannot be stored. They are either performed or not and if they are not the clock cannot be put back. For example, an empty hotel room is a guest/night lost forever. Last night cannot be filled tomorrow morning. Similarly if there is excess demand for the service it is almost impossible to expand production – and the demand is as perishable as the service.

Ownership

Finally, in the sale of a service as opposed to a tangible product there is no change in ownership of the product. The service is performed and paid for. Nothing changes hands but a temporary use of knowledge or expertise.

These attributes of a service serve only to distinguish an intangible service product from a tangible unit product. They highlight some of the special difficulties that a marketer needs to solve in placing his offering before potential buyers (the market). They do not alter the fundamental concept of the core, tangible and augmented product, they merely add some modifiers which assist in defining an offering in the service area.

Products and the property industry

It is conventional within the property industry to think of the business in two ways. First, the practice and the services which it offers; second the types of property which may be built or may need disposal. In this section we will follow convention and consider, first the practice and services and second, the markets for the types of property which may be offered. This is a subtle distinction but one which should yield a far greater return in practical terms.

The practice and products of the professional

For the purposes of this section we shall consider a theoretical general practice firm which deals with both residential and commercial agency. It also provides a range of professional services includes mortgage valuations, structural surveys, lease negotiations and purchase, rent review and dilapidations. On occasion it involves itself in statutory valuations – compensation claims and rating in the main. In other words a fairly typical broad-based general practice firm.

The offerings of such a firm can, broadly, be split into two product areas. These are:

Estate agency – Residential
                Commercial
Professional practice – Residential valuations
                Commercial valuations
                Structural surveys
                Management
                Planning
                Statutory valuations
                Dilapidations

It is helpful to consider the nature of each of these product areas separately but first to establish that each fits clearly into the category of a service product.

Estate agency

'Those acting as an intermediary ('an agent') in the sale or acquisition of land' (Nigel Stephens (1981)).

In common with insurance salesmen and most other salesmen whose activities result in an apparently high commission return in exchange for what appears to be little work, estate agents have consistently had a bad press. This is not particularly surprising. They deal with the public at its most stressful and most vulnerable times and have often, in the past failed to

(a) understand clearly what they actually do, and
(b) market their product and the value that they add to their clients in a way that adequately involves the client in their activities.

So far has this wheel turned that there is a fairly general feeling within the property industry that estate agency – particularly in the residential market is 'not really a professional activity'. As we shall see, it is not – but it probably should be.

The chairman of a publicly quoted property company said recently in addressing an eminent firm of chartered surveyors 'the first thing that you people do is to ask my opinion as to whom we should appoint as advertising/marketing consultants to help in the disposal of my property. I engage you because you are supposed to be the marketing consultants and to advise me. If you're not careful I shall engage consultants directly – then who needs you?' They were suitably shocked, but why? He was right! (Not just because he was a client either.)

Let us consider the nature of estate agency in marketing terms, following the analysis tools identified earlier. What does the product look like in terms of core, tangible and augmented features?

There is little guidance on this from published material. Textbooks have tended to concentrate on how to get instructions, how to sell, how to run a mailing list and on the aspects of the product which can be managed. These areas are, of course, highly important and relevant but, if we were to concentrate on them as indicators of the nature of the product, we would surely be guilty of a high degree of product orientation which, as we saw in Chapter 1, tends to lead the self-indulgent in the general direction of the bankruptcy court. Where then should we look? The definition of marketing given in Chapter 1 suggests that marketing is 'the management process responsible for identifying, anticipating and satisfying customer requirements profitably'.

So we begin at the beginning – with the customer. What are the customer's wants and needs?

In order to answer this question it is necessary to pick our starting point very carefully. It will also be helpful for the sake of illustration to limit our discussion initially to the residential function.

What is the need inherent in the decision to instruct an estate agent? 'To get a property sold' is the pat answer – and this leads quite naturally to the question 'why?' And the moment this question is asked it opens up a whole range of possibilities, one of which is to translate what was previously understood as a 'need' into a 'want'.

How does this happen? Let us consider the question why someone wants his house sold and see where it leads.

There are a number of reasons for selling a house:

- change of financial circumstances
- change of job
- change of life-cycle circumstances
- widowhood
- marriage
- change in number of children
- death
- bankruptcy

all of which lead to an inescapable conclusion. The person wishes to change residence (even in the case of decease where, of course, the residence has already changed).

What, then, can now be perceived as the need which leads to the 'want' to sell the house? The 'need' is to change residence – to move house.

What are the effects on the house owner of this need to move house? One of the major effects is the need to pay for the new property – finance. And where, in most cases does a substantial proportion of this finance come from? From the sale of the house. It should be noted at this point, however, that the sale of the house is not the only available source of finance. It may be infinitely preferable to the alternatives but there are, nevertheless, alternatives. The need, therefore, can be translated into a 'want' – 'I want to sell my house to raise finance rather than taking up alternatives which I could if I had to'. If, of course, there is no alternative finance available the 'want' translates back into a 'need'. Complicated isn't it!

Given the need to change residence what other wants and needs might be generated?

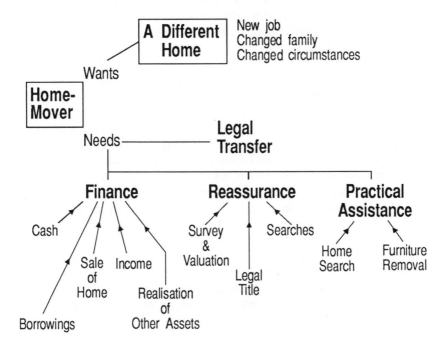

Note: Sophisticated 'new home ' vendors provide most, if not all, of these facilities as part of their 'sales package', e.g. Barratt Homes, Wimpey, McCarthy & Stone

Figure 2.3 The estate agency environment

It will be immediately apparent that the apparently simple statement, 'I want to sell my house', is actually part of a complex hierarchy of wants and needs, most of which interact and which contribute greatly to the stress felt by the client who is trying to move.

In the first place he needs to find a new property – in itself a complex task with powerful financial, social and psychological overtones (as we shall see in Chapter 3). In order to do this he first has to set some cash limits and in order to do this he needs to be able to review his financial situation.

For most people this review of the financial situation is the first contact with an estate agent. Most people's three main assets in considering house purchase are:

the value of the existing home
cash resources
borrowing ability

and they quickly seek to quantify these. Cash resources are fairly easy – they are usually known within fairly close tolerances. The other two are more difficult and usually involve professional help (at least in the eyes of the client). Unfortunately, being the first point of contact for estate agents, particularly if they are also financial service providers, they are also seen as a potential point of sale for service products (estate agency and financial services) so an immediate conflict of purpose is fairly predictable.

Leaving aside for the moment the practical problems for the client in getting at the service which will satisfy his current need (to get information) the client finally satisfies himself as to his financial position and proceeds to negotiate for the purchase of his new home. At this point he needs reassurance (as to whether or not his vendor actually owns the property and as to its structural stability and general condition), legal assistance (to ensure that the specific rules inherent in the law of the land are followed in respect of his transaction) and finally money (in order to complete the purchase).

At this point his troubles really begin. In most cases, as we have seen, he needs to sell his property in order to raise the requisite part of the finance which will allow him to fulfil his underlying need (which is to move to a new home). So he calls in an estate agent (unless he has already decided to go it alone) and asks for his help.

It is here that the confusions really start. The client now needs to sell his house. From the agent he wants (in some cases he might even need)

Marketing advice
– how should I price the property?
– where and when should I advertise?
– how should my house be presented?
– what are the features which add value from the viewpoint of potential purchasers?
– what sort of purchasers might be around?
– what type of sale method and campaign is most appropriate?

Marketing management
– Someone to actually manage the process of advertising, selling and collecting the money.

He also wants from the agent some specific clues which will help him to decide on whether to use the other services of that agent or not.

What are the other services provided by the agent?

Marketing management – normally a standardised pattern of advertising, telesales or direct sales. The agent 'stands in' for the client and manages the presentation of the property to its potential markets. When a purchaser is located he will normally negotiate terms and manage the complex interactions between purchaser chains, lenders and professional advisors on behalf of the client.

Property management – the agent will often be required to maintain some kind of management control over a property at various points within its sales life cycle. For example, if the property is left empty the agent would normally be expected to advise his client of the dangers of its freezing up. Similarly he would often hold keys to the property and control access to it.

Simplified accounting – the home vendor acting for himself deals with a variety of suppliers – board contractors, various advertising media suppliers – each of whom has to be paid, very often in advance, with a consequent effect on cash flow. It is normal to pay an estate agent in arrears, often only in the event of a successful sale by the agent.

We have, therefore, an enormously complex situation to be sorted out, at the inception of the client's potential relationship with the agent.

The client, initially, wants marketing advice. The agent has a product – as yet indeterminate – yet which can be clearly seen to include at least four identifiable sub-products bundled as a product offering.

At the heart of the whole thing is the client's NEED for a buyer with the ability to purchase. Small wonder that there is confusion and lack of confidence on behalf of the client and equally small wonder that there is confusion on behalf of agents in marketing their product offering.

What happens in practice?

The client calls in the agent for marketing advice – and also to assess the agent's potential to provide him with a buyer for his property. The agent sees this, not unnaturally, as a selling opportunity and – sometimes unintentionally – slants his advice to appeal to those elements of the client's make up which he thinks are most likely to affect the client's buying decision.

In its most basic form this 'slanting' of advice results in the agent quoting an asking price which he thinks will be

a) towards the high end of what competing agents might quote;
b) as near as he can possibly get to what he thinks the client already thought (i.e., he tries to reassure the client by reinforcing the client's self-image of cleverness in assessing the market);

both of which lay the foundations for future disappointment as they pay little attention to the achievable, only to the opportunity for the agent to operate.

What, then, does the product offering comprise?

At its most basic level – the core product – the agent is selling his ability to provide a buyer with the ability to purchase. This, however, is the end product of a package which includes some measure of:

- marketing advice
- marketing management
- property management
- simplified accounting

although the distinctions between these areas may not be fully understood or clearly identified.

This package is presented to the client – whether by design or default – as a product offering – 'estate agency', 'real estate brokerage', call it what you will, and the packaging becomes the 'tangible' product. Unfortunately, as we have already seen, the essence of the product offering is, by its nature as a service, intangible, so the 'tangibility' is expressed through inference and implication rather than through direct demonstration.

The essence of tangibility in the product therefore is to be found in:

- design of showroom
- paperwork
  - particulars
  - letterheads
  - business cards
- methodology
  - sonic 'tape'
  - computerised comparables
- mailing list service

and all the other visible manifestations associated with estate agency.

But this is by no means all the story. As we saw in the example of the pen there is a variety of other needs to be addressed in the product offering. These are the intangible needs and the estate agent's product offering leans heavily upon satisfying them (although few agents recognise this or take specific action to cater for them).

For example, we have already seen how, at the initial marketing consultancy meeting, there is an almost overwhelming tendency to 'slant' advice in order to win instructions and that the slant of this advice is to reassure the client as to the sagacity of his own prejudgement of the market place. That such an approach is so often the key to gaining an instruction simply demonstrates the strength of the desire for reassurance in this stressful situation.

But reassurance comes not only from direct confirmation of personal opinion. Reassurance comes also from the implicit approval of one's peers

– if people similar to the client can be seen to be using the service then the client will feel reassured and will be more likely to use the service. Many agents, particularly the better ones, make regular and profitable use of testimonial letters, both in explicit advertising and in the more personal face to face encounter situation.

We shall see in Chapter 3 the importance of social groupings within the buying decision. The importance of social reassurance is not just upon estate agents who either try to be as cosmopolitan (classless) as possible or who consciously adopt the lifestyle symbolism of their chosen market grouping (e.g., the 'yuppie' concept in 1980s Docklands) to generate a common identity with their vendors.

The average private vendor also seeks another form of gratification. He often wishes to distance himself from the 'unpleasant' aspects of the vendor/purchaser relationship. Like everyone else he seeks the best possible deal but often doubts his ability to sell or to negotiate. The agent here performs a most useful function – doing the dirty work. How often have we heard the comment 'XYZ company are a load of sharks. I wouldn't buy anything from them – but I'd certainly get them to sell for me'.

At the same time the agent is the long stop – someone to blame. 'I wouldn't gazump you for the world – the agent told me I had to.' 'You 'told' me to go to auction. Why didn't anyone come to buy?' Someone to blame – a scapegoat.

Our product analysis is then:

Core product – to provide a buyer with the ability to purchase
Tangible product
  – showroom
  – house style
  – corporate image
  – mailing list
  – motor cars and negotiators
Intangible product
  – reassurance
  – scapegoating

Looked at in these terms the promotional efforts of the estate agency world can be seen for what they have traditionally been – very hit and miss – and small wonder.

In later chapters we will consider other products supplied by the general practice firm, together with the marketing initiatives open to the firm in positioning its offerings against the competition.

In this chapter the nature of a product has been reviewed in terms of its core, tangibility and its augmentation and have considered estate agency in these terms. This consideration has opened up a number of avenues for further discussion and these avenues will be built upon in future chapters.

References and further reading

P.F. Drucker (1985), *Innovation and Entrepreneurship*, Harper & Row, New York pp. 22, 23

P. Kotler and G. Armstrong (1989), *Principles of Marketing*, 4th edition, Prentice-Hall International pp. 4, 5, 180, 244, 296, 297, 681

A. Maslow (1985), *Motivation and Personality*, New York Times Book Co Inc, pp. 37, 55, 57

W. Meyers, *op. cit.*

A Mitchell, *op. cit.*

N. Stephens (1981), *The Practice of Estate Agency*, *Estates Gazette* p. 26

V. Packard (1957), *The Hidden Persuaders*, Penguin

G. Zaltman and M. Wallendorf (1979), *Consumer Behavior*, John Wiley & Sons, New York

3 Consumers and their Influences

Case study

In the early 1970s Parkhurst Estate Agents burst upon the South Wales property scene like a meteorite. Based primarily in Swansea it quickly spread to other locations, in particular to Newport, where its growth – and subsequent contraction – provides an interesting study in consumer perception and in the attitudes of the 'establishment' professional firms.

From the very inception of the Newport Office the Parkhurst operation was different. It was the epitome of the differentiated and focused product. At a time when several of the larger long-established firms were still operating from offices reminiscent of nothing more than a social security office, complete with sliding opaque glass shutter in a screen designed to keep the customer at arms length, the Parkhurst offices were open plan, colour schemed in strident fluorescent colours and operated on a 'browse around, take-away' supermarket basis. The whole operation was young, designed for the young and was in tune with the sense of urgency and direction which hung over from the swinging 1960s.

Right from the word 'go' the office incorporated a sense of personality which became closely linked with the carefully cultivated image of its local partner, Alan Darlow, a young chartered surveyor with a highly developed flair for promotion and public relations.

The whole operation was cohesive in its imagery. Fluorescent orange boards, the slogan 'The Go Ahead Agents', personal number plates on a succession of performance cars, a helicopter trip from wedding to reception, the whole operation oozed conspicuous success, bolstered by tales of high earning and even higher spending.

It took the town by storm and within a few short years built up a very impressive market share rumoured in excess of 40 per cent of the total available.

Inevitably it came to an end. The heady growth led to a flagship office, bigger and better than anything seen before; concealed lighting, musac, a fishpond built in – and an overdraft to match.

Partner and firm parted company. The former opened again under his own name and proceeded to build a new business at a pace which soon outstripped the old. The firm, now bereft of its 'role model', gradually contracted into profit under a hardworking manager and its market share slipped as it came under attack from all sides. Finally it moved back to its old premises and was sold.

What happened during that period?

1. A clear strategy of differentiation and focus was brilliantly implemented.
2. Consumers, at the beginning of the consumer boom in owner-occupation for the young, were asked to trade in terms which they were already used to – supermarket style, popular music, no-pressure selling.
3. Consumers were provided with a role model with which they could identify – the free spending high achiever – if they bought some of that it might rub off!
4. Consumers were wooed with overt sales messages clarifying the product offering, 'No Sale No Fee', 'accompanied viewings', 'free valuation for sale', 'the advertising changes' – either new to the business or so old that nobody bothered to mention them any more.
5. Consumers were plied with images of reassurance – the overt success of the principal, 'sold' boards erected within days, slogans like 'just count the boards'.

It is also revealing to consider the attitudes of 'established' firms towards the upstart:

'It's too flash, people won't like it (the people were used to us) and it won't last.'
'Walkround showrooms are too dangerous, so many people will do private deals.'
'They're only saying what we already do, surely people will realise this and come back to us 'professionals'.'
'Advertising is unprofessional – spending all that money and setting themselves up as experts.'
'We'll report them to the RICS for unprofessional (read non- protectionist) conduct.'

and many similar responses.

But what did the consumer think – and why? This chapter addresses some of the influences on consumer behaviour and looks at how consumer perceptions may be shaped by environmental, social and psychological factors, many of which may be modified and stimulated by marketing initiatives.

Consumer buying decisions

The activities of consumers are influenced, in varying measures, by a wide variety of factors. At the extremes an Australian aborigine living in the 'bush' will have significantly different buying requirements from a jet-setting international real estate consultant. At rather less extremes one partner in a firm of surveyors will buy a BMW 320i whilst another in the same firm, with a young family and a mortgage, might buy a Montego Estate.

It has long been a mystery to me why, on a brand new housing development one family will, through choice, buy the right hand partner in an otherwise identical pair of semis whilst another family will choose the other.

On the same development, one couple will buy whilst another will give up, perhaps through frustration at their inability to penetrate the labyrinth of rules and regulations which surround the house purchase, perhaps because somebody 'talked them out of it[1], perhaps because they simply 'didn't see themselves living there'.

Experienced estate agents will recognise that different couples behave in different ways when approaching house purchase. In some the male plays a dominant role, perhaps stressing the investment potential in the site, perhaps moving into aggressive behaviour signalling the start of negotiations. In others the female is dominant, often making similar signals but sometimes bolstering the male's ego – making the bullets for him to fire – but all the while keeping a firm grip on the proceedings.

What kind of factors influence these behaviours? Are there any significant patterns to look out for? Do the behaviours stem from factors which the marketer can manage?

In order to make sense of anything it is usually helpful to impose some kind of structure on the problem. We will do this by looking at aspects of the process in turn, then relating these aspects to behavioural factors which influence them in some practical way.

The structure then, is as follows:

a) The buying decision – what kinds of decision are there? Do the different kinds of decision have different characteristics? What are the lessons to be drawn in dealing with residential property?

b) Stages in the buying decision – before a decision can be arrived at the decision makers go through a number of identifiable stages – inception, interest, information search, information analysis and classification. Buyers within these stages behave in identifiable ways and their needs vary considerably. How can we cater for their needs and manage them to advantage?

c) Buying roles – as we have already seen buyers operate within different, identifiable, roles, sometimes as advocate, sometimes as defendant, sometimes aggressive, sometimes passive. Can these roles be recognised and managed? Does the information we provide need to be tailored to cater for these differing roles? Are there implications for staff behaviour and training?

d) Consumer perception – consumers see life through different spectacles than those worn by providers. Consequently they do not always behave as we would like them to. They even misunderstand what we tell them about ourselves and our products. What kind of factors shape their perceptions and how can we ensure that our messages are understood as we would wish them to be?

e) Product adoption – some people accept new ideas and act on them faster than others. Is this important to us and how can we take advantage of this?

The buying decision

'Where is the problem?' you may ask. 'If someone wants something they go out and buy it.'

Quite true, but that statement begs a number of questions. First of all, what is a want? What does it mean to say that somebody wants something? Secondly, 'they go out and buy it'. What do they actually buy? Where do they get the money from? How do they choose between alternatives?

It would be helpful at this stage to distinguish between 'wants' and 'needs'.

Kotler defines a need as 'a state of felt deprivation in a person'. In other words a need is a state in which a person finds it difficult to manage without something. A thirsty man in a desert needs water in order to survive. An alcoholic needs a drink (an alcoholic drink) in order to avoid traumatic withdrawal symptoms. A businessman needs a car of a certain standard in order to avoid feeling less important than his peers (whom he is trying to impress). A busy housewife needs a washing machine in order to avoid

a) going around in dirty clothes;
b) going to the launderette;
c) doing the washing by hand (and thereby taking up time which she could usefully use on something else).

A need, therefore, is quite clearly a powerful motivation force and also a complex status to recognise and define.

Attempts have been made to do this however, and a most useful graphic description of the nature of needs, which helps to relate them to the host influences which affect them, is found in Maslow's *Hierarchy of Needs*, (1954).

Kotler makes the point that when a person experiences a need, that person is unhappy. In order to avoid unhappiness he will either look for something which satisfies that need or will try to extinguish the desire. In rich societies they do the former, in poor societies they have little choice but to do the latter.

A want, however, is quite a different matter. A want is a need, modified by the culture in which the individual exists. An Australian aborigine, wanting to beautify his body, goes in for extensive body painting using locally available materials. A European lady, depending on social status, economic circumstances, age, lifestyle and a host of other factors will use one or other of the many brands of cosmetics made available to her.

'They go out and buy it'. Always assuming that they

a) have enough money;
b) like going to the shops/restaurant/pub;
c) cannot or do not wish to buy via mail order.

But does every trip to the shops for every different type of purchase follow exactly the same routine? Is buying a car similar to buying a house? Are there differences between buying a house for the first time and buying a second, third or subsequent house?

Clearly, the patterns of buying in these situations will differ and we need to evaluate these decisions at a different level if we are to make headway.

Marketers, generally, describe three levels of buying decision. These are:

• Routine
• Limited problem solving
• Complex or extended problem solving

Routine

By far the majority of consumer decisions are made as a matter of routine. Which toothpaste to buy, which breakfast cereal, how many apples, how many oranges, which cigarettes – acres of consumable products are bought every day 'on the nod'. 'This is what we always buy'.

It also happens that these purchases constitute the bulk of the profit making capacity for the firms that supply them so it comes as little surprise that consumer-orientated suppliers dealing in mass markets with routine decision making spend a very high proportion of their product budgets in:

a) persuading people to try their wares, and
b) persuading people to stay with them rather than be seduced by the opposition.

An elementary consideration of the human animal is enough to highlight the difficulty of getting people to change – hence the importance of brand names, brand images and brand reinforcement through sophisticated and innovative advertising, particularly on television.

Limited problem solving (LPS)

In this situation people have a broad understanding of the type of product to be purchased but may be unfamiliar with 'state of the art' design, techniques or features. Here we start to approach the world of the residential estate agent dealing with sophisticated purchasers who have moved home within an area on a number of occasions. They are familiar with the broad mechanics of house moving but need to catch up with modern trends in display, current commission rates, impact of the multiples, availability of finance, upgrading their endowment policies etc. at the same time as forming new judgments on which estate agent (if any) to use.

They are alert to ideas in advertising and corporate image and are likely to look quickly through the clutter of information provided, focusing sharply on the new information which they need as a basis for their decision making.

Engel et al. in *Consumer Behaviour* postulate that this type of buyer is likely to perceive competitive offerings as broadly similar and that they are likely to be influenced more by point of sale initiatives than by complex explanation.

Extended problem solving (EPS)

Here the buyer confronts a completely unfamiliar product and needs to go through a complex learning and assimilation process before he can even begin to approach sensible decision making. This process can last quite a long time and will obviously vary considerably from person to person.

The first-time house buyer is clearly within this classification. He confronts a momentous decision which could affect his standard and quality of life for many years to come. He very quickly becomes aware that he is in a minefield and seeks help and guidance wherever it may be found. At the heart of his search is the need to reduce anxiety by minimising his risk and clever marketers aim their appeal messages at this need.

Decisions, then, within the property industry, tend to be of the limited problem solving or complex varieties and it is to these classification of purchasers that residential property marketers should focus their attention. The imagery needed to sell soap powder differs greatly from that required at more complex levels and we should remain aware of these differences.

Stages in the buying decision

At every level of purchase decision making the buyer goes through a number of stages which should be recognised by the marketer and reflected in product design. The stages apply in even the simplest of decisions but tend to become more marked as the decision type becomes more complex. They are, therefore, of considerable interest to marketers of both property and property brokers or estate agents.

The Five Stages have been identified as:

- Problem recognition
- Information search
- Evaluation of alternatives
- Purchase decision
- Post-purchase behaviour

and we will follow this convention.

Problem recognition

As we have seen buying behaviour starts when a potential consumer recognises a need. For example, a young couple becomes engaged. After the initial euphoria wears off their thoughts turn to the practical problems of where to live. There is a basic need for them to live somewhere but that could be satisfied by them living where they are, that is, staying apart. However the act of becoming engaged was the result of their recognition of a need to be together – so that is not a viable solution.

The next possibility is to live in a parental home – but that gives rise to difficulties with privacy and other unwelcome social problems so the need becomes more clearly expressed as 'living together and away from parents'.

This now requires research into what might be available and the research will result in recognising that the alternatives are (not exhaustively!):

- Rented flat
- Rented house
- Rented fixed caravan
- Purchased flat
- Purchased house
- Purchased mobile home
etc.

At this point social considerations come into play and some of the alternatives – e.g. the rented mobile home – may be rejected without further consideration. The problem is narrowed down. The want is now for a house or flat, rented or purchased.

It should not be thought that this preliminary decision making is rapid. It often evolves over quite a long period and will include reading – magazines, advice leaflets, books; taking soundings and advice – from parents, friends, other family, maybe even a foray to the local estate agents or a 'friendly' insurance salesman ('Take the policy now, we'll get the mortgage when you're ready').

Clearly, there is considerable potential overlap between the first stage and the second stage – information search. In the example, which relates to an extensive problem solving situation there were three clear stages before sufficient clarity could emerge in the problem recognition stage to allow the purchases to move on. The example also shows clearly the nature of the problem to be solved (living together and not living with others) and some of the product alternatives open to the consumer (often forgotten as competition by the marketer).

Information search

At this point our young couple will have established

a) that they do not want to live with mum;
b) purchase (or still, possibly, renting) is their probable preferred solution – and they would like a house or a flat.

A lot now depends on how urgent the situation is becoming for them and two levels of attention or activity can be distinguished. Heightened attention: if the young couple are still happy to drift along for the time being, whilst they carry on looking at each other and saving their pennies, they are likely to enter this state and here they are interested in making a move at some time in the future but are doing nothing specific to make it happen. They will, however, become more sensitive and receptive to information regarding mortgages, house purchase, estate agents, house prices and comments about the property world in the consumer press.

At some point, however, they are likely to move into active information search; here the situation is becoming much more urgent and they will actively seek out information which they think is relevant. They might do any of the following – talk to the building society, visit estate agents' offices, drive around looking at 'For Sale' boards, look over a few properties, bore their friends to death with questions and with stories of the latest properties viewed or the 'shady tricks' of the estate agents (offering them properties which are – too dear/already sold/under offer/suffering from structural problems...).

It is quite clear that during both of these phases our young potential consumers are likely to be relatively open to the effects of persuasive messages – and are equally likely to be influenced by adverse messages – which relate to their areas of interest. It is necessary for marketers to consider, therefore, the source of such messages and their likely effects on the recipients.

The main sources of information for the consumer are:

Personal sources – family, friends, workmates
Commercial sources – advertising, sales people, PR
Public sources – media, consumer associations
Experience – use of the product, part-trial

The impact of information from each source will vary with the complexity of the decision, the degree of risk perceived by the consumer and the sheer volume of data received but, in general, it can be said that the consumer uses data from commercial sources for information about the product but that he uses data from personal or independent sources to evaluate the product or to test its social acceptability. Hence the importance to the estate agent of avoiding the likelihood of their meeting a dissatisfied ex-customer or of the disgruntled media undermining positive images carefully engineered in promotional activity.

Evaluation of alternatives

At some point in the process our young couple will progress towards resolution of the problem. They are now forced with imposing some kind of order on the potential chaos of images, information and messages to which they will have been subjected and in order to do this they have to, consciously or unconsciously, classify the information in some way so that it can be evaluated.

Psychologists can suggest a number of alternative problem solving methods used by consumers in decision making. The activity is further complicated by the likely use of differing methods to sort out sub-problems within the main problem. In practice, and this is very often true in the purchase of a first home, a rule-of-thumb method which satisfices the decision, rather than optimising it, is utilised.

Some examples of this approach would be in limiting the areas to be considered, number of bedrooms, conditions, affordability etc. until a manageable subset of the available offerings emerges. Experience suggests, some in other consumer areas, that a short list of four or perhaps five is the preferred size.

Further consideration of this process suggests that a series of variables are considered by the consumer. These can be identified as product attributes.

Property product attributes: location, nearness of shops and facilities, types of neighbours; size, number of bedrooms, number of living rooms, kitchen fitments, bathroom fitments, central heating, double glazing, size of garden, garage space – all the familiar catechism as listed in millions of house details over the years.

To this list can be added a number of intangible attributes: reputation of the agent, personal experience of the agent, attitude (as perceived by the buyer) of the present owner, propensity of area values to increase/decrease, likelihood of demographic changes affecting the area, lender recommended by the agent, attitude of professional advisors to the property – a host of factors.

Different consumers will append different weightings to the importance of each product attribute, depending on the consumer's experience and the specific influences to which he has been subjected – social, economic and psychological.

Clearly, there is a fruitful field for the property marketer to identify the likely attribute of the property as perceived by a potential consumer and to influence the consumer's perceptions in a favourable manner. He could do this by:

a) modifying the property in some way – arranging for the outside to be redecorated, persuading the vendor to keep it tidy, asking the vendor to be absent whilst prospective purchasers view it – a greenfield site for the creative marketer;

b) altering beliefs about the property – if there were a popular belief (folk memory) that 'they play tag with hatchets in Feering Street' the marketer might highlight the memory then attempt to replace it with a more acceptable image – 'of course, that was all a long time ago, the area has been completely renovated, more people now own their own homes, there is a flourishing playgroup and everybody belongs to the neighbourhood watch scheme';

c) altering beliefs about competitors – 'of course, 20 years ago that was a very popular area but the houses are so big that they've all been turned into flats, I wouldn't like to bring up my children there';

d) altering importance weights – 'I think you're very wise in considering three bedrooms as being the most important thing – of course, if you bought a 2-bedroom you could always change it when the kids come along, in the meantime you'd have less to look after so you'd both have more time available to enjoy yourself – and there's always a waiting list for 2-bedroomed houses if you wanted to sell it again;'

e) call attention to neglected attributes – 'do you know that we're only 2 minutes walk from Beechwood Park if you use the footpath around the common';

f) changing the buyer's ideals – 'of course there's a lot of sense in taking two moves to get into West Town but you could do it now if you gave up cigarettes/beer/extra bedroom – let me show you how'.

Of course, in the examples face to face selling expressions have been used, but they illustrate the principles and could be incorporated into other message channels, perhaps more subtly.

Overload

It should be noted at this point that, particularly in a complex decision making situation, information overload can occur. In this situation the consumer receives more information than he is able to handle successfully.

Research has shown that when this happens:

a) consumers feel more certain, more satisfied, less confused and desire less additional information;
b) but they make poorer decisions.

Most experienced property professionals who have dealt with first time buyers will have personal experience of this phenomenon. It is nowadays not unknown for an agent to set up a 'first time buyer briefing' on some low priced flats which take the prospective purchaser smartly through the mechanics of buying and finish with depositing him in the hands of a solicitor complete with mortgage application and draft contract. This has become a recognised marketing approach but the systematic overload of vulnerable consumers in the full knowledge of its psychological effects would seem to stray close to the bounds of ethical acceptability.

Purchase decision

By the end of the evaluation stage the purchaser will have ranked the available offerings and formed an intention to purchase. This, however, is still subject to modifying factors, in particular the attitudes of other people – family, friends, professional advisers; and unanticipated factors, loss of job, loss of spouse, etc.

The decision to buy 'at this time' is also still subject to variation and the likelihood of variation is closely related to the buyer's perception of risk in the decision.

In the purchase of property there is clearly a high potential for risk. There may be hidden faults, the neighbours might be horrible – or even worse be lovely, then move! – friends may not like the area so may not come to visit, the whole thing may prove crippling financially, particularly if interest rates rise. In such a complex decision there is risk at every turn.

People become adept at dealing with risk in their lives and evolve personalised strategies for risk reduction. In consumer markets they may choose to purchase only nationally branded goods – there was considerable consumer reluctance to purchase 'own-brand' goods when they were first introduced by the supermarket chains. They may choose to avoid making decisions at all; they may choose to buy 'one like mum's'. It is essential that at the point of sale, the marketer recognises the potential for non-purchase and takes steps to manage this stage in the buying process very carefully.

Viewed in this light it is small wonder that most residential agency firms experience a sizeable proportion of post-agreement drop-out. The wonder is, surely, that it is not even greater.

Buying roles

- Gatekeeper
- Influencer
- Decision maker
- Buyer
- User

Within the study of marketing the concept of roles is central, and particularly so in considering the marketing of property and property-related organisations. We shall consider roles in an organisational context in a later chapter but, at this point, we should consider the major roles which people play in the consideration of a purchase.

In considering these roles it is important to remember that:

a) roles may exist side by side
b) individuals or groups may fulfil the roles
c) an individual or group may occupy or take part in any or all of the roles.

Gatekeeper

A gatekeeper is, quite literally, someone who controls access – in this case normally to information. For example, mother, picking up property details, may discard some thus excluding those properties from consideration by the buying group. Similarly, mother or father, out shopping for details, may consciously choose to exclude the offerings from one agent from consideration – for whatever reason. A child in the family, noticing an advertisement for a property which he personally, does not like for some reason, might find ways of excluding that property advertisement from the consideration of the group.

In a more formalised setting the recently emergent relocation specialist companies act as gatekeepers in excluding non-appropriate properties from their clients.

Naturally, whilst this idea may be beneficial to the family unit as buying group it is often not beneficial to the activities of the marketer who must, therefore, be careful to allow for the gatekeeper's activities in pitching his product offering, perhaps by presenting his proposal in a number of alternative ways, to ensure that at least one may filter through to the buying unit.

Influencer

Any person or group which helps to shape another person's perception of evaluation of a product. For example, a disgruntled ex-customer might successfully defer a potential purchaser from picking up property details at the office where he or she felt badly treated. As we saw in the previous section a skilled sales-person at the point of sale might influence the way the buying group perceived the relative values of particular product attributes. A child may influence his parents not to consider properties in a new area because, 'I would have to go to a new school away from my friends'. A friend may influence a member of the group by passing on his own perceptions (valid or not) about product attributes – 'I wouldn't have a timber-framed house – remember those stories on the TV'.

It is worth restating here the high importance which attaches, particularly in a high risk, complex purchase decision, to personal testimony or opinions as opposed to 'managed' product information. The role of the local press as influencer, particularly in the information search phase, can be crucial in the buying decision.

Decision maker

A person or group who decides to purchase. The function of decision maker will vary considerably from group to group, depending upon the relative power structure and the allocation of responsibilities within the group. In car purchase, for example, the decision is likely to be male dominated. Similarly, in the purchase of a trousseau, the decision is likely to be female dominated.

Mention of dominance in the house purchase decision, however, tends to raise hackles on both sides. It is seen as both a financial decision (with a tendency to male dominance) and a lifestyle decision (with a tendency to female dominance).

There is little or no published research but discussions with experienced estate agents tends to suggest that any suggestion of male dominance in the decision is more illusory than real. The decision appears to be fundamental to aspirational lifestyle – and the men, whilst their opinions might be listened to on the periphery, do not really get a look in.

Buyers

There is often a confusion in the two roles, decision maker and buyer. The buyer is the person or group who actually implements the mechanics of the decision – the person who does the deal. Again, prediction of the actual person within the group can be tricky. Choice of buyer by the group will again depend upon inter-group dominance factors and there is some evidence that traditional roles are changing gradually. The role here, though, is relatively visible and whilst dependent upon social factors, is likely in most circumstances to remain male dominated.

Case study

An interesting example of differing role participation was seen in an estate agency staffed mainly by women. Although it was quite clear from the outset that the women performed very well in selling houses – almost always to other women as the decision makers – instructions remained slow until it was realised that the menfolk were predominantly the decision-makers as to which agent to use. The marketing images were adjusted to provide a greater empathy with the male decision-makers and instructions improved dramatically.

It is also useful here to consider the mechanics of the buying role which tends to be adversarial rather than consensual; stress is heightened through both size and complexity of the decision and the lack of confidence of most people in the role. Both of these factors tend to require the male to play his 'traditional' roles as the provider for and protector of his family.

User

Any person or group who participates in the use of the product. In the context of property this will include the resident family but may also include non-resident family members making occasional visits, family friends as visitors and tradesmen visiting for specific purposes. Clearly the influence of their respective views as users will relate to the circumstances of use. The window cleaner who refuses the task of window cleaning on the grounds of excessive danger from the glass conservatory under the bedroom windows creates considerable problems for the property owner and if such a view were considered prior to purchase, might significantly influence both the purchase decision and the decision process.

Consumer perception and behaviour

We have several times in Chapters 1 and 2 referred to the 'buyer's perception' of product offerings and contrasted this to the 'seller's perception'. That they tend to be different is easy to demonstrate – and this difference in perception often leads to confusion in interpreting the various images provided to consumers by marketers.

For example – to a person of 5'1" anyone over 5'6" would be perceived as tall. To someone of 6'0" anyone under 5'8" would be perceived as short. In this example there is a clear absolute difference in perception. Those of 5'7" and 5'8" are seen in diametrically opposite terms. But there are shades of this difference outside the parameters which are grey areas. Clearly there is a problem for communicators and their audiences!

Similarly, different people will behave in different ways relating to messages or ideas fed to them. For example, one person may be excited and motivated to purchase by the racy image of a 'hot hatch'. Another may see the same image as 'flashy' and superficial and be repelled by it.

What sort of factors affect the way that a consumer perceives product messages and the way that he behaves in a buying situation?

There is, by now, an enormous body of literature and research which examines aspects of consumer perception and behaviour. Not surprisingly much of it conflicts as different studies yield different results. There are, nevertheless, identifiable influences which can be seen to point consumers in particular directions, often on a scale large enough to be recognisable and approachable by marketers.

This is the basis of market segmentation, which seeks to break markets down into target sectors with recognisable consumption patterns.

In Chapter 1 we saw that consumer markets are segmented into geographical, demographic, psychographic and behaviouristic groupings. We should now seek a more detailed understanding of why consumers should behave differently within their groupings.

The buying patterns and activities of any individual consumer are shaped by a unique combination of factors. These relate to his upbringing, his education, self-image – a host of interactions. These interactions are best identified as a series of layers, much like onion rings. As one is peeled off so others are uncovered, each shaped by what has gone before and shaping the ones that follow.

These factors can be classified under a series of headings:

- Cultural
- Social
- Personal
- Psychological

Culture
By far the most important factor which determines a person's buying behaviour is the culture in which he or she lives. At its most basic, the buying habits of a person who lives in a drainage pipe on the approach to Bombay airport are going to be drastically different from those of a high earning, free spending city 'Yuppie'. On the one hand the culture is one of basic survival, on the other, one of survival at a materially different base point.

Case Study

Hong Kong RICS students were shown photographs of a country cottage and asked to suggest a method of sale, giving reasons. None of them picked auction and were clearly mystified when this was suggested. They could not relate to the UK desire for out- of-town living when their whole cultural base was geared to city dwelling – only the peasants lived in the country.

The culture in which we live determines the base points, the ground rules, for the way we live – and it is upon these ground rules that we build our patterns of consumption.

Sub-culture
The overall culture of our environment is often modified by sub- cultures. Within the UK is to be found a variety of clear sub- cultures – racial groupings, religious groupings, nationality groupings. These tend to set their own internal standards of behaviour and enforce them in subtle and exclusive ways. Their behaviour standards, in turn, lead to identifiable buying patterns – Kosher and Halal butchers, for example, cater to very specific identifiable sub-cultures as do synagogues and mosques.

Social class
It appears to be a basic human trait that societies exhibit a class structure. Such structures are readily identifiable within the UK as a whole and clear sub-structures exist within the identifiable sub-cultures. In many cases the maintenance of overt class structures implies distinguishable spending patterns. It is worth mentioning, at this point, that social class, even in the inherently conservative UK, is not a fixed situation. There is continual movement between classes and, whilst social class is, itself, used as an indicator of buying behaviour, there are some grounds for suggesting that the class-moving group and the pressure to move between groups may also be a significant indication.

Social factors
Human beings are social animals and their behaviours, therefore, tend to confirm patterns acceptable to others within their immediate environments. We need, therefore, to examine the broad mechanisms that signal the rules for conforming as it is these mechanisms and signals that can be influenced by the thinking marketer.

Reference groups

Social influences are exercised through the mechanisms of reference groups. A reference group is any grouping to which a consumer relates for social norms and for guidance as to the propriety or otherwise of a purchase. The influence exercised by reference groups is very strong on the consumer and it is essential for marketers to recognise both the existence and the potential effect of such groupings.

Reference groups can be further analysed as primary groups and secondary groups. Primary groups are direct, face-to-face groupings such as family, friends, work-mates, local church etc. Secondary groups would include professional associations, trade unions, WI, school old pupil's associations, Rotary, Lions etc. Generally these groups would have a much wider membership and tend to exercise impersonal communication and control channels. Groups to which consumers belong are called affiliative groups, those to which the consumers would like to belong, aspirational groups, and those which positively repel in some way, dissociative groups. For example, few Rotarians would wish to be know as Hell's Angels and probably vice versa.

Very little research data is available into the effects of reference groups upon property decision making but most practitioners can readily recall instances where there appears to be group influence.

Case study

Whilst working in the steel industry in Cardiff in the early 1970s the author decided to live in the country rather than in town because he did not want his children to grow up believing that milk came out of bottles. The reactions of a city-based peer group were very negative and disbelieving, in some cases almost violently so. The decision was outside the group's norm and served to reinforce their perception of the author (working at that time in computers and therefore already perceived as different) as a non-conformist. It did not stop the decision being taken but it certainly made things more difficult!

It is also probable that the influence of aspirational groups to the property buying decision is very pronounced. Experience suggests that the buying decision relates to an aspirational lifestyle for the family group. The group is likely, therefore, to be heavily influenced by its perceptions of the benefits of lifestyles to which it would like to belong. Indeed the strength of aspiration – as suggested in the case study above – is such that the consumer is likely to disregard criticism from his/her current affiliative group – probably on the grounds that this grouping is becoming a dissociative group – changing the ground rules completely.

In this context think of the advertising campaigns run by Barratt Homes and Wimpey Homes where the opportunity of joining aspirational groupings is subtly suggested.

Family groupings

Family groupings have similar effects upon perception. They are particularly important in the formation of the consumer's underlying relationships with the world, in particular attitudes towards culture, sub-culture, general morality and politics. In combination with school and other educational groupings there is also a considerable impact upon problem-solving weightings which influence decision making methods and bases for aspiration.

Personal factors

The buying needs and patterns of a consumer will be affected by a variety of personal factors.

Age and life cycle stage

Young married couples buy small houses 'ideal for first-time buyer'. They also buy washing machines, tumble driers, cookers and a host of similar 'first-time' purchases for the home. They are clearly perceived as an important segmented market and property professionals are well aware of this. In recent years demographic changes have meant a dramatic increase in the number of senior citizens. Catering for this increase has led to the development of sheltered housing schemes targeted specifically to the needs of an ageing population.

The human animal passes through a variety of life cycle changes, from childhood to the grave, and exhibits considerable – and well documented – change in consumption patterns at each point in the cycle.

Occupation

An acquaintance (self-employed) recently commented that it costs the average employed person in a white collar occupation anything up to 20 per cent of gross income just to keep the job. In other words pursuit of a particular occupation tends to imply not only a standard of living but also the parameters within which that standard of living can be enjoyed. Few social groupings tolerate more than a token maverick – the majority must conform. The young bank manager is expected to be mobile, get involved with his peers in the professional community, be personable and available. He is likely, therefore, to have housing needs that allow these criteria to be met and the 'executive ghetto' estates – with an 'executive' company car in the drive plus a 'latest model' second car for the (growing) family, fair sized garden, double glazing, luxury kitchen, dinner party circuit, social concern for the (less privileged) local village environment plus the baby sitting circle and well publicised local playgroup fits the bill very well. (New homes marketers are well in tune with the needs imposed by people's occupations – particularly where a ready and valuable market can be identified.)

Economic circumstances

Age and life cycle and occupation are identifiable factors which impose fundamental boundaries upon purchasing choice. They are, however, very much modified by the economic circumstances within which individual consumers find themselves. Clearly, within a grouping of apparently similar consumers there will be wide variations in gross incomes and in both the proportion and distribution of disposable incomes. Size of family, availability of inherited capital, self-image choices – a host of factors come into play.

Lifestyle

The picture is further complicated by freedom of choice. Pressures to conform pile up on an individual almost from the moment of birth. School, family, friends, workmates, union colleagues, ideas gleaned from books or other media all exercise some degree of attraction or coercion over a person, often pulling in competing directions. The balance achieved by a person within these pressures is expressed in his lifestyle.

The measurement of lifestyles relates to an individual's balance of preference between activities, interest and opinions coupled with his demographic profile (age, occupation etc.) and is known as the science of psychographics. Various researchers have identified a range of lifestyle classifications, perhaps the best known of which is the VALS (values and life styles) classification developed by Arnold Mitchell in 1983. These were further synthesised in to five groupings by William Meyers (*The Image Makers*).

These groupings suggest areas of possible market segmentation. For example, there is a clear targeting of the 'Yuppie' products of the late l980s towards those who would be seen to achieve – the value of success is measured by its external trappings – the XR3i and the Filofax being perhaps the prime examples. In the same way the small country house market tends to relate to the highly conservative English belonger – identified at one time as the Young Fogy – recognisable by the tweed jacket, cavalry twills, Barbour, green wellies and Range Rover – all products aimed specifically at his important market segment.

Personality

It would be very helpful if everyone in the categories so far identified behaved predictably, the marketer's job would be made much easier.

Unfortunately they do not – and the reason is that each individual's personality relates to the specific factors, chemical, genealogical and environmental that have shaped its development. This is further complicated by the fact that each individual has a 'self-image' of both what or whom the individual would like to be. Quite clearly the existence of differing personalities, even within an outwardly similar grouping of people, will lead to differing behaviour, making it, at the least, difficult to predict overall behaviour patterns with specific subsets of the group.

Psychology

From the world of psychology come four elements which are fundamental to the marketer. These are perception, learning, motivation and attitudes.

Perception

We all see the world through different eyes – and through different ears, noses and taste buds. Having seen the world we react to what we see in different ways – dependent on what our other senses tell us, what we already know, our personality and our response to all the other factors which we have considered above. Perception is the process which allows us to make sense (in our own terms) of the world around us and of the various stimuli provided by that world. It is not surprising, therefore that we not only 'see things differently' but that we do not always see everything that happens to us. The typical result of 'seeing things differently' or individual perceptions, is that most arguments between people, particularly violent arguments, tend to involve the two protagonists actually saying exactly the same thing but not 'hearing' what the other says – or at least not recognising that the other is actually agreeing but in different words.

Estate agents will readily recognise that perception of their function differs dramatically from person to person and also from group to group and this perception is shaped by a variety of previous experiences, the media, Auntie Mary and so on. Some, who may perceive the agent as a necessary evil, spend their time arguing about fees, complain at the drop of a hat – and often end up with a less than perfect job which reinforces their original prejudice. Others perceive the agent as honest and professional, there to assist in a difficult area of life – and receive a service to match. Some interesting aspects of perception are relevant to marketers.

- Perception is unique. As mentioned above no two people perceive a situation in exactly the same manner. To take the most obvious, their viewpoints are physically different. They stand in different places. They perceive from different standpoints. No two consumers, therefore, will behave in exactly the same way. Every kitchen salesman knows that one man's luxury fitted kitchen is someone else's nightmare. A friend of mine recently bought a house with a beautifully fitted kitchen then ripped it out and replaced it with one of a different colour. (The same friend returned a brand new Rolls-Royce bought for him as a present by his wife – it was the wrong colour!) Every salesman knows that the clinching factors in a deal vary from person to person – and takes great pains to find out exactly what these factors might be.

- Perception is selective. We see what we want to see. It has been estimated that the average person is exposed to over 300 commercial advertisements per day. How many do we see or remember? At the same time we are subjected to literally millions of stimuli, voices, perfumes, noises, light and shade, written words, pictures – the list is endless. Perception, as we have seen, makes sense of these stimuli; but to do so it has to be selective. The vast majority of stimuli are analysed at a superficial level – screened, if you like – and only those judged by the unconscious mind to be of interest to the individual are allowed through into the conscious mind. That does not mean that they have not been seen, they are simply suppressed.

It is worth mentioning at this point that it is to this subconscious area that subliminal advertising claims to aim. Claims that consumers are being unfairly manipulated by such advertising continue to surface but recent research suggests that the claimed effects are, in fact, illusory.

Kotler identifies three consequences of selective exposure upon perception. These are:

(1) 'People are more likely to notice stimuli that relate to current needs.' Earlier in this chapter we identified the increased susceptibility to advertising that our young couple would experience when they entered a stage of information search. People looking for offices do not normally notice advertisements for factory space – the advertisement is screened out by the perception process;

(2) 'People are more likely to notice stimuli that they expect.' Our young couple shopping at Dixon's would not expect to find property details there – and might not notice them if they were shopping for a camera even though they were in a state of active information search. In a walkround showroom a property placed in the 'wrong' price range becomes almost invisible – even to the shelf filler who has 'lost' it.

(3) 'People are more likely to notice stimuli that deviate a lot from the normal.' A 4-bedroomed house stands out amongst 2- bedroomed houses for the first-time buyer. A small price reduction does not catch the eye like a large one.

The practical implications of this for marketers are in promotion and we will return to them in other areas of the book.

- Perception can distort. As we have seen perception is both subjective and unique. It is an attempt by the mind to impose order on a large variety of information being received by a variety of senses. It is not surprising, therefore, that the mind tries to make sense of information by relating it to what is already known. The effect of this is that there is a tendency for information received about a topic to be moulded or twisted so that it fits with information already held in the mind and relating to that topic. For example, in a debate on estate agency which gives two sides to the arguments there will be a tendency for a listener to be reinforced in his preconceived ideas by the data provided and to discard any information which conflicts.

  An interesting example of this is the debate over water privatisation. If there is already a preconception that privatisation means profit and profit means minimal expenditure or lower standards for the consumer then any debate on water privatisation will tend to pick up the existing preconceptions and reinforce the idea that privatisation means lowered standards of water hygiene.

- Perception can discard. We saw earlier that not all data passing the senses gets transmitted into the conscious mind. In a similar way the mind will discard information that it does not particularly want to keep. Everyone has experienced learning problems at school or in their professional life. The mind tends only to remember what it – often at a subconscious level – considers important.

In a nutshell, then, perception can be a major enemy for the marketer. Even if his image, so carefully planned, manages to penetrate the screens set up to avoid overloads it is very likely to be distorted and/or quickly forgotten – a problem indeed!

There is a further problem. Because of the factors already discussed perception tends to be inherently unstable, it will vary with the state of mind of the perceivers and with the circumstances under which the message is received. Little is known about stability although some research suggests that perception of frequently purchased products tends to be relatively stable. It is interesting that the stable perception of estate agency as being a necessary but undesirable evil, one step above motor traders in the commercial demonology, relates to the constant repetition of 'knocking stories' in the popular press, thus making it very difficult to alter through conventional promotional techniques.

Learning

Learning has been defined as 'the more or less permanent acquisition of tendencies to behave in particular ways in response to particular situations or repeated stimuli'. An enormous body of literature has built up over the years which attempts to describe the processes of learning. In more recent years there has been a concerted effort to relate these processes to the activities of the consumer but much remains to be learned as only a small proportion of the basic literature and research is directed at consumer activity.

It is more helpful at this stage to consider some of the effects that learning has upon consumer reactions than to review the basic literature – a study of a lifetime. I propose only to suggest some areas which may have relevance to marketers in the property profession.

Zaltman and Wallendorf identify the principal variables which appear to relate to learning as Stimulus, Drive, Incentive and Habit. Each of these is relevant to consumer activities and we shall consider each in turn.

Stimulus
A stimulus is anything that makes something else happen or begin to happen. For example, noticing a large pile of washing-up on the draining board is often a cue to pick up a cloth, dry the lot and put it away. This activity often leads to a reward – 'thank you for doing that'. Failure to perform the activity can lead to an unpleasant experience 'thank you for not doing the wiping up – I work my fingers to the bone, you just sit there and don't even notice ...', which might be sufficient to ensure that next time that stimulus occurs, the appropriate action will be taken.

This is the base point from which theories related to stimuli and activities develop. Pavlov's dogs pressed the right button – they got a reward, they pressed the wrong button – an electric shock. Positive and negative reinforcement of their response to a stimulus – the bell ringing. From this base springs a large quantity of variations and modifications. Pavlov and the early experimenters thought that all learning activity could be explained in terms of reflex actions – and that these reflex actions could be 'taught' or 'conditioned'. Later experiments became aware of broader implications. Actions were not simply automatic. Courses of action could be inferred from surroundings.

Stimuli need not be specific. A stimulus similar to the original will produce similar responses. This is known as generalisation and has some interesting effects for the marketer. Many are upset to think that their carefully planned images might actually help a competitor. Yet this may well happen – particularly where the product offered and the stimuli used in promotion are similar. Fortunately, as in most things, nature provides checks and balances. Properly applied stimuli can be used to discriminate rather than generalise if their reward structures are carefully organised.

Comparative advertising, which tends both to change behaviour and be memorable, uses both generalisation and discrimination in applying its messages.

A stimulus need not be primary. It can act as a secondary reinforcer to another stimulus. For example, a housebuyer wants to buy a home. In doing so he will very likely come into contact with an estate agent – or at least with an estate agent's promotional activities. The estate agent here acts as a secondary stimulus. If the customer has a bad experience with the agent he is unlikely to go there again, whatever the other attractions of the property which might have interested him.

Remember that consumers, particularly in the world of property where they are almost always involved in relatively complex decision making, are subject to a wide variety of stimuli. The property marketer must, therefore, be aware that different stimuli have differing weights of importance to the consumer and they operate, therefore, with different strengths. The level of contrast between different stimuli is, therefore, very important. It is also worth remembering that the stronger the initial stimulus, the greater must be the difference between the initial stimulus and a subsequent stimulus for this difference to have an effect on the consumer.

How many times has a negotiator, listening to a customer who has

a) looked at several houses with him;
b) spent several hours in his car;
c) looked at 20 or 30 sets of details;

heard the words 'Which estate agents are you, then?' and wondered why?

His product (the estate agency) was not sufficiently differentiated and was, in any case, subservient to the product under consideration – different homes.

Let us return to the case study at the beginning. The stimuli were differentiated clearly, they were consistent – and they were clearly projected. They achieved their effect – and in doing so made it almost impossible for their competitors to use similar stimuli without succeeding in reinforcing the original images to the benefit of Parkhursts'.

Drive

Any basic motivating force acting within an individual can be termed a drive. Learning theory suggests, quite simply, that the greater the drive to learn, the greater the chance of learning. In marketing terms this is the basis for the idea that once a person enters a state of active information search (that is, they decide that they would like to consider the purchase of a home) they show an increased susceptibility to marketing images, persuasion and general information related to the topic. The practical implications of this have already been discussed.

Incentive

In the discussion of stimuli we touched upon the application of incentives to reinforce the effects of the stimuli. Pavlov's dogs received a reward if they pressed the right button. They also received a disincentive – an electric shock – if they pressed the wrong one. People react in much the same way.

Marketers have used incentive in both obvious and subtle ways. Perhaps the most obvious is the price discount for quick settlement. Estate agents, and many others, have used the '14 days free holiday accommodation' vouchers provided free to those who sign up for sole agencies for a fixed period. Slightly less obvious, and closer to the borderline of professional acceptability, is the 'quid pro quo' arrangement often offered to solicitors and other professional advisers in respect of mutual introductions. The more covert use of incentive lies in the promise of some intangible benefit if the product is used. Examples here are the 'Wimpey Welcome Home' – 'You too could enjoy this desirable lifestyle', and the promise of relative security offered by alarm systems for the elderly.

Habit

We are all, to a greater or lesser extent, creatures of habit. Once we establish a pattern of activity we are difficult to shift into an alternative. Even if the habit does get broken – say by a competitor managing to establish a foothold in a simple activity, for example, the one-off sale of a probate property on behalf of a solicitor's client – the habit is relatively easy to re-establish by the firm which the solicitor habitually used. A habit, once learned, is hard to break and easy to start again – ask any smoker (or ex-smoker). A marketer of professional services, therefore, must be aware of this and seek to establish the use of his firm's services as a matter of habit with his clients. Once this is established his firm, whilst not totally immune to competition, is in a far better condition to deal with it (and to win back the occasional errant client).

A look with open eyes at the nature of the professional property services market supports this view. Firms pay great attention to establishing ongoing relationships with clients and potential clients. The key factor for success within the business is contacts. For contacts read 'habitual relationships'.

Motivation

Before any conscious human activity can take place the person involved has to be motivated to undertake that activity. What is motivation? Motivation is the force that drives a person to satisfy a need (a state of felt deprivation). The greater the need, the greater the motivation to satisfy it.

We touched upon needs earlier in this chapter and referred to Maslow's Hierarchy of Needs as an attempt to identify them within a human context. This, however, is not the end of the story. There are a variety of theories which relate to needs in man and the explanation of these theories forms a body of research in its own right. Early research tended to polarise between needs analysis as suggested by Maslow and concealed needs as suggested by Freud. A leading exponent of Freudian analysis in marketing problems was Dr Ernest Dichter whose research led, indirectly to publication of *The Hidden Persuaders* by Vance Packard (1957); a journalist's exposé of the frightening new tools which were supposedly becoming available to marketers.

The problem with Freudian research – which seeks to express consumer motivation in terms of more or less sexually related desires and repressions – is that of interpretation. This is often as much a product of the quality of the researcher's imagination as of testable results and can easily arrive at conclusions which may be, to say the least, bizarre.

– Customers resist prunes because wrinkles remind them of old age.

Conversely, another analyst's view was that

– People do not wish to risk the laxative quality of the prune.

The problem here is that both may be right, both may be wrong, either may be right or wrong and nobody can actually prove the statements anyway.

This is not to suggest that motivational research is of no value. Far from it; it may often produce insights, instantly recognisable as sensible, which can be of great value in product design and promotion.

Maslow's theory is simpler to deal with and suggests approaches to thinking about products and promotion which can be readily used by the marketer.

Maslow suggests that human beings have a hierarchy of needs, ranging from the most basic – hunger, thirst – to the most ethereal – self-actualisation! He also suggests that satisfaction of these needs follows a hierarchy. Once basic needs are satisfied needs at the next level of the hierarchy become urgent and their urgency increases the motivation to satisfy them.

One of the more interesting ideas contained within Maslow's theory is the thought that human needs are never exhausted. As a low order need is satisfied – e.g. thirst is slaked – so the nature of the need translates into a higher order – consumption of tea with its social implications replaces the need to satisfy basic thirst with water.

In the UK and US environment the majority of low order needs are, generally, satisfied. It is not surprising, therefore, that product marketing images tend to relate to the satisfaction of middle or high order needs.

Once again the 'Wimpey Welcome Home' is an example of an appeal, not to the basic need for shelter, solved long ago as a problem within the UK culture, but to the much higher level needs for social status, belonging, family and self-approval – perhaps with an implied appeal to the very high level of self- actualisation (a warm house allows you to make the most of yourself).

In looking at how a need translates itself into motivation to take action it is important to consider the intensity of the need. Clearly, the more intense the deprivation felt, the greater the drive is likely to be to satisfy the need. Unfortunately, this does not translate directly into motivation which must allow for the effects, often competing but sometimes complementary, of other unsatisfied needs. A person has limited resources to put to the relief of needs. His motivation to satisfy any particular need will relate to his personal assessment of the relative balance of needs at any particular time.

This introduces a further interesting idea for marketers. Needs can be subdivided, for the individual, into central needs and peripheral needs.

- Central needs: are the basic, fundamental needs identified by Maslow; hunger, thirst, security, belonginess, status, self- expression.
- Peripheral needs: are the preferences for alternative methods of satisfying these central needs.

This helps to make some progress towards understanding motivation. Motivation arises from the balance of competition between central needs as modified by the balance of preferences for solving competitions between peripheral needs.

What sort of competition can take place between these needs and how might competitions be resolved? Central needs tend to be at the heart of the idea of the triangle. They also tend to be at the heart of a person's ability to live. A need to drink, whilst it may be satisfied by a number of types of drink, is nevertheless a fundamental need. If it is not satisfied then sooner or later the person will die. Clearly, therefore, it is very important to survival and generates a correspondingly high motivation to satisfy it. Similarly, whilst social status is very important to the individual who is well fed and watered, feels relatively safe, is well able to propagate the species and is well accepted as a part of his family, the need for status would cut little ice in a life-threatening situation. Even lifelong subscribers to private medical schemes are happy to accept the services of a faith healer when conventional medicine fails to help.

Logic suggests, therefore, that the closer a need is towards the survival level, the stronger that need will be in its ability to create motivation. Logic also suggests that central needs – i.e. those basic to the human condition – tend to be mutually independent – i.e. satisfaction of one need is not a substitute for satisfaction of another. The basic needs still exist. For example, satisfaction of the need for food does not alter the existence of the need for water.

Peripheral needs, preferences for alternatives, are quite different. In particular they are preferences – that is, a choice between alternatives – so are, by definition, capable of substitution. Secondly, the allocation of preferences will vary considerably between individuals. Preference allocation will relate to learned factors, habit, environment, culture – all the things that we have previously discussed as being determinants in consumer perception. It is at this focal point of the person – development of motivation from preference competition – that these factors can be seen to interact.

This divergence between central and peripheral needs is of great interest to marketers as it allows researchers into consumer behaviour to isolate (hopefully) salient preferences within consumer groupings which can then be applied as reinforcement to appeals to basic central needs.

Again the 'Wimpey Welcome Home' appeals to central needs – shelter, family approval, reproduction of self-image/status – but reinforces these images through more subtle appeals to the peripheral needs – car type, executive suit, suitably personable and desirable wife (shades of the 'Stepford Wives'), warm colours glowing against a dark background – all of them reinforcing the wisdom and desirability of this model lifestyle.

Summary

Motivation, and its theories, is central to the development of ideas in modern marketing. Like many other psychological factors motivation itself cannot be measured. Only its effects are able to be seen.

Motivation arises from the pressure to satisfy needs. The more basic the need, the more pressing the drive to satisfy it. The more powerful the drive related to other drives at that moment, the greater is the motivation generated.

Needs can be separated into central needs and peripheral needs. Central needs tend to be independent in their actions. Peripheral needs shape the preferred methods of satisfying central needs and relate to a wide range of formative influences.

Whilst central needs form the basis of drives and motivation their satisfaction is modified by peripheral needs and it is to these peripheral needs and their satisfaction that marketers should and do turn their attention in their attempts to modify behaviour in favour of their products.

Attitude

The final area of psychological research of interest to the marketer concerns attitude. Market researchers pay great attention to establishing the attitude of potential purchasers towards their products. Attitude is perceived to have a bearing upon the likelihood of potential purchasers to actually proceed to purchase.

What is attitude? Attitude can be defined as 'a learned predisposition to respond in a consistently favourable or unfavourable manner with respect to a given object'. Key words in this definition are:

Learned – an attitude doesn't just happen. It evolves as the result of specific experience and can therefore be modified;

Predisposition to 'behave' – once an attitude has been formed it will influence its owner's responses, in a similar way whenever a similar situation arises;

Favourable or unfavourable – the attitude may be either positive or negative towards the object.

It should follow that, as an attitude exercises some control over responses, then a modification to behaviour will also follow. Unfortunately this doesn't always seem to be the case where buying behaviour is involved. Buying behaviour is probably too far removed from the attitude to be consistently predictable.

For example, an attitude (held by many people) that 'large companies do not provide as good or as personal a service as small companies' would not necessarily result in a house seller using a small agent rather than a national one. Similarly, a favourable attitude towards Mr Major as Prime Minister does not necessarily guarantee a vote for the Conservative Party any more than a favourable attitude towards Mr Kinnock would guarantee one for the Labour Party. Nevertheless it would certainly help!

And this is the important point. Whilst an attitude is not necessarily a guarantee of related action there is considerable evidence to suggest that the more strongly an attitude is held the more likely it is to be a reliable indicator of active behaviour. Marketers, therefore, strive to influence attitudes and to build up strong positive attitudes in favour of their offerings.

It is interesting to look at some of the reasons that attitude might not lead to behaviour changes.

Behaviour is a compromise: buying behaviour is often the result of compromises between alternative attitudes. For example our first-time buyer will learn, or have already learnt, a number of attitudes which are relevant to his purchase.

'I don't like the idea of negotiating with a professional' – might lead to a preference for a private deal;

'Solicitors charge far too much for conveyancing services' – might send him hot-foot to a licensed conveyancer, or in an extreme case to a DIY manual;

Timber-framed houses are a fire risk and can fall down through dry rot because of poor practices on the building site' (picked up years ago from the World in Action programme) – might lead to exclusion of any timber- framed houses from consideration;

'XYZ Estate Agents are tough to deal with' – might direct interest to the competition in a multiple agency situation;

'House prices normally increase every year' – might tip the scales between purchase and renting – even where recent experience (for the professional) suggests otherwise.

Clearly the decision to buy at all, the decision as to who to buy from, the decision as to which house to buy, are all compromises based on the relative strengths of the attitudes learned and strengthened during the buying process.

We will return again to the question of attitudes later where we look at promotional activities. Strategies for changing attitudes are clearly import-ant to marketers, nowhere more so that in property. The reader will readily appreciate the implications for the commercial property marketer. Here attitudes are not simply learned through experiences, but are often the result of conscious formal learning activity. An interesting example of this is found in the area of dilapidations as a professional discipline. General practice surveyors (who lack detailed knowledge of building technology) tend to see dilapidations as the province of the building surveyor, whose training considers technology in depth. Building surveyors, however, generally lack detailed training in the legal aspects of dilapidations and see the work as being more suited to the GP. The net effect is that either the work goes to a specialist or it gets done badly. Both surveyors have a learned attitude that is only partly adequate. Neither sees their own development as a high priority.

This leads to an interesting problem for the marketer. The human animal appears to prefer to maintain consistency in its beliefs and attitudes. This preference leads to the perceptual distortions discussed earlier in the chapter and these perceptual distortions tend to have the effect of reinforcing attitudes rather than promoting change.

As usual the marketer is up against it.

Conclusions

Within this chapter we have introduced some of the variables which affect the way that consumers approach and take purchase decisions. A vast body of consumer research now exists, much of it impenetrable and much of it apparently contradictory. What does come through very strongly is the complexity of factors affecting purchase behaviour. Property marketers often rely on experience, built up over a lifetime of activity within their chosen markets. Unfortunately they are not immune from the behavioural problems which affect their clients. Their attitudes are just as likely to be formed, moulded and reinforced by perceptual distortions as anyone else's. It is quite revealing that the major advances in consumer marketing of property products have, over the past 10 years, come from the private housebuilding sector rather than from the 'professionals'. There is little published research available into purchase behaviour within the property market and there is both great scope and need for such research to be done. In marketing, perhaps more than in any other discipline, knowledge – and the flair to use it properly – is power, and to the powerful go the rewards.

References and further reading

J. F. Engel, R. D. Blackwell and P. W. Miniard (1990), *Consumer Behaviour*, Dryden Press, Orlando, Florida

P. Kotler and G. Armstrong (1989), *Principles of Marketing*, 4th edition, Prentice-Hall International, pp. 4, 5, 132, 180

A.H. Maslow (1970), *Motivation and Personality*, 2nd edition, Harper & Row, New York, pp 80–106

W. Meyers (1985), *The Image Makers*, Orbis Publishing, London

A. Mitchell (1983), *The Nine American Lifestyles*, Macmillan Inc., New York

V. Packard (1970), *The Hidden Persuaders*, Penguin

G. Zaltman and M. Wallendorf (1979), *Consumer Behavior*, John Wiley & Sons.

4 Organisational Buying

Management Today recently ran a feature article which dealt with the benefits and problems of relocating firms from the high-cost South East of England to other parts of the country. Within the article they considered availability and costs of property, staff, benefit schemes and a range of other topics of specific interest to chief executive officers considering costs and benefits of corporate relocation.

Only one firm of property advisers took advertising or editorial space in that edition – regardless of the likelihood that its readers would be well motivated and quite possibly in an active information search mode whilst reading the issue.

This immediately raises some valid questions for the marketer dealing with commercial property and commercial agency.

a) Has the commercial property marketer become blinkered in his approach to promoting his services?

b) Has the commercial property market become so inbred that it fails to recognise creative opportunities outside its narrow sphere of inter-professional activity?

c) How much thought is given by commercial property marketers to the nature of commercial buying decision?

d) How close do they get to the 'real' decision makers – i.e. the ones who actually pay the money?

e) Has the apparent simplicity of dealing with other property professionals stifled the creativity which can open up new market opportunities?

f) Do corporate managements have an awareness of the competitive capability of the advisory sector of the property industry? Should they?

Introduction

It is always invidious, in considering any activity, to generalise from the specific and it may well be, of course, that the example referred to in the case study is an isolated one. That, however, should not deter the reader from asking the questions nor from trying to answer them. In discussing the nature of organisational buying decisions with student groups at all levels it becomes very clear that little or no concept exists that the world of property relates to the real world where organisations buy other kinds of asset – capital or consumable.

Yet it does – particularly in the areas where property is purchased as a means to a trading end (the value resides in its use value) and in the area where the services of property professionals are retained – whether for buying, selling, advising, valuing, surveying or for any of the multifarious activities offered by firms of commercial property specialists.

The purpose of this chapter is to examine the nature of organisational buying decisions, drawing on the ideas already projected in the previous chapter, so that a framework can be laid for the later consideration (in Chapter 5) of the activities of the commercial agent.

The nature of organisational buying

In money terms markets for organisational buying are much larger than those for private or consumer buying. There are, nevertheless, far fewer organisations than there are individuals. This means that

a) there tend to be less purchases by volume;
b) each purchase tends to be larger in cash terms.

In many organisations the sheer size of the purchase in cash terms tends to be intimidating to individuals. The purchase is larger than is met in a private capacity. Decisions tend to affect a wider range of other people, not all of whom will be under the direct control of the decision maker. As the decision may affect a range of people and functions it is probable that it will impinge upon areas where specialist considerations arise which are outside the specialist knowledge of the decision maker. Organisations being, by their nature, competitive environments, the decision maker is likely to feel vulnerable in both decision making ability and in the potential consequences which can spring from 'bad' decision making.

The practical effect of the size of decisions, complexity and need for specialist knowledge tends to be that decision making becomes more formalised and becomes spread throughout a number of people in the organisation. This multiple involvement and 'spread' effect has given rise to the identification of the group involved as a 'buying centre'.

In the previous chapter we have considered many of the factors which affect the buying decision for individual consumers. It is important to realise that although there are a number of factors which relate specifically to the activities of a buying centre, the buying centre is, itself, composed of individuals and that they, both individually and as a group, are still subject to the same perceptual influences that affect them as individuals.

The organisational buying process

Considerable research effort has been devoted over the years to identifying the stages in organisational purchase decision making. These are broadly similar to the stages found in consumer decision making but tend to be more clearly defined, as would be expected in the rather more rigid structures needed to run a business and to share responsibility and expertise.

The number of stages identified vary from researcher to researcher depending principally on the researcher's viewpoint and specialist interest but it is reasonable to take an amalgam of the stages identified and look further into these.

Problem recognition

- establish objectives and specifications
- identify vendors and obtain bids
- evaluate proposals and choose supplier
- purchase the product
- evaluate supplier and product post-purchase

Every purchase begins with the recognition of a problem or need. Organisational decisions are no different in this respect. There are simply more potential points at which the problem or need can be identified. In property terms these can range from the operational need for more space, different space or simply more modern space through to the sophisticated needs of the investor/manager for a new profit-earning vehicle. It is important to note, however, that the process of identifying the need will vary considerably with the type of need identified.

It is also important to note that the type of person or department identifying the need will vary in different organisations and situations. For example, the process of identifying a need for more operational space in, say, an engineering workshop, could extend over a protracted period in which lack of space starts by being a nuisance – often overcome in the short term by reorganising work flows, workshop layout, production schedules etc. – then gradually becomes increasingly urgent until the harsh fact is faced by a hard-pressed production manager 'we need some more space!'.

Even at this point the solution may not be a foray into the property market. Short term solutions may include relocation to other parts of premises already owned. Eventually the penny drops. 'We have to move.'

In this situation the need will have been partially identified by a number of people within the organisation. The production foremen will have experienced problems, the production manager will have lost sleep, operatives may have started leaving thus bringing in the personnel manager. Eventually the problem will have exercised the minds of senior management faced with continual interruptions to delivery schedules, even in the worst cases leading to a loss of orders or a loss of capacity to keep up with the level of potential orders available. None of these people, it should be mentioned, are likely to be property professionals. The realisation will have evolved through a combination of irritants. No wonder that in many cases the decision is shelved until it is almost too late to avoid serious financial losses.

It is easy to see how a similar proliferation of participants might arise in the decision to seek alternative or additional retail premises. This could arise from a local shop manager spotting a gap in the local market, from a regional manager 'Managing by walking around', formally through a market research study, or simply through the managing director being unable to shop in his own local High Street. From whichever source the result is likely to be the same – a wide range of people involved.

Expressing this idea in more formal terms, the organisation is subjected to pressures on a number of fronts. Economic situations change. Local demographics change. Technology changes. People change together with their ideas. All or any of these factors can affect the balance of profitability for a company and for the many alternative courses of action open to it.

So far we have dealt with recognition of a problem or need arising from within the company. It should not be forgotten that the onlooker can often see most of the game and that the initial clues that lead to recognition of a problem can arise from outside sources. A passing rep, can often alert a company to new horizons, sparking off ideas which can have far reaching effects. A casual visit to a competitor, or a chance word from a customer (particularly for those companies who actually listen to what their customers really have to say) can be the spur for a completely new business direction – and with it the need for a wide range of new products – property, technology, staff, office space etc.

Objectives and specifications

Once a basic need has been recognised, through whatever source and by whatever route, it must be satisfied. Maslow's triangle applies just as much to commercial organisations as it does to individuals. A spot, once itching, must be scratched.

Buyers and bids

A number of factors now become relevant. First, the size of the decision. Clearly there is a world of difference between satisfying the needs for supplies of toilet paper and for buying a new office building. The size of the decision, both in cash and complexity is different by several orders of magnitude. Decisions, as in the consumer sector, can be identified in terms which relate to these factors. The differences have been classified by Kotler as:

> **Straight rebuy** – where a product is regularly purchased and the general parameters of purchase are well known to the buyer;
>
> **Modified rebuy** – where the general parameters are known but where the buyer wants modifications to the product at a general level e.g. price, specific feature;
>
> **New task** – where the substance of the decision is outside the normal run of buying activity and where extensive search and evaluation is likely to be needed.

In the context of commercial property the buying activity will normally be 'new task' although purchase of investments or development opportunities by specialist companies could operate at a level rather nearer the modified re-buy.

The important point to notice in all of these classifications is that the basic process, although modified to suit the purchase's importance, remains the same.

In order to make progress towards satisfying the need, therefore, it must be clarified and, if possible, quantified so that its scope can be examined and related to the overall commercial objectives of the company. Input is needed from any sector of the business which might be affected by the decision.

For example, in our engineering works it would be shortsighted to rush off and buy just the exact amount of space that is needed to solve the immediate problem. Murphy's Law would ensure that if that approach were taken, the need for substantial additional space in the adjoining warehouse (which now cannot cope with all the output from the expanded production department) would become critical the moment that contracts were signed for the (inadequate) acquisition. Nobody does things like that – do they? As many people and functions that might be affected must be considered as is possible within the logistics of the organisation. If they are not specifically consulted, their needs, through the planning process, if one exists, or through the flair of the CEO and the perseverance of those who 'happen to get wind of things', must be taken into account. It is interesting to reflect on how stated needs become modified, often to the point where they become almost unrecognisable, in this part of the process. On a practical note, what a fruitful sphere of activity this period can be for the skilled creative marketer if he can only get himself involved early enough.

From this phase of activity emerges, in formal or informal guise, a specification of what the company believes would best fit its needs (now modified to become wants). This specification may emerge as a formal document setting out the detailed technical specifications. More often, in the world of property, it emerges as a general statement of requirements – 'x'000 square feet or square metres of warehousing, minimum entrance height 10'(3 m), 3 mile (5 km) radius of junction 8 on the M4, easy access for articulated vehicles. Maximum price £y00 000.'

Evaluation of supplier

Identifying buyers and obtaining bids
In a conventional discussion of organisational buying this stage of the procedure refers to the activity of trawling through potential suppliers of a product, comparing their offerings and suppliers, then inviting bids for the supply of the product. Clearly this is a fairly straightforward task in respect of the toilet rolls but increases in scope and difficulty as the spectrum moves towards the new purchase problem.

It is tempting, and would be very easy, to think that this phase does not apply when considering property purchase. In fact, of course, nothing could be further from the truth. Not only is there the basic need to satisfy – the purchase of a property interest – but also, in many cases, the purchase of specialist advice from various property advisers. And this is where property marketers face their continual dichotomy. On the one hand they have to sell property on behalf of clients. On the other they want to sell their services to potential clients.

In addition, many commercial agents act on behalf of purchasers in the acquisition of property. In this situation, they are very likely to become the subject of supplier investigations and their offerings will be the object of considerable scrutiny, particularly in a 'new buy' situation. It is noticeable that within the past few years there has been a considerable increase in 'beauty contests' as part of the acquisition process for professional services – leading to a noticeable growth in demand for professional training in presentation skills and techniques.

Because of this it is worth considering at this point some of the formats under which quotations may be invited for business. These are often informal quotations, gained as part of an interview or presentation. They may, however, be more formal, requesting full tender particulars, either closed or open. Again at this point, it is worth highlighting the marketing opportunities available to a firm. Any purchase of services is risky. The risk relates to several factors – the perishability of service products, inseparability from the provider, lack of anything tangible to own if the thing goes wrong.

Purchasers, therefore, are likely to undergo increased stress when making this type of decision and the marketer or presenter should be aware of every opportunity for part delivery of the services or other activities which add credibility and reassurance to their offerings. (See Chapter 5 for a fuller discussion of this topic.)

It is also worth stressing the importance of contact with the purchaser during this phase by agents acting for vendors of property. An important function of the agent acting on behalf of a client in a purchase situation is to distance his client from the ministration of sales agents. This is fine as it keeps everything neat and tidy. Unfortunately it also shuts out the creative sales agent who may be able to add additional dimensions, both about the property itself and the local constraints surrounding it, either of which could be of great value to the purchaser if applied sympathetically and which could allow the agent to conclude a sale on behalf of his principal. The obvious danger is that the purchaser's agent, in safeguarding his client's interests by shielding him, could actually shut out relevant information simply through an inadequate knowledge of the client's full requirements. The selling agent should therefore make every effort to deal direct with purchasers rather than with any kind of middle man. We will return to this topic later when we discuss buying roles in property. It is not just opposing agents who shut out the real decision makers.

Once again it is necessary to look separately at the evaluation of suppliers and of property. Although there are superficial similarities there are considerable differences between the supply of services and the supply of tangible products. As we have already seen, the service does not exist until it is performed. It cannot be seen, touched or sampled until it takes place. A tangible product already exists. It can be experienced, sampled, seen, tested.

During the process of evaluation, in a service product, the purchaser has to determine the likely ability of the supplier to perform. In order to do this he has to make a range of assessments, many of them dependent upon the submission provided by the supplier. Because of the range of uncertainties this can be quite a difficult process and the supplier must make every effort to ensure that non-supportive information is not supplied inadvertently. As we have already mentioned, particular attention must be paid to the areas of the company that interact directly with the customer. The attitude, presentation and appearance, not just of the responsible representative, but also of receptionists, telephonists and other staff coming into contact with representatives of the purchasing company can all have a crucial impact on the decision process. If documentation is supplied, it is essential that it is clear, concise, unambiguous and that it supports the specific image that the company wishes to present to the customer – i.e. it must be tailored to meet the customer's needs, not to some general needs which may or may not be appropriate to the specific case.

In the case of the tangible product the supplier will be concerned not solely with the physical attributes of the product. He will also be concerned with a range of intangibles. The ability of the provider to service the product, the reputation of the company in providing accurate information about its product, the ability of the company to provide back-up in terms of training, installation and after sales service, will all be factors in the decision.

Property is a rather unusual product, even in its most tangible form. As we saw in Chapter 1 property products, whilst they are superficially tangible, actually have a high degree of intangibility in that they are bought in response to derived demand, i.e. they have no intrinsic value. The marketer must, therefore, be very clear as to the specific needs of the company making the purchase so that the matching benefits are presented to the decision making process.

The evaluation process itself will vary from company to company. In some the decision will be made in a committee environment, in others, by a single person. Whichever mode is adopted it is essential for the seller to try to get an understanding of both the type of process to be used and the identity of the participants to the decision. Many deals have been lost by concentrating on the wrong person, at the wrong time and giving the wrong cues or information.

Selection of a purchasing routine

In many larger companies there will be separate purchasing organisations. These will have specific procedures through which they can control the purchasing activity. Issue of purchase orders, requisitions on call-off orders, a range of alternatives. In even larger companies, particularly where production facilities are distributed geographically, further decisions come into play as to whether all purchases are handled centrally, whether some may be handled locally and so on.

Knowledge of these systems is important to the marketer as there is scope to influence procedures to the benefit of the vendor, particularly in the area of terms and payment controls and systems.

In the case of property purchases it is critical that the procedure for dealing with the sale is fully understood by both sides. In many cases the sale will be coordinated by property specialists, either in-house through a property department or externally by surveyors in private practice. The period between agreement and signature can be very fraught and repeated access to the effective decision maker may be required relatively frequently. It is essential to be aware of the latitude and authority for decision making enjoyed by the negotiators in this interim stage if maximum momentum in the progress of the sale is to be maintained. Many sales fall through at this point through the inability of the seller to communicate adequately with the effective decision maker.

Evaluation of a product and supplier

Once a product has been purchased, as in consumer markets, the purchaser is likely to question the wisdom of his decision (buyer's blues). In organisational markets this questioning often extends to formal appraisal of decision making. Purchases are readily accessible to such formal appraisal techniques. Fortunately for many suppliers, selective perception once again rears its head, this time generally in favour of the supplier.

As long as there is a reasonable correlation of expectation to performance the purchase decision maker is likely to distort minor (and sometimes even major) malfunctions to support the wisdom of his original decision.

Unfortunately (for the marketer), firms and managements are well aware of this phenomenon and review tends to be undertaken by a third party with no axe to grind. This means that evaluation, particularly in larger firms and in the better run small firms, is likely to be relatively rigorous.

The performance of property, both as an operative unit and as an investment or development, is measurable through a range of techniques, most of them well documented within the property-related professional literature and the property professional is trained and experienced in doing this. Rather less easily measurable, except in the obvious 'achievement/no achievement' terms, is the performance of professional advisors. How does an observer measure whether an acquisition was made on the most favourable terms available? The parameters of measurement are highly complex and not susceptible to standard criteria. The property professional, therefore, is likely to be judged on those intangibles once again. Was the representative helpful/friendly/available/good at ringing back/knowledge-able/personable ... all those things that we try to be but don't necessarily manage deliberately. Measurement in these intangible areas is likely to be highly subjective so the property professional must be constantly on the lookout for personality clashes, tendencies to be insular or inward looking and any other factors that might affect the personal relationships which build up during an assignment. Awareness of problems is 70 per cent of their solution. Clearly the professional should be aware of the likelihood of assessment and make an effort to retain contact with his client on a regular basis even after the job has been completed. In doing this he will readily become aware of any coolness creeping into a relationship which might give an early warning of adverse comment arising from the process and allow him to take corrective action before any real damage occurs which could torpedo his chances of being asked again.

The ultimate aim of any supplier is to achieve a loyalty to him, as a source, from the customer. The odds start in his favour, selective perception works for him, the emotional and often financial commitment made in the original purchase decision works for him, inertia works for him and often the sheer pressure of work in his customer's organisation works for him. Why then should any professional lose a client? But they do!

Participants and buying roles

In considering the consumer buying decision we identified a number of roles played by various participants within the life of the buying activity. These were:

- Initiator
- User
- Influencer
- Buyer
- Decider
- Gatekeeper

These roles operate in a similar manner within the organisational purchase decision and it is worth examining them a little further in this context.

Initiator

As we have already seen the decision to initiate property purchase or sale activity can arise from a variety of sources. In the case of retail, for example, this can range from a shop manager who requires extra space right through to a specific policy decision taken as part of a strategic business initiative at high level. It is important to identify the source of the initiative as this will often provide a great deal of useful information to the property professional, not least of which is an increased understanding of the degree of priority which may be given to the decision by the client or purchasing company. It is also important as the initiator of the decision is very likely to become its sponsor or champion within the company's decision making activity and may probably exercise considerable influence on the progress of the decision through the relevant corridors of power.

User

Property, as a corporate asset, has a relatively high profile. It can tie up large amounts of capital and its performance is likely to be closely monitored. It also exercises a considerable constraint upon those who have to use its facilities. Indeed the monitoring of property as an asset is the foundation stone for the discipline – so important to surveyors and other property professionals – of property management.

In order to get the best results from any asset it is essential that its

features are closely matched to the needs which led to the purchase of that asset. The importance of the user in influencing property decisions, therefore, cannot be overemphasised and every effort should be made to ensure that the needs of the user are adequately met.

This has important consequences for property advisors who should make themselves fully aware of operational constraints imposed by the user before they can sensibly advise on sale or acquisition matters. This, however, poses something of a problem. Property research tends to be concentrated into property related areas; yield, underlying demand, economic trends are regularly promulgated by the pundits but we hear rather less about workplace layout, external lighting for shift workers or constructional constraints imposed by the revolution in information technology.

Few surveyors have direct experience of retail activity, shop floor working or any of the other activities to which commercial property lends itself. Equally few go and ask the right questions of users who do have this experience. Small wonder that property professionals – surveyors, architects, managers – can be seen as remote and detached from the realities of commercial and industrial life.

Influencer

Yet in the final analysis the user of property often has a major influence in property acquisition. The surveyor who ignores this influence does so at his peril. An unsuccessful acquisition (unsuccessful in terms of the needs of its users, however successful in 'pure property' terms) is unlikely to generate further acquisition instructions. Similarly the surveyor acting in the sale of a property will achieve less than ideal results if he fails to establish clearly the potential use benefits of a property and to match these to the needs of potential purchasers.

Buyer

As we have seen above purchasing routines will vary from company to company and from situation to situation. Once again it is essential that the property professional is aware of the specific constraints that apply to his client in the specific situation if expensive mistakes and potential heartache is to be avoided. The assumption of a standard situation is often at the heart of a failure to communicate with the 'right' person at the 'right' time. This kind of failure can result in a deal going off or, perhaps less obviously but as importantly, to a loss of confidence between agent and client.

The professional does not take chances. He finds out the facts and ensures that the client is properly serviced – even if that takes a little longer. This kind of professional gets reinstructed – again and again.

Decider

In an organisational context it is often difficult to establish just who is the real decider in a transaction. This is partly a result of the need to spread responsibility, particularly in the relatively high value purchase decision which normally relates to property or property professionals. Once again, however, it is essential that the property professional gets to the heart of the matter and finds out precisely who will be making the relevant decision. It should always be remembered that people do not cease to be people just because they are at work, nor do managing directors or chief executive offices become any the less subject to consumer influences by virtue of their high office. They suffer like the rest of us from selective perception and are likely to perceive a purchase decision quite differently from the way that the professional would like.

It should also be remembered that, although a decision may be apparently taken by a committee, there will always be one individual with whom the buck stops and who has ultimate responsibility. This is the person to whom most attention should be paid and it is essential that he or she is correctly identified if a great deal of abortive work is to be avoided. Unfortunately, as we shall see below, it is not always easy to isolate the decision maker, and even if he can be identified, not always easy to get at him. Still, if it was easy we would all be millionaires, so that should not stop us trying.

Gatekeepers

We met the concept of the gatekeeper in the section on consumer purchase decisions but in the context of organisational buying, particularly in the property sector, it assumes a much greater importance. The idea of the gatekeeper is an integral part of an organisation's operational structure. The control of access to information also controls to a large extent the ability of people within that organisation to exercise operational freedoms. The gatekeeper function becomes part of the power system.

Gatekeepers operate at many levels, most of them to the detriment of external agencies (except in special circumstances as we shall see). Secretaries control access to the boss, engineers control the flow of information to purchasing agents, purchasing officers control the flow of information to engineers. The greater the ability to control information, the more chance there is of proscribing action.

Partly because of the complexity of property purchase, the practice has evolved of using specialist property professionals as agents for the purchase as well as for the sale of property. Not unnaturally these agencies act as gatekeepers over the supply of information to their principals and are likely to guard access to their principals as savagely as any mother shielding her baby from a hungry lion.

The road to decision makers is, effectively, blocked at every turning. The best selling agents overcome these blockages. The majority are happy to work within the constraints.

But that is not creative or active marketing – and it is not the way that skilled marketing consultants and marketing managers (which is what we are paid for) should act. We must be aware of the whereabouts of gatekeepers, the scope of their actions and we must evolve strategies and tactics for overcoming them in our marketing campaigns.

In our preceding discussion the impression has been given that gatekeepers are the bane of the property professional's life. This can often be the case for the reasons which we have discussed but there is also a powerful plus. Used to its full potential, the gatekeeper system can be a powerful asset to the professional by, effectively, locking out competition and strengthening existing power and influence bases.

We start with a considerable advantage. As we can already see, organisational buying is, itself, a potentially complex and stressful activity. It can also tend to be expensive in terms of manpower and the penalty effects of poor decisions. Once a satisfactory relationship within a buying situation has been created, therefore, there is a considerable and valuable investment for the company to protect and a corresponding reluctance to go through the whole thing again without compelling reasons.

This, of course, works to the considerable advantage of the 'sitting tenant' who is able to perform to a lower level than would normally be accepted for a 'new starter' yet retain instructions against a demonstrably superior performer. (Note – this is not meant to suggest that firms, once established, can afford to relax and worry less about the client's wishes, but it might help to explain some of those disappointing occasions when you 'know' that you are the best by miles but the dozy firm that's always 'done their business' carries right on doing it!)

This phenomenon, once appreciated, can be strengthened by ensuring that the client firm's internal gatekeeper system is kept well oiled and excludes potentially conflicting information and people to the mutual benefit of client and agent.

This is the battleground for the professional marketer to organisational buyers. It is hard to get in, but once you are in it is just as hard for someone else to get you out. Firms lose repeat instructions through their own inability to perform, not just professionally but also in the management of their marketing and their client relationships. (They also lose through changes of key personnel in the client company bringing with them their existing well-managed relationships from their previous employment – just make sure that 'your' gatekeepers can cope if this happens.)

Organisations and the world of property

A considerable body of research now exists into the way that organisations behave in a buying situation. Much of this is theoretical and attempts to identify the essence of what actually happens within organisations when they are faced with buying problems. The trouble with this research, from our point of view, is that it is too general in its application and we can, therefore, draw only tenuous conclusions from it. This is not to say that the research is unhelpful to us. Far from it – the basic research suggests a variety of avenues for further exploration within the industry.

Recent research has considered organisational buying as an interactive approach between buyers and sellers rather than as a purely internal activity with marginal external interruptions, stressing the idea that both marketers and purchasers are receptive to, and vary their behaviours according to, input from the other party. This is true within consumer markets to an extent but that extent is necessarily limited by the fragmentation of the consumer base and the sheer practical difficulties of obtaining a meaningful dialogue. In organisational markets the situation is very different. Purchases tend to be high volume, high value, repetitive and tend to generate an ongoing relationship between supplier and purchaser.

The property business is not unique in its interactions but it is unusual in that a large proportion of the time of its practitioners is involved with advising and participating in the acquisition and disposal of assets for its clients. Property professionals are thus involved in very close relationships with their client companies and assume roles which are both internal and external to them. It is worth considering further the effects of interaction within organisational purchasing in more detail within a property context.

Research identifies (Turnbull and Cunningham 1981) that

– Both buyers and sellers actively participate in the transaction. Each is therefore affected by the other's initiatives.
– Long term relationships tend to develop and these relationships base themselves increasingly upon mutual trust, built up over a long period.
– Interactions between the buyer and seller companies tend to operate at many levels, some of them formal and others informal. Interaction is not confined to formal 'buying/selling' departments.
– The participants to the relationship tend to become more involved with the maintenance of the relationship than with the mechanics of transactions.
– Over time, the various links forged tend to become institutionalised.

A brief review of the activities of the property business is sufficient to suggest, empirically, the fundamental validity of these propositions and on that basis we can consider some of the implications for property-related marketers.

Relations between property advisors and clients, whilst they are ongoing in the sense that business tends to repeat, tend not to be ongoing in the sense of a continuous dialogue. They tend, rather, to be episodic in that a purchase now might lead to a rent review in six month's time. The rent review might lead to a sale next year. The sale leads to further purchase, rent reviews, dilapidations and so on.

Each of these encounters, whilst apparently unconnected, leads to increased knowledge of the other's motivations, practices, processes and so on. In the same way each encounter, dealing as it almost invariably will with risk and uncertainty, tends to develop greater understanding of the other's mechanisms for dealing with individual and corporate stress and this, in a well managed relationship, leads to the almost imperceptible development of strategies for minimising these unpleasant effects. As a result a measure of mutual trust and confidence develops.

As time passes these strategies tend to become incorporated into the 'normal' way of dealing with each other and, as the individual participants progress through their organisations, the relationship becomes formalised. The obvious danger in this behaviour, of course, is that the individuals may change, leaving behind a set of routine responses that are no longer relevant or tailored to the needs of the current participants. In many cases, of course, the new individuals, recognising the value of long-established relationships at a corporate level, evolve updated strategies which modify the relationship to their revised mutual advantage.

The second danger to these established relationships is the effect of external change upon the parameters within which both parties have become used to operating. Failure of either party to appreciate mutual benefits from revised industry thinking can lead to strains, sometimes to the point where the parties part company. The purchaser seeks an alternative supplier more in tune with its needs and the supplier seeks purchasers that will be able to benefit more fully from its perceived increased abilities.

In recent years this process of structural change has been very evident in the property profession itself where the RICS has found it difficult, if not impossible, to come to terms with the new regime imposed upon a large section of its membership, firstly through court decisions increasing the power of consumers to seek accountability for negligent advice and secondly through commercial changes springing from the decisions of major financial institutions to enter the fields of residential and commercial estate agency. The latter change, indeed, has been so fundamental that the very basis of professional ethics for the chartered surveyor – once based on mutual protection but now having to take on board essentially different concepts of professionalism – are being questioned.

What does this all mean for the professional? It means that the professional firm, and in particular those responsible for marketing it, needs to pay a much closer and more informed attention to the nature of the agent/client relationship. It can no longer be left to chance and the hope that going to the right school/university/club will achieve the desired effects. They might – but it's risky. More risky than the sensible businessman will allow. These relationships must be identified, planned and managed with a clear aim in view.

Consumer industries manage their client relationships. The stars of the 1970s and 1980s pour enormous resources into this area of management. McDonald's – possibly the most seminal force in fast food retailing – concentrates on relationship management. In the US the control of physical layout, personnel policy, services provided and even raw materials purchase is enshrined in the franchise agreement. Tom Peters has reported that if an IBM rep loses an account (where equipment is normally placed on a rental basis) he automatically loses all commissions previously paid to him in respect of that equipment. That's a tough line – but IBM is synonymous with excellence in their business achievement and in its reputation for client relationships throughout the world.

Some of the estate agency chains are going down this route. The Prudential and Black Horse Agencies have well established training departments. Their objectives? Managing the agent/client relationship to mutual, and hence to corporate, advantage.

We will look further into the management of client relationships in a later chapter. For the present suffice it to say that the agent/client relationship is at the heart of most of our activities. We neglect its management at our peril.

References and further reading

P. Kotler and G. Armstrong (1989), *Principles of Marketing*, 4th edition, Prentice-Hall International pp. 171–2

Management Today (May 1989)

A.H. Maslow (1954), *Motivation and Personality*, Harper & Row, New York

T. Peters, *In Search of Excellence* (Audio tape – Secrets of Success), Hamlyn Books on Tape

P.N. Turnbull and M.T. Cunningham (1981), *International Marketing and Purchasing*, Macmillan Press, London

5 Service Management

Case study

Seated at my table in the local steak house I was approached by the waiter who asked 'How would you like your steak, Sir?

Answering immediately 'medium rare', it did not occur to me until I sat in my bath considering the general state of the universe that I had actually become part of the service management system which operated within that steak house.

The steak house could just as easily have presented me with a steak done to their particular specification. In some circumstances that might have been quite satisfactory. In this particular operation, however, they felt it important to involve me, as the customer, in a specific element of delivery of the service. In their particular service environment my involvement at this level was deemed to be an important element of the service which they wished to provide, and from which some of my enjoyment would be derived.

In other words they managed my involvement with the service delivery.

A few days later I received a plastic card from my bank. Under separate cover I received, also from my bank, a 'PIN' number. Accompanying both was an instruction leaflet that explained how I could use these two pieces of equipment to get money, at any time of day or night, from a 'hole in the wall'.

In this case my bank's function was to provide me with access to cash. Considering the expense of employing 'round the clock' cashiers they found a way to move some of the 'mechanical' aspects of delivering this service further into my (the customer's) domain. In doing this they

a) made the service more accessible to me;
b) improved my perception of their service.

By managing my involvement with the delivery of the service they added value to my experience of their service.

Yet I ended up doing more work in my interaction with the bank (the service provider) than I would have under the old system.

Both of the examples in the case study clearly identify the interactive roles of providers and receivers (suppliers and customers) in the contact areas of service products. They also identify the crucial nature of this interaction in defining the service itself at the point of delivery. In defining the crucial nature of the interaction the importance of managing it so that the desired perceptions are generated can be readily identified.

Within this chapter we consider further

the nature of service products;
the client's role in providing the service;
implications for winning and keeping clients;
quality;
some perceptions which relate to the client/supplier interface.

The nature of service products

We introduced in Chapter 2 the ideas that service products only differ from tangible consumer products in their balance of tangible and intangible product attributes. At the same time we identified that service products are, fundamentally

- Intangible – in the sense that they cannot be physically touched;
- Inseparable – the service exists only at the point of contact between supplier and receiver;
- Perishable – in the sense that they cannot be stored;
- Not heterogenous – in that the individual participants and their perceptions will be different every time the service is performed, however carefully managed;
- Not subject to change of ownership – the service is a one-off event. Once it has happened it is defunct so no change of ownership can occur.

Some implications which spring from these aspects are:

– a service cannot be patented. Aspects of the method of service delivery, particularly 'hard' images such as brand names, service agreements, franchise agreements may be copyright and therefore capable of a measure of protection but the actual service itself, existing as it does in such a restricted format, cannot be exactly replicated. There is, therefore, no protection available against attempts at replicating the service delivery system.

– a service cannot be stocked. The service only exists when it happens.

There is, therefore, by definition, only one of it and it does not exist in advance of its delivery. It cannot, therefore, be held in stock. This does not mean that aspects of it cannot be manipulated as if they were stock. There are many ways available in which participants to the service can be manoeuvred so that production factors can be applied as if they were, effectively, stock and some of these factors will be addressed below.

– a service cannot be sampled. The service only exists when it happens. Sampling can therefore only take place whilst the service is being delivered. This gives rise to a number of creative opportunities for the service manager and these will be explored further.

– a service cannot be precise. The interactions between supplier and recipient are extremely complex and are always individual. The extent of these interactions is unpredictable so a service can only be specified in general terms. The effect of this imprecision in specification is that whilst the service management system can be replicated, the individual service experience cannot be. There is always, therefore, a need for responsive interaction between people at the point of service delivery which, in effect, 'tunes' the service provided to the specific needs of the consumer or client.

It is worth, at this point, distinguishing between the service itself and the service delivery system within which the service is actually provided.

The service product

As we have already seen in Chapter 2 a product can be identified in terms of its core, tangible and augmenting factors. A service product can generally be described as a package of activities, all of which 'bundle' to provide the core benefit to the client.

For example, a residential agency has its mailing list, its computer systems, accompanied viewings, market appraisals etc. each of which is readily identifiable as an activity and which contributes to the core activity – finding a buyer. The total service provided is made up of a 'bundle' of individual activities.

It is this 'bundle' of activities which form the service which can be identified as a product. The environment within which this bundle of activities is delivered can be described as the service delivery system. This, however, can be further identified as the series of interactions between people, equipment and the client which define the total service experience.

It is important to realise at this point that the service delivery system is, in effect, akin to a manufacturing system in that it

a) produces the product required;
b) is capable of being managed;
c) is capable of being qualitatively assessed.

Hence the term 'service management' which applies specifically to management of the service delivery system which leads to production of the service product.

Client involvement

A key variable in the delivery of a service product is the activity of the client. We have seen above how the involvement of the client is a specific contributor to the delivery of the service itself. The degree of involvement, mode of involvement and expectations of the client significantly influence the client's perception of a second key variable, quality, and it is the client's admittedly subjective perception of quality that shapes his perception of value for money or satisfaction.

We should consider in more depth the scope for client involvement in the service delivery system in the light of its important contribution to such fundamental variables.

At what point might the client participate? Clearly the client participates at each point of direct interaction with the provider. The agency client participates in his interactions with the valuer, receptionists, partners, potential purchasers, specialist related advisers. He also participates, if only unilaterally, in his perception of the intangible augmenting factors, reassurance, arms-lengthing, club membership. Each of these contributions affect his experience of the service and are assessed by him in his review of the service quality which he experiences.

It is a truism when considering these interactions that the client's perception will always be shaped by them. The trick is to ensure that this perception corresponds as closely as possible to the perception that the service provider would like the client to receive. In other words every interaction – or as many as can be identified – should be carefully managed or the client will draw his own conclusions – possibly very different conclusions from those intended or favoured by the service provider. Management is about making things happen not letting them happen.

In this context it is worth repeating the old chestnut that 'it takes 12 pluses to balance 1 minus'. Some authorities think even more than that (if it's capable of being measured at all!).

Some examples

Two examples of client involvement were quoted at the beginning of this chapter. Others spring readily to mind illustrating a variety of degrees of involvement in the design of service delivery for different market segments.

Take self-service restaurants. Within this system the client participates directly not only in his choice of menu but also in the transfer of food and utensils from 'service point' to table. In university canteens this process extends to cleaning away used crockery and waste food once the meal is finished. This mode of service relates primarily to costs and the need for low cost meals. It also serves as an important indicator to the 'standard' of service – and this contributes to a perception of the meal as a utility function (filling a hunger gap) rather than as an event – an 'eating experience'.

(Note at this point that in writing the previous paragraph, and, I suspect, in reading it, there is a great temptation to imply 'quality' of service into the example. This temptation was, and should be, resisted. Quality is implied but there are a number of levels and types of quality to consider and we shall return to these later in the chapter. Suffice it for the present that the system implies a different core product.)

Contrast the self-service restaurant with the gourmet restaurant where the client participates in a different way altogether. Here the core product is very clearly the eating experience. Tableware, decor, standards of dress for the waiters, soft lights, background music, all set the scene. The client participates in his standards of dress, table behaviour, conversation and background knowledge and experiences.

Very difficult to manage? Yes, but there may be manageable elements.

Informed choice and education at the table from knowledgeable staff assist the client with decision making. Choice of the lobster living happily in its tank involves the client in the meal's preparation. Invitations to the kitchen to discuss nuances of the menu and its preparation with the chef widen the scope of the client's eating experience. Hostess systems for lone diners contribute to conversation. Informed proprietors make a point of chatting with their clients thus enhancing self-image and therefore enjoyment.

Once again the images conjured up suggest a standard of service and relate to the perception of quality received by the client. Again the use of the term 'quality' is potentially misleading and detracts from the precision of thought necessary to target the management of service delivery to the point where it makes a competitive difference.

The telephone system illustrates the idea of client involvement very clearly. At its heart the telephone system provides a means of voice communication between two remote parties. In its early days a connection was hand-wired and direct. As the concept spread so networks were set up, linked by operators who could identify individual subscribers and their contacts. As the networks spread so directories became necessary, originally scanned by telephone operators. These eventually became unwieldy and local directories were published 'for the use of subscribers'. At this point subscribers not only 'looked up the numbers they needed' but often dialled them direct – both direct examples of client participation in the system. How long before directories became re-centralised but with direct inter-rogation from client-based terminals – a sophistication of the client's involvement?

In this example, of course, there is a further level of client involvement. The client interacts directly with the hardware in the system, the actual telephone lines – as we all know a source of potential irritation when the line is not very clear. All these are indicators of 'quality' which affect the client's perception of the overall system.

Let us turn closer to home. In residential agency (where there have been significant attempts at making the delivery system more marketable) we find self-selection showrooms. The client participates directly in locating and choosing suitable properties from display racks, often 'managed' or directed by the display sequence of the properties or by similar cues.

In other offices clients are 'qualified' by negotiators trained to assist the client in identifying suitable properties through analysis of needs, and so on.

In both cases the client participates but in significantly different ways. Once again there tends to be an equation with 'quality' levels, particularly in the eyes of estate agents and again this equation can be seriously misleading.

At the extreme of client involvement is the activity of a client in showing prospective purchasers around his property. This can often be a critical activity, both to the likelihood of a potential sale and to the standards of service experienced by both client and potential purchaser, with all that this entails. Key areas repay management effort, yet little more than lip service is paid to managing the client's involvement by many agencies.

Quality and the client

A significant element in the client's perception of quality in the service product derives directly from his experiences within the service delivery system. This area will be explored in detail later in the chapter but it is relevant at this point to identify quality as a concept from the client's viewpoint. Quality can be both a subjective and an objective concept. At the objective level specific aspects of a product can be measured against objective yardsticks. For example, the time from instruction to sale agreed can be measured accurately and compared against the times achieved for other, similar transactions.

At the subjective level, however, quality is measured as a perception of the service experienced against a perception of the service expected. Clearly there is a wide range of potential for perception of each event, both yardstick and actual activity, to be influenced by a host of extraneous factors. There is, therefore, considerable potential for things to go badly wrong at this point.

There is a further complication in that quality can be perceived simultaneously at several levels. For example, the gourmet dinner, perceived as a specialised eating experience and, by association, high quality, can also be delivered badly, thus creating a perception of a low quality offering of a 'high quality' service.

Problems with the old perceptual difficulty of differing word meanings abound in this area making it even more important to pay close attention to the management of the client's experience to ensure that it corresponds as closely as possible with that intended by the provider.

Creating clients

A number of effects arise from the inherent nature of service products, most of which operate at an intangible level and which affect perceptions directly or indirectly. A service cannot be handled physically, it cannot be sampled, except in the most limited of terms, it cannot be stored or transferred from someone else. From the client's point of view the whole thing is decidedly incompatible at the point of choice.

Any purchase decision carries an element or elements of risk. The purchase decision for service products is one big risk. The client's purchase decision is based, fundamentally, in the elimination of risk (see Chapter 3). In order to win and keep clients, therefore, the service manager – and marketer – must be aware of the risk elements to the client and must devise methods of minimising decision making risks both as part of the product itself and, more importantly, as part of the product offering and promotion.

Key areas for minimising risk

So far as a client is concerned a company bears a marked resemblance to an iceberg. In other words, the bit that he sees represents a much larger bit that he does not see. He also does not know how much of it he cannot see and so long as he does not run into a submerged bit he is unlikely to be unduly concerned. (There is, however, the uncomfortable feeling that unless he makes an effort to identify it he might go the same way as the Titanic!)

From the company's point of view it is a matter of some sorrow that 90 per cent of the qualities it possesses in terms of expertise, experience, ability to add value, industry profile and all the other things it may treasure, are represented by a mere 10 per cent of its contact personnel – and this is on average! It is worth just reflecting that in some circumstances the whole company could be represented by the cleaner – or for some residential firms, the board man (who probably works for someone else!).

On this very limited range of contacts a client (in a high risk situation) will be basing a large proportion of his decision making relating to the possible use of that company's services. Whoever makes that contact had better get it right.

All potential contact personnel are signals to potential clients. Their dress, their appearance and most important of all their attitudes to clients are a visible representation of the company's attitudes. The company's attitudes shape client's perceptions.

This is a key area which needs to be carefully managed. How, we discuss below.

Contact

Every time a client interacts directly (or sometimes indirectly) with a person who represents the potential supplier (in the client's eyes) we have contact. More than any other single factor, contact – in the form of personal relationships – shapes perception. Each contact made by any person within a company with a client or potential client is 'dynamite'. Effects out of all proportion to the nature or importance of the original contact can ensue.

It is at this point of contact that delivery of the service (as perceived by the client) actually takes place. It is from this point of contact, therefore, that the client's perception of quality (and hence satisfaction and value for money) and service stems and it is from the client's perception of value for money that repeat business (or even payment for present business) arises.

Once again, this is a key area which needs to be carefully managed.

Service presentation
As the client tries to minimise risk in making his purchase decision he evaluates, both objectively and subjectively, a range of quality factors and indicators.

Nevertheless, however strong the indicators, he is left with a product that he cannot see, touch, feel, hear and can only experience once the services takes place. This, as we have seen, is likely to make him uncomfortable. This lack of comfort increases his perception of risk, making him even more uncomfortable.

It is essential, therefore, that presentation of the service addresses the 'unsaid' factors which augment the core product and which are often the main elements which allow the client to discriminate between competitive offerings. In the residential agency world, as we have seen, the concepts of reassurance and club membership plus 'blameability' are often key factors in the decision.

There are, however, other, more direct weapons available to contact people, particularly those operating at the 'professional' level of service delivery.

One possibility is an 'instant sample delivery' of some aspect of the product which can be taken by the client as a indicator of the 'level of professionalism' to be expected and sometimes as an example of the client/provider relationship which may develop.

An estate agent, for example, taking instructions on a property, can say volumes about his experience and knowledge by such simple expedients as his dexterity with using a tape measure single-handed. In a similar way, a sensible discussion about development possibilities can demonstrate a range of knowledge and expertise, thus involving the client (or potential client) in a partial experience of the overall service.

Creative thought about the nature of the service being provided often suggests areas where creative use of such 'instant part delivery' can generate dividends.

Creating clients, therefore, is about:

  – realising that clients are uncomfortable about their potential risk in decision making;
  – identifying the true nature of risks which the client faces;
  – managing carefully the aspects of service presentation which a client may use as criteria in evaluating supplier suitability.

It is worth restating at this point that the client's perception of quality, in whatever dimension – and we shall explore several possible quality dimensions – is created, shaped and reinforced by his personal contacts with the supplier. The perception created can be individual or it can be corporate, where the effects of a range of contacts are absorbed into a 'corporate opinion' or 'corporate culture'.

Concepts

'Quality is the difference between what you got and what you expected!'

Fundamentally, quality is a subjective concept. It relates to the extent by which actual experience deviates from expected experience within an activity or range of activities. Discussion of quality therefore is a fruitful area for mutual misunderstanding, misinterpretation and downright cussedness. The whole thing is compounded by alternative and conflicting language usage so merits extremely careful analysis and consideration when quality problems rear their ugly heads.

A few simple examples will illustrate the dilemmas.

Most people have attended dinner dances where it is uncomfortable to carry on conversations because 'the band is too loud$_1$. The people trying to talk experience a sense of frustration with the band for interfering and, if this frustration continues, they are likely to translate it into feelings of 'I don't think much of the band'.

This, of course, begs the question of whether talking is the primary object of attending a dinner dance. The band's objective (and core product) is to provide music for people to dance to. If they played quietly enough for people to talk to (i.e. not at all, as any music is potentially disturbing) people trying to dance would experience a lack of quality ('the band didn't even play').

Both groups experience quality at a different level which relates to differing expectations.

A university professor delivers a lecture, dealing with research at the forefront of his specialised field. He is one of the leading experts in his field and the lecture is regarded as a keynote address. His content is superb and represents a significant advance in knowledge. His delivery, unfortunately, is introspective and not at all friendly to his audience in terms of his choice of words, visual aids, pace and timing. His listeners experience conflicting quality feelings. At the one hand his content exceeds expectation and is perceived as high quality. His delivery, on the other hand, does not come up to expectation and is perceived as low quality.

Both perceptions are balanced by the listener in a qualitative verdict of 'good' or 'bad'.

Quality, then, is in the eye of the beholder and relates to a variety of factors, of which expectation and perspective are probably the most important.

The factors which apply can be described as 'hard' and 'soft'. Hard factors tend to be the tangible elements attaching to a product. 'Soft' factors tend to equate to the intangibles.

'Hard' factors

A client approaching, or being approached by, a company is confronted by a variety of images. Obvious amongst these are:

Premises – external appearance, facade, window display, state of repair, location, neighbours, décor, internal layout, even workspace design, all convey messages, often conflicting messages. For example, a prestige premises where workspaces are cluttered and confused says, at the same time:

'I am important and would like to be thought so', and 'I do not manage my internal affairs very well'.

A client will receive both messages and will draw conclusions biased towards whichever negative aspect best relates to his previous conceptions or expectations. (It takes 12 pluses to balance 1 minus.)

Paperwork – letterhead design, grades of paper used, typefaces and standards of typing (particularly spelling) convey images which the client adds to his subset of perceptions. Once again, confusion of images will lead to emphasis of the negative aspects.

Cars – the types of motor car used by personnel create images (in line with the images carefully generated by their marketers as we saw in Chapter 3).

If these images are marred (by untidiness, lack of washing) conflicting messages are produced.

People – people create images in the way they dress, the way they talk, even by their body language. The little things make the difference and create very powerful signals to the client.

Soft factors

People again. In addition to the obvious hard factors – standards of dress, body language etc. people create powerful images through behaviour. Actions speak louder than words and the obvious image confusions created by smart receptionists who say 'How can I help you sir' or 'Have a nice day' and then forget to ring you back speak volumes about real intentions and attitudes. Behaviour is the key factor. Deeds, not words are perceived to be the true indicators.

It is important to remember that, as mentioned earlier, every people contact is a contact point and that it is from behaviour at the contact point that quality, however subjectively, tends to be judged.

Consequently, the effects of contacts by 'back-up' personnel, who may not have been chosen for their social skills, should not be underestimated in considering clients' perceptions of quality. An ill-judged remark by a board man has lost many instructions and sales for estate agents, often without their ever knowing.

Corporate image

Many companies pay close attention to the managed signals that contribute directly to the carefully engineered external image which they wish to present to the world. This image is generated and supported by advertising, public relations and promotional activities and contributes to the level of expectation that clients develop towards the company.

It is worth remembering again that the perception of quality relates to the divergence of performance from expectation rather than from any objective measure and that a corporate image which creates expectations substantially different from performance levels can simultaneously create quality problems. Of course this can also work in the opposite direction but thereby lies strategic danger.

Nevertheless, the client has to make judgements – and judgements in a high risk situation. In an ideal world the messages sent and received by each of the factors discussed (and by many others readily identifiable by the readers in their own businesses) should be cohesive and mutually supportive. Too often they are not. It can be repeated that every time conflicting messages are sent they create conflict in the receiver and that the receiver is likely to interpret conflict in a way which supports unflattering prejudices rather than supporting positive images.

Many of these images can be managed. If they are not, the client or potential client will form his own images and these are unlikely to be helpful. Attention to detail, both in preliminary thought and in execution, is essential.

'Sloppy detailing costs clients.'

Measurement

We have already touched on some of the problems associated with the idea of quality. We turn now to problems of measurement so that the fundamentally qualitative assessment can be placed on a more manageable footing.

Where can quality be measured or identified? The concept of quality, as we have seen, is broad and exists, primarily, in the eye, or experience of the beholder. The beholder, or client, may interact with a service product at a variety of stages in receiving the product offering and may exercise different standards of assessment at each stage. How can these stages be identified?

It is helpful to reconsider the product/client relationship in rather different terms from those which we have used before. Basically, the client can relate to quality in:

the core product
the process which produces the core product
the service delivery system
the general philosophy operated by the company towards its clients.

Core product

Quality can be experienced in terms of whether or not the core product is actually provided; whether or not the objective of using the service is actually achieved and to what standards.

For example, a client using the services of a residential estate agent to sell his home either finishes with a sale or he does not. There is an absolute measure, either the core service is provided or it is not.

This distinction, however, is capable of further subdivision. Did the agent provide a buyer that meets the client's perceptions of reasonableness – i.e. was the expected price achieved? Did the buyer appear within the projected timescale? Was there undue delay in completion? Was the buyer 'difficult' to deal with? Was the client able to achieve external objectives which depended upon the 'right' buyer appearing at the 'right' time.

From the client's viewpoint all of these factors affect the perception of whether the agent 'did a good job', i.e. did the client experience high quality as a result of the agent's endeavours?

Process

Quality can be identified, both objectively and subjectively, in the process which leads to the end (core) product. At this level quality perception passes from the domain of the client much more firmly into the internal domain of the provider. Quality within the process can generally be identified within close limits and can be readily controlled by the provider.

Delivery system

Crucial to the client's experience and perception of quality in a service product is the detailing of the delivery system. It is within the delivery system that client contact is most likely to take place and it is from these contacts that the client's quality perception is shaped.

General philosophy

Underlying the provider/client relationship is the corporate philosophy which relates to quality. A corporate philosophy may evolve or it may be managed. However it is developed it will be reflected in client contact at all levels and will materially affect the client's quality perception (often very different from that which was intended). It is important to realise that it is from the company's management style that staff take their cues in dealing with clients. Style is about deeds not words – 'Never mind what I say, do what I do' is the action phrase that staff react to and which is received by the client as 'quality'.

What kind of measurement systems and approaches are available? Once again the concepts of 'hard' and 'soft' can be applied.

'Hard' measurement applies to activities which can be 'identified' and where physical responses or activities can be counted in some way. For example, it is feasible to measure the average time taken to answer a ringing telephone and it is equally feasible to specify maximum time limits for the activity. Similarly it is possible to measure and set standards for the average time from receipt of instructions to despatch of a completed valuation.

Care is always needed, of course, in analysis of results and in action taken to deal with obvious variances. When a phone is answered after an excessive delay the person who answers is almost always the one who is currently answering three other phones whilst less able and less committed staff stand idly by.

Care is also needed in choosing attributes to be measured and controlled. Standards for the number of eye contacts made with an office caller can lead to some very strange office activities that can easily generate confusion (and hence low quality perception) in the client.

'Soft' factors are considerably more difficult to measure – although no less influential. The 'degree of friendliness', 'degree of helpfulness' in an office is measurable only by inference although sophisticated marketing research can help. In most cases such factors can be measured only by observation – leading to a subjective assessment of divergence from personal and corporate 'norms' or standards.

Note that it is in this area that training can go sadly awry. Implicit within any training programme, particularly in the direct areas of sales, customer care or process, there is a subjective standard of corporate culture. The problem lies in that the trainer may

a) not subscribe to the corporate culture;
b) not be aware of any specific culture;
c) train to a personalised culture.

the net effect of any of which is likely to be a role confusion leading to lack of clarity in presentation and finally to a reduction (through conflict) in the customer's perception of quality in the overall product.

Consistency

The role of consistency in the subjective measurement of quality cannot be over-emphasised. The service manager – and the service marketer – should be aware of all areas of interaction which condition the customer's perception of quality and should pay special attention to the potential for lack of image consistency diminishing the quality experience.

For example, if the senior partner in an 'upmarket' commercial firm arrives for a meeting in a 5-year-old Ford Escort there is a mismatch between his role and the trappings which surround it. Unless this mismatch is 'squared' with the client in some way (I'm using my daughter's car while mine is in for a service and the wife has gone to her mother's for the week') the role confusion is likely to undermine the senior partner's (and hence the firm's) image, leading to a reduced perception of quality in the firm.

Similarly, if a junior negotiator appears in a Ferrari the resulting mismatch between expectation and performance is likely to undermine the confidence of the client.

Images, however, may be inconsistent in much more subtle ways. Most people will be familiar with 'alternative definitions' of well-meant phrases

– the popular press' image of estate agents is full of them.

'Compact gardens' – means 'a window box'
'Needs attention' – means 'rampant dry rot, roof in a state of collapse etc.'

But the words we say at our reception points can be equally two edged.

'Have a nice day' = 'Thank God I've finished with you'
'How can I help you Sir?' = 'Not another dumbo who wants 20 per cent too much for his house'.

In all of these cases the interpretation depends not just on the words but also on the body language that surround them. And body language – the underlying meaning – comes straight from the contact person's experience of the corporate culture or management style.

Quality is difficult to measure. Some aspects can be relatively straightforward but detailed and continual informed observation is essential if consistent images are to be presented to the client – and the client is the judge.

Client management

Very clearly, in a service environment, the importance of the client to the external perception of a firm's quality cannot be over-emphasised. How, then, can it be managed, even improved?

Some clues come from the nature of the interaction.

– the client is an active participant in service delivery;
– quality judgements are firmly based in contact experiences;
– quality judgements are based on the difference between expectation and reality.

A number of factors derive readily from these statements.

– If the client is an active participant can the nature of his participation be improved?
– If judgement is rooted in contacts, can the contact experience be improved?
– If quality refers to the difference between expectation and reality then:

a) Can (or should) expectation be altered to approximate more closely to reality?
b) Can reality fit more closely to expectation?

– Can the nature of participation be improved/altered?

An interesting example of a change in client participation was the move, at the end of the 1970s, from a closed office system in residential agency to the self-selection system. (See case study Chapter 3).

It was recognised that a new breed of client was emerging, nurtured in the consumer supermarkets, who was used to helping himself in a purchase situation. Many of them actually enjoyed the experience. The balance of client involvement shifted considerably in favour of their experience and clients reacted positively to their increased involvement. They felt more in control, un-pressured and perceived a high degree of satisfaction and comfort within the buying experience.

Augmenting this 'do it yourself' experience booklets were issued, free, which allowed the client to educate himself in the basic mechanics of the service thus improving his ability to participate still further and reinforcing his general acceptance and thus his quality perception of the service offered.

What actually happened with this change was that:

a) The extent of client participation increased significantly;
b) Some effort was put into training the client to participate
   more fully;
c) the expectations of the client were shaped by the promotional material, providing a yardstick against which the agency could perform, often better than the client expected.

So – areas in which participation can be changed:

– can the client play a more active role at any point in the system?
– can the client be trained in any way to participate more fully?
– can the client's expectations be shaped to correspond more closely to the delivery system?

Can the contact experience be improved?

– are all contact staff adequately trained for dealing with clients?
– are staff picking up the right 'corporate' messages from management?
– is there any mismatch between images generated and received within the system?
– is there a clear internal concept of the kind of experience which clients should be receiving?
– is there any mismatch between corporate culture and staff training?

Can expectation be fitted more closely to reality?

– do the 'expectation' images exceed ability to perform?
– is there any advantage to re-aligning images so that performance exceeds expectation?
– is the failure in reality based in failure to perform to internal standards?
– are internal standards capable of being achieved?

Other areas can usefully be addressed in this context.

Does the system 'creak' under excess pressure? If so can demand problems be realigned in some way? For example: sending out a weekly list of new instructions to mailing list clients on Wednesday, the newspapers on Thursday and Friday, allowed related activity – sales, valuations, viewings – to be 'staggered' throughout the week rather than being compressed into the weekend. Does the delivery system fit preferred buying patterns amongst clients? Are manning levels geared to internal rather than external convenience? Do clients try to do things for themselves, thus bypassing contact staff (and then blaming them for not doing the job properly)? Could some of this 'preferred work' be passed to the client? Can clients choose between different service levels – thus suiting both their pockets and their personal competencies – with a resulting improvement in satisfaction levels (hence a better perception of quality)? Are there financial advantages in doing this – alternatively, would they pay the same for their own increased involvement? Is there any system for monitoring satisfaction levels which clients receive from contacts? Can a system be envisaged/installed?

Quality circles – positive and negative

Throughout this chapter we have stressed the crucial role of the client in the perception of quality and identified clearly that the client's perception is closely shaped by personal experiences in contacts with the firm, both person to person contacts and person to object or image contacts. As with any perceptual experience the strongest impressions are normally made by contacts between people.

In the context of service delivery this opens up some interesting creative avenues. Before exploring these, however, the interactive role of the client's activities upon the firm should also be mentioned.

Any contact between two people has a degree of interaction built into it. At the corporate level we saw in Chapter 4 how an ongoing client relationship can build, through interactive contacts, into an 'institutionalised' contact system and how such a system can work to the advantage of a careful service provider dealing in organisational markets.

At the individual level the effects of interaction can be just as powerful and can be turned to the advantage or allowed to turn to the disadvantage of the firm.

Basically, a circle is formed. The client takes an initiative. This receives a counter from which a further, modified, initiative results. When attitude is added to the equation the effects upon the quality experience become clear. If a client is happy and generates 'happy' initiatives the contact person – receptionist, sales person etc. – is likely to respond in kind. This reinforces the happy feeling and the whole dialogue proceeds in a mutually satisfying and supportive manner. On the other hand, if a client is unhappy this will show in his initiatives and is likely to result in a less-than-helpful dialogue which will reinforce the client's dissatisfaction and hence decrease his perception of quality in the system. The message is clear: positive messages generate positive responses. Negative messages generate negative responses; unless the cycle can be broken.

At this point the importance of careful management of client contact becomes clear, particularly the management of complaints or potential complaints – where careful handling can often turn a potential complaint into a quality bonus. Some firms, in fact, base much of their client management upon complaints as a trigger. Whilst there may be the appearance of short term success in such an approach it is unlikely to have lasting long term benefits, particularly as it is likely to be based in avoidance of true client management and will, consequently, fail to pick up all the dissatisfied clients who do not complain.

Yet here is another problem. The purchase of service products is, as we have seen, a relatively high risk decision. There is, therefore, considerable investment built into the system which tends to make clients stay with their providers even though they are dissatisfied and though they perceive a lack of quality in the offering. This system inertia can often mask the effects of a deteriorating situation well after the point has been passed at which the provider would have normally been excluded in a 'first purchase' decision.

Complaints management – or even worse, service management by complaint – is a very dangerous strategy.

Other quality circles, operating in much the same reinforcement mode, can be identified. Good service management leads in the long run to a strong market position which in turn leads to good economic results. Good economic results should lead to improved service management (through better training, better management and better marketing). Poor service management, however, can quickly lead to economic decline, in the same kind of vicious circle.

The importance of internal personnel relationships has already been identified – staff take their attitude and behaviour cues from management – it follows, therefore, that alterations in internal relationships will lead to alterations in external relationships – once again positive or vicious circles result, with a long term effect on market share and profitability.

Most things which happen within an organisation have interactive and far-reaching effects. Effects upon customers in a service organisation can be diagnosed directly at the contact point, within the service delivery system. This is, therefore, a key indicator both to customer and managements, of the basic state of a company's long term health and should be given appropriate management attention if the company is to prosper.

'Managements neglect quality indicators at their company's risk.

The client-based culture

Management philosophies have undergone a series of changes in emphasis over the years; from the days of Urwick and Gilbrth's 'Scientific Management', through the 1960s with their concentration on organisational analysis, the 1970s with Management by Objectives and matrix management, into the 1980s where Tom Peters and others have preached the importance of people and the client.

It is to this culture that service management ideas direct management thinking.

'The client pays the wages.

No clients = No wages
Poor quality = No clients
Quality = Clients' perceptions.

(No mention anywhere here of managements, products, selling or any of the other accoutrements of the management commentator. Just a simple recognition that if clients do not want to buy what you make then you cannot survive as a business. Everything else springs from that.)

We have also identified many times that the crucial indicator of quality to a client is the experience generated by people contacts, hence the idea 'People make the difference'. People contacts make or mar the perception of quality in service products.

So in order to make the best of clients we have to make the best of our people too. Otherwise we get the client orientation that we deserve.

Service management – the main points

Manage the contact point – the point at which the client experiences the service. Manage it through training, coaching, monitoring, encouraging, but remember, quality starts at the top.

Manage the customer's expectation – quality is perceived as the difference between expectation and reality. Don't create disappointment. Don't promise what you cannot deliver.

Manage the client's involvement – the client perceives quality in personal experience. Help the client to help you help himself.

Look for positive and vicious circles.

'Accentuate the positive'
'Eliminate the negative'.

Manage the signals.

Confusion = uncomfortable experience = poor quality.

Make the signals match – all of them!

Measure the measurable – but don't confuse measurement with management – measuring simple things can indicate behaviour designed to avoid facing real problems. Your staff will know exactly what you mean!

Set the style – your staff are boss-watchers – they will do what you do not what you say.

Win the wages from the client – he pays!

The best

Advertising
Present business
New business
Repeat business

comes from satisfied clients.

References and further reading

R. Normann (1988), *Service Management – Strategy and Leadership in Service Businesses*, John Wiley & Sons, pp. 54–5

T. Peters and N. Austin (1986), *A Passion for Excellence*, Fontana/Collins, London, p. 40

6 Commercial Property People and their Products

In two separate areas a leading potential client for property professionals judged the industry and found it wanting. Comments like these addressed to a leading firm, noted for its professionalism and commitment to high standards of conduct and operation, are not hugely encouraging to the rest!

From where do such perceptions derive?

Take the first case – 'which advertising consultants should we use?' The context here is clear. The client wishes to dispose of property or a property portfolio and is seeking the professional marketing advice of a property advisor. Yet the response is not that of a marketing consultant – who would evaluate the product, define a disposal strategy and seek the services of a specialist consultancy if they were appropriate. It is the response of a property professional – who apparently purports to undertake property disposal without the requisite marketing expertise.

Take the second case – the property portfolio offered through a merchant bank. The perception here is that property people don't identify property in terms that investors relate to; they don't consequently have the intrinsic financial credibility that will enable them to dispose of a high value portfolio adequately.

Let's take another situation. During the latter part of 1989 and throughout 1990 it has become obvious – to the point where it has become a subject for debate in both leading articles and letter pages of the main property journals – that leading management consultancies are targeting property advice as being their 'natural' territory. The growth in property values and the increasing importance of property underlying corporate asset values identifies property as a vital strategic asset with wide ranging implications on financing and stock valuations. Unless property professionals identify their own importance in a wider strategic context they must remain vulnerable to such threats.

Some firms already identify this changing role and are both recruiting experienced management professionals and sponsoring their own senior staff through post-graduate management training. The professions as a whole, however, are slow in realising their new role and show little interest in extending their competencies into such new areas.

A senior consultant property valuer specialising in licensed premises bemoaned the fact that, whilst in order to value public houses successfully his knowledge of public house operations needed to be wide ranging and specific, he did not pretend to operate as an operational consultant in the area. At the same time ex-regional managers and the like from the licensed trade retail sector were acting as consultants – and then calling upon his services as a valuer. The problem was that he identified himself primarily as a valuer, not as a consultant. His potential clientele took him at his own valuation, and in doing so restricted his potential market place into a relatively narrow field of activity.

What products do commercial property professionals offer?

We have already referred to two areas of professional expertise offered by property professionals; property marketing and valuation services are the stock-in-trade of many commercial firms. The case study referred to two separate aspects of property marketing, advice and perceived range of expertise. Our licensed trade valuer positioned himself as a narrow specialist (through his own attitudes) rather than as a more general consultant (a role which he was well able and well positioned to fulfil).

Property professionals offer a range of specialised and specialist services

– Property marketing
– Valuations
– Rent review
– Property management
– Dilapidations
– Project management
– Planning

are just a few examples from a broad spectrum.

Let us examine some of these areas in more detail, starting with property marketing – the commercial agent.

Commercial agency

The activities of the commercial agent, whilst superficially similar to those of the residential agent, may be significantly different. Differences tend to arise in

a) the levels of technical knowledge needed by practitioners;
b) the operation of commercial agency as a market between professional operators rather than as a market between professional salesperson and lay buyer;
c) the cash values of properties being traded in the market place;
d) the activities of specialist buyers trading in a mix of property interests incorporating a range of values derived commercially from use investment and development values as a matter of course.

The markets also differ significantly in that agents act regularly in the purchase of commercial property interests on behalf of clients, rather than on the rare occasions met in residential.

The complexity within the market stems from the fact that property is owned in the UK as a series of interests, most of which are capable of subdivision and therefore multiple ownership. For example, a freehold office block may be divided into a number of physical sub-units; each of these may be subject to a variety of legal property interests and each of these is capable of separable ownership. The top floor may be let on a long lease as one unit. The second floor may be let as two units on short leases, one of which is subject to a sub-lease. The ground floor may be owner-occupied by the freeholder who nevertheless derives rent from the rest of the building. Each occupier may be liable for rates and for a proportion of both the maintenance and running costs of the building.

In such a scenario the identification of the effects of such a mix of interests upon the value – and therefore the disposal or acquisition of such interests – can be a highly complex exercise which tends to imply a sophisticated level of expertise and training in those who purport to advise.

It is not surprising, therefore, that this professional expertise has been called upon by would-be buyers and sellers of such interests, however skilled they may be in their own business activities, and that a recognised trading pattern has developed between professional advisors. Neither is it surprising that the marketing tools and disciplines used by such professional advisors have tended to relate to the needs of their fellow professionals rather than to those of the clients which they service. The danger, of course, is that such a closed market place is likely to become inward looking to the point where the needs of real users, investors and developers are forgotten.

There are indications that this may be so within the commercial property market. At the start of Chapter 4 we referred to a number of questions raised by the failure of professional property advisors to take advantage of opportunities to reach decision makers which were obviously available by association with influential articles on corporate relocation yet which were largely ignored by the property industry. This surely points to a dangerous level of introspection.

In the same vein it is still usual to find the majority of commercial property advertising budgets spent within the pages of the two leading property journals, Estates Gazette and Chartered Surveyor Weekly. When the number of corporate decision makers (as opposed to property professionals) who religiously scan the advertising pages of Estates Gazette is considered, it becomes fairly easy to identify the real targets of this advertising.

Yet is this the appropriate medium for future property promotion? Property is increasingly traded as a commodity. Investors, in particular, frequent the auction marts buying on clear investment, rather than property-related criteria. Businessmen are becoming increasingly aware of the potential that property holds for significantly creative accounting opportunities which materially affect the viability of their companies and the perception of their companies' values in the world's stock markets. Is the time approaching where the needs of the primary decision maker will, necessarily, figure in the marketing approaches of the commercial agent? Has it already come, but passed the commercial agent by?

Commercial agency includes the purchase and disposal of all kinds of commercial property on behalf of clients. In order to do this adequately there may be a need to draw upon specialist expertise from within a variety of the disciplines of the property profession. Sometimes these specialist expertises are 'bundled' with the main product. Sometimes they are sold as separate disciplines. These will emerge during our analysis.

In order to identify the nature of elements of any product it is first necessary to examine the environment within which that product is supplied. In the case of residential agency it was seen that the need for residential agency arose from a need for money which, in turn arose from a need for an alternative dwelling (see Chapter 2). This can often be the case with commercial agency. A company needs more space so it buys some and in order to finance the transaction sells its existing space.

But is this an adequate explanation? Many companies buy space without having to sell other space. Equally, many companies sell space without showing any desire or need to replace it! Perhaps space is not the driving force at all?

Perhaps we would be better turning to the concepts of added value to explain the situation.

Why does a surveyor practise his profession as a sole trader? Many could earn more money as employees, at the same time gaining extra security from the synergy of other people's earnings. Certainly this is often the case in a partnership which combines some of the costs and benefits of both situations.

The sole trader surveyor sacrifices a possible loss of income and security for the chance of a higher income and the independence of action that only a sole trader enjoys. He derives significant added value from the uncertainty and from the feeling of independence.

In the same way he derives an added value effect from combining his personal and financial resources in such a way that his total return is greater than it would be in any other scenario. (In the partnership he might receive higher rewards but at the cost of restricted freedoms. As an employee his increased security would be paid for by even greater restrictions – although for some this may be counterbalanced by the power derived from dealing from an increased financial base.)

The reason for a businessman being in business at all, then, derives from a subtle equation by which added value is received from a personalised mix of resources in an earning situation.

Tom Peters says 'Business is easy. It's about making things and selling things'. True, but these two activities must result in a profit and profit is a naive expression of the total concept of added value.

The use of the word 'naive' here is deliberate. Added value is a total concept which implies benefits which do not necessarily appear in the balance sheet. In the small business, indeed, these benefits may well outweigh the balance sheet expression of each profit. As the business grows, however, the relationship between continuing profit and added value becomes more closely equated and it becomes increasingly realistic to express resource values in cash terms.

'But what has all this to do with commercial agency?'

We identified earlier that the provision of a home – or space – did not seem, necessarily, to be the guiding motivation in the buyer and selling of commercial property. What, then, could be?

If the nature of business outlined above is realistic then the answer becomes clear. Space, or the lack of it, is simply a resource, the use of which may or may not be appropriate in terms of adding value to a business at a particular point in time. Following this line of logic, if space is a resource, quantifiable in money terms (as represented by the, incorporation of profit into the concept of added value), then space is simply an alternative use for money in a business context.

This has some interesting implications. The residential purchase decision – and hence the activities of agents within the sector – relates to the disposal of property as a means to moving house, an idea which is hedged around with a mass of personalised intangibles. In the commercial decision the activity can be reduced to a financial context – making it susceptible to analysis to the same degree as any other operational commercial decision. Commercial buyers, therefore, are likely to view commercial agents as contributors (or adders of value) to financial decisions; put another way the core product of the commercial agent is to act as a solver of business problems – the role identified and played by IBM to its enduring competitive advantage.

The tangible product

As in the residential sector the tangible product of the commercial agent is the visible expression of his activities. Office location, décor, board styles, staff qualifications policies, range of advisory activities offered, all provide visual and, to an extent, tangible clues as to the nature of the product on offer.

Within the commercial sector many of these clues are likely to be more subtle indicators and will be accompanied by even less tangible factors which relate to the structural nature of the relationships inherent in the commercial decision making process (see Chapter 4).

It should not, however, be forgotten that whilst corporate buyers are subject to special factors which relate to corporate buying they are still, nevertheless, subject to the same kind of fundamental influences, as individuals, that exist in the personal buying decision and that apparently intangible factors may therefore become an integral part of the perceived tangible product.

Few commercial agencies have yet taken these factors closely to heart. There is no equivalent – yet – to the staff man who can wear any colour suit as long as it is dark grey, any colour shirt as long as it is white and any colour tie as long as it is black. Few organisations yet go further than promoting the use of the company tie or the RICS tie as a badge of office conveying respectability.

Perhaps there is scope in this area for sensitive and profitable management of service delivery (see Chapter 4).

The augmented product

As we have seen, the commercial agent is in the core business of providing an advisory service. He provides this advisory service in a sophisticated market place, dealing either with other property professionals or with business people accustomed to making value judgements on the basis of incomplete information.

Buyers in this type of environment are generally operating in a limited problem solving mode (LPS) (as opposed to an extensive problem or routine purchase mode). In this type of buying mode some interesting behaviour is likely to occur.

– Product alternatives are perceived as being essentially similar – i.e. one agent's offering is perceived to be very much the same as that available from another.

– Evaluation of alternatives tends to be non-rigorous – the effect of this being that decisions may well be taken on the basis of subtle cues (which match preconceptions) rather than on the basis of an extended evaluation of alternative offerings.

– Buyers are likely to use a limited set of criteria in their decision processes and to focus on the most salient – which makes it potentially more difficult to change emphasis away from such obvious factors as price into the more rewarding areas of added value.

The cumulative effect of such factors is to increase the importance of intangible augmenting factors and consequently to increase the importance of identifying these factors and managing them to advantage.

Many of the augmenting factors will be similar to those inherent in the residential agency product – reassurance, 'arms-lengthing', blameability. Their effects, however, may be more direct.

Reassurance

In the commercial world decision risk tends to be spread throughout the buying group, thus diminishing the need for individual reassurance. Individuals, nevertheless still need some reassurance in decision making and will look for the cues, visible and subliminal that support or undermine the correctness of their decisions. These cues may be in the form of modes of dress, figures of speech or even as part of body language but in an environment which has tended to become inbred, are of great importance to the decision maker.

'Arm's-lengthing'

In the commercial world the concept of dealing at arm's length has different considerations from those in the residential decision in that there is often need for secrecy in dealings. Part of the skill of negotiation lies in assessing the relative strength of the opposition. If the opposition remains hidden from view relative strength can be judged only in the person of the negotiator – and this bland stance effectively removes many of the important clues.

Blameability

No-one likes to be blamed for making mistakes. Corporate decision makers are no exception to this general rule. The saying 'the buck stops here' is only valid when there is no-one else to pass it to. One compelling reason for taking professional advice is that the advisor can carry blame if things go wrong – even if his advice was good! Commercial agents owe their existence to this aspect of their job as much as to any other aspect of their function.

Summary

The commercial agent, then, in broad terms provides an advisory service which, at heart, is a management consultancy role. Many agents recognise this role and take pride in their ability to provide responsible and effective advice. Few, however, recognise it as a primary role and even fewer design their marketing initiatives to emphasise their consultancy abilities. In the absence of a developed appreciation of this consultancy role they must remain vulnerable to market attacks from predators – consultants, merchant bankers and the like who can position themselves more directly to the underlying needs of the potential client.

Property people, however, tend, if they are to be at all successful, to be instinctive marketers and to manage ongoing relationships well. This is particularly appropriate in an industry where the vast majority of firms are relatively small. It becomes less appropriate as firms grow and activities are delegated, even to professional staff.

Until relatively recently (1987), marketing was not a discipline included in professional examinations and generations of surveyors and valuers have grown up without a formalised understanding of marketing as a discipline. This has led to the situation where, whilst many professional advisers are able to give valid marketing advice to their clients, they are unused to giving this advice in terms which a client, formally trained in or exposed to marketing ideas, would understand and this contributes to a perception of property professionals as narrow specialists which in turn reinforces their isolation from mainstream commercial developments.

The product analysis which we made above suggests a number of crucial insights into the nature of the product provided by commercial agents. Some of these involve a fundamental rethinking of the agent's role vis-à-vis his client. Some provide pointers to aspects of the function which can be reinforced by careful attention to detail in product design, packaging and promotion.

There is no 'one right way' for a firm. Every agent has different potential strengths which can be managed to advantage. Those who rely on instinct alone, whilst they may remain successful, do so as amateurs rather than professionals and are vulnerable to attack by professionals.

Professional services

At the beginning of this chapter we identified a list of potential products provided by commercial property professionals. These can, in the main, be identified under the more general heading of professional services, for example valuations, development appraisal, rent review, dilapidations.

These products will be readily identified by property professionals as the core areas to which their professional training relates. They are, nevertheless, products which have to be 'sold' in an increasingly competitive market place.

Some professions have built-in advantages. For example, legal constraints surround a person's ability to sign an audit statement for a limited company or to appear in the High Court on behalf of a client.

No such legal parameters surround the services of property professionals. Subject to the laws of negligence, anyone can practice as a surveyor, valuer, auctioneer, estate agent or whatever.

In many areas there is considerable overlap between the specialist skills of different professions. For example, cost accountants perform many of the functions of the quantity surveyor, financial accountants and investment analysts overlap directly with investment surveyors; many potential clients identify solicitors as the primary advisor on commercial leases; there is an ongoing misconception about the complementary roles of structural engineers and building surveyors and so on.

Professional institutions have, traditionally, discouraged competition amongst their members by restricting advertising claims, presumably on the basis that 'a professional is a professional...'.

The market for professional services in the 1990s is no longer a clear-cut area where surveyors do surveying, accountants go accounting, solicitors go 'soliciting'. It is a complex arena for conflicting professional pretensions and will increasingly be judged on competitive advantage to be derived from specific individual skills.

The product

'At the heart of professional advice is a very simple concept. Professional advice is based on an opinion. The core product therefore could not be simpler. What clients buy from professional advisors is, at heart, an opinion. A bank manager buys an opinion of value from a surveyor. In legal proceedings it is actually spelt out. If times get rough or a problem is difficult, solicitors recommend that 'we should take counsel's opinion'.

But opinions can be differentiated. One person's opinion is not at all the same thing as someone else's opinion. Many factors came into play in assessing the quality of the opinion. Method of delivery, circumstances of delivery, persona of the deliveror all affect the degree of credibility which attaches to the opinion.

Prima facie a chartered surveyor's or an incorporated valuer's professional opinion has built-in credibility by virtue of his professional credentials. But we all know that the relative credibility of different advisors varies – according to circumstances, reputation and the topic on which advice is sought.

The factors which affect the perceived quality of professional advice are part of the tangible and augmented product and need to be identified as such.

Tangible product

Once again we are in the area of what can be seen, heard, felt, touched, smelt – all of those things which impinge on the tangible sensors.

Most obvious amongst these, in considering professional advice as a product, are the report and reporting mechanisms. Many opinions are delivered in both written and verbal forms. The recipient or observer will be influenced in his quality perception by the quality of delivery which he encounters. For example, a report which is delivered with confidence and with adequate explanation of reasoning and technicalities is likely to carry more weight than the same opinion delivered in a hesitant manner and with little or no demonstrated ability to explain the process by which the opinion was formed. The report, in either format, is a tangible expression of the credibility which can be attached to the opinion and will be judged as such.

Once again more subtle clues come into play. An opinion which is provided by somebody who conforms to the recipient's preconceptions of what the opinion provider should appear to be is more likely to be considered authorative than a similar opinion proffered by someone who does not conform. It should be noted, however, that preconceptions can encompass a wide range of behaviour. For example, the opinion of a Solicitor who appears somewhat eccentric in dress and behaviour would probably be accepted if preconceptions include the idea that some solicitors, often very good ones, indulge themselves in such dress and behaviour.

The tangible product incorporates elements derived from brand imagery. A large professional firm takes pains in its projection of self-image and a client expects the tangible offering to conform to the standards projected by the imagery. The old bugbear of conflicting images is particularly important here and the potential damage which can be caused through a failure to manage service delivery closely cannot be over-emphasised.

Augmented product

Chartered surveyors, incorporated valuers, solicitors, accountants – most professional people have traditionally practised in firms with unlimited liability, that is, they put their necks (and potentially their wealth) on the line every time they pass a professional opinion.

Such a commitment, however tenuous it might have been, commands respect, both at a conscious and an unconscious level, and has been jealously guarded as a principle, up to the last decade (when cracks started to appear in the professional edifice).

Within the last decade it has become fashionable to litigate – to look for scapegoats. Professionals nowadays are generally subject to onerous rules covering professional indemnity insurance, and professional rules are being relaxed to allow incorporation with limited liability and even, for the future, mixed practices.

There are signs that many professional institutions are losing clarity in their roles and that the potential product benefits of professional institution membership are also eroding.

It is important that the professional person should identify professional status with its important role at the augmented product level. In our analysis of residential property sales we identified reassurance as a critical augmenting factor.

For the professional product reassurance as an augmenting factor is probably even more important. Refer back to the core product – an opinion. An opinion is only as good as its credibility – hence the crucial nature of reassurance at the augmenting level.

Many property professionals trade daily on the strength of their professional qualifications and membership, yet do little to involve themselves in critical debate on future directions of their professional bodies – which they increasingly perceive as archaic, bureaucratic and out of date. (Note that we are not simply referring to surveyors. One has only to read the 'house journal' of any of the professional bodies; they are all suffering from similar problems.)

The danger with a 'detached' viewpoint or attitude is that clients may also begin to view the reassuring aspects of professional membership with suspicion. If and when this happens the power of institutional membership to reassure – and inevitably the perceived benefits springing from that membership to clients, will be reduced, with potentially uncomfortable effects on professional pockets.

Professional membership is but one aspect of reassurance that relates to clients. Clients derive reassurance from reputation, track record, perceived success levels, appearances – all the things that affect those same clients in a consumer purchase decision. A problem for professional service providers lies often in the fact that they may be competing in organisational decisions where perceptions of reassurance and risk are likely to be magnified and distorted through multiple interactions.

Every problem is potentially an opportunity! When the client is an organisation his needs are likely to be recurrent. Supply of personal, professional services is often well suited to the creation of ongoing institutionalised purchase and supply procedures – and just as vulnerable to changes of personnel!

Most surveyors in provincial private practice are aware, if instinctively, of the opportunities for new business presented by a change in local bank managers, building society managers and so on. Many become aware by default, when their cosy relationship with 'Fred' is not carried forward by 'Fred's' successor – who is of a different age group and background and is wooed assiduously by aggressive competition more in tune with his personal aspirations.

Times change. Behavioural aspects that are reassuring to one person are not necessarily reassuring to another. This moves us neatly into club image.

The residential purchaser reacts to a club image – 'people like us buy from people like us'. The 'professional' purchaser reacts similarly. He has not only to convince himself of the probity of his buying decision but may also need to be aware of the needs of his own client to whom he may have to justify his decision making.

For example, the solicitor that commissions a structural survey on behalf of a client may have to justify his own actions to that client if the surveyor subsequently proves to have been negligent in making or reporting on his survey.

There is, therefore, some likelihood that the 'nobody ever got sacked for recommending IBM' principle may apply to professional advisors. This is, of course, the principle behind the development of professional institutions! Is there a danger that, as major providers grow and increase their dominance over the industry, that the operation of this principle will contribute to hastening the decline, or eventual demise, of the professional institutions?

Specialist expertise
Professional opinions are purchased when people have to deal with topics which are outside their normal range of activity and which are perceived to have built-in specialist complexity. We have already seen that property – as a concept – qualifies well on both counts for most people – and most organisations.

We have also seen, however, that property advice is, itself, being channelled into increasingly specialised areas – building survey, dilapidations, rent review, for example – where the level of professional expertise required is increasingly departing from the generalist education most property professionals receive.

A client, therefore, particularly as he becomes more aware of the specialist nature of his needs, is likely to require additional demonstration of specialist skills in the areas of advice which he seeks. He is likely to look for track record of achievement in the specific area before he can attach sufficient credibility to an opinion to want to buy it.

We see demonstrations of the importance attaching to track record all around us. Commercial agents' boards decorate commercial property, hopefully with 'Sold' on them – a demonstration of track record. Quantity surveyors and architects erect hoardings publicising their involvement with building projects. Even arbitrators are delighted when their cases are referred to the Court of Appeal on a matter of law (particularly if the courts find in their favour). Other technical specialists demonstrate their track record and involvement through publications. A learned article in an influential magazine – or even better, a book on a technical topic (like this one) – can help to establish not only credibility as a specialist pundit but also track record in selling advice – and we all know that we feel happier about our television or car if someone whose opinion we trust has one just like it!

Blameability

Does the purchase of professional opinions have its element of blameability attached? Perhaps even more strongly than within the residential decision, particularly if the decision is institutional in nature.

Here again we reiterate that no-one ever got fired for buying IBM. People are likely to take the safe course. One reason for buying IBM is that if things go wrong they are likely to move Heaven and Earth to put them right – and they have the resources to see it through.

In the property world clients are often taking decisions or buying advice upon matters which are of crucial import to the conduct or continuation of their businesses. A rent review 'missed' by a property management firm, for example, has considerable potential repercussions upon cash flow and upon corporate capitalisation in the short term. Few individual corporate managers will wish to attract the ire of his peers or his board of directors without the longstop of someone else to blame – preferably someone well covered by insurance.

Summary

Once again, the product turns out to be not what it seems at first. Intangible factors have a huge influence upon product design and upon the buying decision. We reiterate that marketing is a management function. Management in this context implies that things are done deliberately, not left to chance. This in turn implies careful attention to detail in the design of product packaging and in the management of service delivery to ensure that quality signalling does not create confusion in the mind of potential buyers. Confusion leads directly to mistrust – or at least unease – and in the relatively high risk buying decision for property advice there is ample opportunity for a buyer to seek alternative suppliers.

Commercial property

The book *Modern Methods of Valuation* introduces the concept that there are three principle reasons for buying property. These are:

a) The buyer wishes to take advantage of the commercial or trading opportunities presented by the property
   – Users
b) The buyer wishes to utilise the property as a vehicle for financial investment
   – Investors
c) The buyer wishes to realise a profit through the development and resale of latent opportunity within the property
   – Developers

These categories apply to both commercial and residential property but commercial professionals are concerned, primarily, with buyers for commercial purposes and it is to those that this section is directed.

Users

Land has no intrinsic value. The statement that land has value as a scarce resource is true but misleading. Land has only a value derived from its ability to contribute to value-adding activities. This may be self-evident to most readers but bears repeating as it is only by direct attention to value-adding potential that value – in the shape of potential purchasers, however notional, can be identified by the marketer or valuer.

If illustration were needed to this fundamental concept consider the relative values of a 10 000 sq ft (930 m^2) warehouse unit situated half way up Snowdon and an identical warehouse unit in the vicinity of Heathrow airport. Every valuer will immediately recognise a large potential difference between these two units and many, if asked, will assign the basis of difference to 'demand'.

But what makes demand? The answer to this question is the basis for the property marketer. What makes demand is an amalgam of potential benefits – passing trade, access to suppliers, access to communications – roads, railways, canals, airports – access to raw materials, fashion in building style – a host of factors which bear – and require – further examination.

It is worth remembering that considerable research material, both public and private, is available within these areas. Some of these we identify in Chapter 8 on marketing tactics. The property professional needs to be aware of relevant research and how it can be assessed.

But what is relevant research? A number of major property advisors either maintain in-house research facilities or sponsor academic research, often both in an effort to improve their own advisory capabilities and as part of their market profile. Much of this research, however, tends to concentrate on property matters – new starts, yields, rental and capital values, rather than in the primary demand areas from which these factors and trends derive.

Marketers – and the astute property professional – should direct their attention to the primary factors if they wish to stay ahead of the field and offer the professional service which their clients expect.

So, let us examine some of these value-adding features in more detail, using our notional warehouse/office unit as an example.

Physical facility

Our unit has some fundamental physical attributes – which can be more or less duplicated in any location. Size, method of construction, access doorways, electrical facilities, colouring and so on. Even at the physical level, however, there are value-adding factors – state of repair being an obvious one.

But the real differences start to appear at the next level. The old saw suggests that there are three factors which affect value – location, location and location. But what is implied within that statement is the important factor. What does 'location' really mean?

Location

Access to customers

In the case of our B1 unit access to customers may not be of great importance. After all, how many customers wish to visit a warehouse and how many base their buying decisions on such visits? As usual, the answers all depend. They depend on the nature of the trade concerned, the type of product involved, the type of buying decision and the position of the warehousing function within the end-product marketer's distribution network.

Some customers, for example office equipment buyers, computer or other hi-tech buyers, may include warehouse visits as part of their decision making. Some suppliers, indeed, may maintain a sales demonstration suite as part of the warehousing facility. To these, access is important, bringing with it a need for parking space, communications and so on.

Others, for example food retailers – vendors of similar consumables, may be content to be serviced by representatives and have no need or desire for warehouse access.

Similar constraints apply in other trading areas. A newsagent often relies upon passing trade to supply a significant proportion of his customers. A specialist antique dealer, whilst happy to sell retail, would not welcome the flow of unqualified customers that would be generated by a high-visibility High Street location.

Access to communications

Our B1 unit, situated near Heathrow, has potentially good access to the airport. To the enterprise that deals regularly with overseas customers this may be a most attractive option. To the high-tech computer systems design organisation, seeking office space, the prospect of a jumbo jet passing overhead at 45-second intervals may be less than enticing.

Access to trading areas

In the not-so-distant past auctioneers' offices were typically located close to the cattle market which they served. They were easily accessible to farmers on market days and the market was easily accessible to the auctioneer. As estate agency became an increasingly important aspect of the auctioneer's business many chose to move their operations to High Street positions more accessible to their new clientele.

Similarly, barristers' chambers are located within easy distance of the law courts lest business opportunities should be missed.

Major fine art salerooms today attract clusters of specialist antique dealers who both hope to benefit from the flow of customers attracted by the saleroom and take advantage of the saleroom's nearness to ensure that they do not miss possible stock opportunities.

It is important to notice here the changing nature of trading relationships. The astute marketer looks not simply at things as they are today but also at things are they are likely to be tomorrow. The advisor must research his markets as closely as the trader.

Access to raw materials

Throughout the eithteenth and nineteenth centuries vast tracts of the UK, particularly in South Wales, Yorkshire and the North East, were developed into thriving communities, their wealth based primarily upon the coal trade. Some areas, for example Tredegar in Gwent, were developed even further through the additional iron ore resources to be found close at hand. Industry was attracted to the raw materials and support industries were attracted to these industries as potential customers.

Today many of these areas are crumbling away through dereliction as the principal industries close, their raw materials exhausted. The reason for the communities existing has been removed and the industries attracted by those industries have, in turn, collapsed.

The 1990s equivalent of such industries is to be found in Cumbria. The nuclear reprocessing plant at Sellafield exists primarily because the raw materials it feeds upon are found in quantity on site as a by-product of the primary reactor. Feeding on this raw material is, to a large extent, the viability of West Cumbria's economy – and any investment or trading decision based upon it.

Access to workforce

One positive benefit of industrial dereliction is the availability of a labour force. Humans are territorial to a degree and, once established in a location, are reluctant to give it up. The Japanese have taken advantage of this in locating Hi-tech industries in areas of high unemployment – notably in South Wales and the North East – and have taken full advantage of reduced wage levels in their product costings.

There is another dimension to the concept of access to a workforce. The question of physical access must also be addressed. Mobility patterns are changing rapidly as we approach the millennium. Those who once walked to work or used public transport are now conditioned to the use of private transport thus enabling the use of workplace sites which would, even 20 years ago, have been considered too remote to be viable.

A workforce implies living conditions – workers need somewhere to live. Their choice of somewhere to live brings in a range of other constraints – the infrastructure of the areas from which a workforce can be drawn becomes an important variable. Availability of medical care, education, shopping and leisure facilities all become important criteria in assessing the earning power of a potential trading site.

As a workforce becomes more sophisticated – engineers, say, in a Hi-tec manufacturing and development plant – so their needs become more sophisticated. An important 'keynote' project in the development of a region as a centre for high technology development was almost scuppered when key development personnel refused to recognise the area as culturally acceptable and declined to move there. The dilemma for the developer (a Government-sponsored agency) was solved only through a 'fudge' – an accommodation which allowed these personnel to be settled in more 'acceptable' area.

Benefits
Other factors came into play in the availability of grant or other aid from central and local government initiatives. In its early days the Welsh Development Agency made successful use of grant aid in attracting new industrial users into a regenerating South Wales – so much so that in 1990 they are faced with a shortage of space against increasing demand.

The study of location, as a value-influencing factor, is complex and is a regular subject for research. It contains within it important keys both to current and to future trends in property values and must remain a staple of research for both the property valuer and marketer.

Other factors
In the preceding section we examined location as a prime value influencer. The reader may be forgiven for thinking that this is more than enough. Surely, given size, basic facilities and location, there is sufficient data for sensible conclusions to be formed.

Property valuers and marketers, however, know differently. Other more subtle factors affect value – because they affect peoples' ability to do business (i.e. derive added value) from a property.

Fashion
An important influence upon value – and therefore upon the marketer – is fashion. Different types of property tend to go in and out of fashion – both as trading and investment vehicles. For example, the London Docklands development was the forerunner of a rash of similar schemes, albeit on a smaller scale. The initial success of London Docklands pointed the way to a series of lookalikes based on a 'waterside living and working' concept. It is important to recognise here that, whilst the schemes produced may not have fully acknowledged this, it was the concept rather than individual schemes which became fashionable and which fuelled financial and media support.

Similar fashion influences are discernible in the growth of 'Hi-tech' building. Discussions with surveyors and students readily recognise hi-tech buildings as ordinary sheds with red or electric blue cladding – and possibly some extra internal trunking! The fashion for hi-tech as a concept produces the well-known 80:20 principle – where 80 per cent of the results are produced by 20 per cent of the effort.

Style
Building style can contribute greatly to the 'earning power' of a building in certain circumstances. This relates to discussion elsewhere in the book dealing with the importance of care in matching quality indicators.

For example, a retail outlet specialising in Art Deco-style lamps will benefit from being housed in an Art Deco building, where the general ambience of the building's style will enhance the effect created by the displays. Similarly, Harrods would not command the same prestige if it were housed in a 1950s or 1960s tower block. An up-market estate agent's office will draw added value from the ambience and external appearance of an attractive Regency building which would detract from a sparky 'modern' agent's offices more at home amidst the neon signs of a High Street replete with Dixon's, MacDonald's and Curry's.

Summary

The experienced reader will readily recognise in the preceding paragraph the essential factors considered by a competent valuer in making his evaluation of a commercial building. He will wonder, no doubt, why such factors are included in a book on marketing.

The point is that marketing is based upon potential added value – and to recognise a property's potential for adding value it is first of all necessary to understand clearly the factors that allow it to add value. For the valuer it may be sufficient in most circumstances, to agglomerate such factors and utilise the agglomeration implied in the use of comparables, exercising his skill and judgement based on experience in what can easily become a subjective application of the general to the specific.

For the marketer, however, each factor should be carefully weighed and examined so that the property's potential to add value to the most appropriate (and highest paying) purchaser is fully explored.

It bears repeating that the value of a property, to a purchaser and hence, as a security, derives from its ability to add value to the earning power of the purchaser. Valuers are traditionally aware of the potential and, indeed, utilise it as a principle in what is termed a 'profits' valuation.

Unfortunately, even in 1991, many aspiring valuers are taught that profits valuations are mainly used in such arcane and specialised areas as pub and petrol station valuations, thus perpetuating a predisposition to depend upon comparables rather than to look, specifically, at the potential of an individual property to add value. This, in turn, works against the ability of such a valuer to make a thorough investigation of these factors when considering marketing advice. And a critical glance through any representative property advertising will demonstrate that it shows!

We have dwelt at some length on the factors which affect the ability of a property to add value – and thereby justify rentals and capital value. This is deliberate as these factors underpin the two other basic reasons for buying property – investment and development.

Investment

Investors in property have no interest in property except as a vehicle for financial investment. Its utility as a vehicle, of course, is circumscribed by its ability to generate income and capital growth and this ability is derived from the use factors outlined above.

It is worth considering the motivations of an investor before proceeding too far down this road. An investor uses his money to buy money in an alternative form, hopefully ending up with more (or at least as much) as he started with. The chances of his not doing this are the risks attached to the investment.

How does an investor derive returns on his money? He can do one of two things (hopefully both at the same time). He can

a) draw an income from allowing someone else to use his capital – for example by investing in a bank or building society;
b) grow this capital in some way.

Property is particularly interesting to an investor because it allows a wide range of permutations to be made on these basic themes. The inherent flexibility of property, deriving from the legal potential for limited ownership of property rights, allows interests to be created which earn in the short term, the long term and all stations in between.

In the first place property interests can earn an income – conventionally in the form of rent (which derives, of course, from the property's potential for adding value, in some way, to its tenant). In modern leases the rental paid is subject to review, normally every five years, at which point the rent is expected to increase.

As a rental increases the second part of the equation, capital growth, comes into play. Assuming that risk remains unchanged a higher rent justifies a higher capital value. For example, a shop let at £10 000 per annum and costing originally £100 000 (i.e. bought at a risk factor or yield of 10 per cent) will, assuming that nothing has changed, be worth £150 000 if the rental increases at review to £15 000 per annum.

But there is a second factor to the equation. Our assumption was that yield remained unchanged at 10 per cent. What happens if the rent remained unchanged but the yield changed?

An improvement in yield from 10 per cent to 8 per cent results in a capital value of

$$\frac{100}{8} \times 10\ 000 = £125\ 000$$

Similarly a falling of the yield to 12½ per cent would result in a capital value of

$$\frac{100}{12.5} \times 10\ 000 = £80\ 000$$

And this is a key factor for the investor. Not only can he achieve capital growth in the normal course of events through rental growth but can also influence capital value to a marked extent through the manipulation of yield.

How can yield be managed – and grown? Yield is, quite simply, an expression of risk so if risk can be reduced then yield can be improved.

What affects risk in a property investment? Quality of tenant's covenant, type of interest, lease terms – in some cases quality of portfolio management. A wide range of specialist factors which form the substance of the professional valuer's training – yet few advertisements for investment properties allude even obscurely to inherent potential for yield growth in an investment or portfolio.

Developers

A developer's needs are simple. He wishes to realise the potential latent within a property and turn the difference in values created into profit. There are, as always, complexities and varying degrees of risk inherent in differing levels of development.

These risks are tightly bound up with both investment criteria and use criteria – from which underlying value springs.

Marketing initiatives for development property should, therefore, focus upon potential and should attempt to minimise risks – or at least quantify risks – if maximum interest is to be aroused.

Summary

People buy commercial property for one, or more, of three basic reasons – to use it, to invest in it, or to develop it. Fundamentally, all property value stems from its ability to be used to earn money, i.e. it is a derived demand.

The marketer focusing on buyers' needs must take account of these detailed factors in the design of marketing initiatives if he wishes to attract a level of attention which ensures that his client's interests are best served.

Conclusion

Within this chapter we have attempted to identify the nature of buyer needs in the principal areas of activity of the commercial property professional.

The marketing of commercial property is a skilled activity which relies upon contact networks, technical knowledge and, not least, the flair and perception of the individual professional. Our purpose is not to tell such people how to suck eggs but rather to explore the area at a level of detail which may open up new avenues to be explored and from which the basic ideas which lead to successful sales, PR and advertising activity may flow.

At the same time the chapter demonstrates the use of a rigorous questioning approach to what are, for many people, daily activities, well learned and easily taken for granted. Similar questioning may be made of specific functions with often interesting and illuminating results.

7 Strategy

Case study – The birth of the majors

From the middle of the 1980s the estate agency world – and much that was the province of the professional surveyor – has been racked by the birth pangs of the major conglomerate companies.

Leaving aside obvious differences in management styles set by their respective chief executives it is readily apparent that the groups have taken, often radically different, approaches to their developments of brand image, corporate identity, internal training and projected profiles. These differences have provided a continuing theme for conversations amongst estate agents throughout the land and interest still continues.

'Why did the Pru throw away the goodwill that it had bought so dearly by its policy of immediate rebranding?'

'Why did Black Horse Agencies and Nationwide Anglia have a policy of partial rebranding?'

'Why did General Accident and Royal agencies hesitate about branding?'

'What are the building societies after?'

'What's going to happen to the independents?'

It is very interesting to take a detached view of the motivations behind the early development of these groups. We stress 'early' because as each group develops so it gains a momentum of its own which can easily outweigh the original strategic constraints which led to its birth.

It is tempting to assume that these large groups were formed to take advantage of the profits to be earned through estate agency. The synergy of a large branch network allied to the management expertise that can be brought to bear from a centralised matrix, sharing marketing and development costs provides an alluring scenario for cash-rich institutional managers looking for fresh fields to till. But this would be only telling part of the story. House purchase is the point at which many people become prime targets for the sale of financial products – mortgages, life assurance, pensions, house contents insurance...the list is long!

Different types of institution can be discerned amongst the major buyers. There are bankers, insurance companies, financial service intermediaries, building societies – and even, at one stage, an attempt to grow a chain by a firm of motor traders.

Does the nature and needs of the buyer give any clues to their likely future behaviour? Let us consider some 'generic' buyers.

- 'The classical expander – Classical strategic theory says 'Find a product area that complements existing core activity. If that product is provided by a range of producers over whom you have a significant competitive advantage – go for it.'

  One area of significant advantage is normally available to a strong, cash-rich corporation in a market with a large number of small, relatively weak providers – economies of scale through synergy and centralisation. If the market has high entry barriers in some way – for example, technological knowledge or market place experience – which can be quickly acquired to the detriment of other large potential competitors, so much the better.

  A moment's reflection suggests a familiar scenario. The traditional order of the estate agency and provincial surveying profession was an industry which mainly comprised small firms operating from a maximum of 10 or 12 offices and more often from a base of one or two. Whilst many had an element of dominance at local level there was no single powerful national or even regional firm. These small firms nevertheless held a strong market position since they often held prime trading positions – often in areas where local planning opinion was firmly set against extension of 'non-retail' users – and their senior partners were often pillars of the local establishment thus ensuring a regular inflow of quality business through professional and personal contacts.

  So, high entry barriers, some financial, some logistic, but a market place inhabited by potentially weak competitors. Also a market where, if strategically situated, locally strong competitors could be 'cherry picked', then the entry barriers for other predators would be raised. A tempting target for the right opportunist, expansion-minded conglomerate.

  Lloyds Bank rose to the challenge identifying both the market place itself as intrinsically attractive and its synergy with the Bank's core product – financial services – as a source of multiplied profit.

  First into the foray it bought wisely and well, picking up, in general, the well rounded, general practice firms of established reputation, often with a county connection through their agricultural arms. As the firms were similar so were their local market images and these images positioned BHA de facto, at the quality end of the volume market.

In line with its general strategy of growth through acquisition the Bank chose to maintain local connections as far as possible by sub-branding BHA against the established 'local' name.

Only later did the BHA brand become the major image but even now, in some cases 5–6 years on – the original local name is still retained in most acquisitions.

A careful and accurately implemented strategy took advantage of the strategic options and has secured BHA as one of the top three or four operators in the market place with notably less outlets than some of its major competitors.

- 'The channel builder' – Not everyone saw estate agency as a profit earner in its own right. For some it had a much more important role to play as a distribution channel for other, more profitable products. The insurance companies were able to view estate agency in this light, but with emphases which differed according to their starting positions. For example, Royal Insurance and General Accident were already well established in the mortgage markets as providers of life insurance linked to house purchase. For them a strategy based upon the maintenance of market share was appropriate, hence a relatively relaxed approach to rebranding and imposing a corporate image.

  For the Prudential Corporation, however, the stakes were different – whilst they were long established as a household name within the UK their image was principally that of 'the man at the Pru' calling at the door for the small scale endowment or funeral benefit. They were not established as a 'first-choice' product for house purchase linkage.

  The importance of house purchase as a trigger for the purchase of longer scale life assurance was obvious and a two-pronged strategic objective emerged – a) using house purchase as a link to the sale of (profitable) insurance; b) utilising a High Street branch network to reposition 'the Pru' as a provider to a more prestigious and lucrative market than it had hitherto enjoyed.

  This is not to say that estate agency did not have to pay its way. It would need to do this if only to maintain the impetus of the staff. But the prime objective and profit potential lay in increased market share for its core products – insurance.

  It is entirely consistent with these strategic objectives that the Pru rebranded outlets immediately upon acquisition. Residual goodwill was lost but attempts to maintain it would have detracted from the primary objectives.

- 'The protectionists'. The other main contenders in the rush for acquisition – although late into the frame – have been the building societies, in particular Nationwide Anglia, Abbey National and the Halifax.

In each case the strategic objective is clear – protection of their existing mortgage markets against perceived threats arising from organised control at the point of sale. Encouraged by market research suggesting that people would prefer to deal with building societies rather than estate agents they plunged heavily into the market.

Unfortunately, there was a down-side to the research in that as soon as the building societies became estate agents they ran the risk of being tarred with the same brush.

Nationwide Anglia felt the repercussions when a trading loss on estate agency was perceived as a loss by the building society thus denting its image somewhat. The Abbey National exercised caution and distanced themselves from their unruly child by branding their operation as 'Cornerstone' – sufficiently distant to avoid undue opprobrium if their fears were realised. (Unfortunately, of course, this distancing also worked against the synergy for which they might have hoped.)

The Halifax, in the meantime, watched and waited, rebranding quietly through acquisition under trading titles. For example Hartnell Taylor Cook in the South West became the vehicle through which the Halifax built its network for Wales and the South West; then measured the effects of branding or gradual loss of established names. Finally, when some of the initial bugs were out of the system, a full-scale national rebranding to use the full weight of the Halifax name, by now secure in the knowledge that common standards could be applied and that a corporate culture was firmly in place, was implemented.

Introduction

In the case study three radically different strategies for the development of new markets by major companies were explored. Obviously a limited case comparison of this nature can only take a simplistic view, commenting upon clearly visible differences in approach and linking them, in retrospect, to underlying objectives.

The case study does, nevertheless, demonstrate how differing objectives translate into often radically different solutions and therefore radically different market place initiatives. It also demonstrates, particularly to those who have lived through these traumatic times, how easy it is to misread the actions of a company in the absence of a clear understanding of its strategic standpoints. For example, the Pru was heavily criticised for its rebranding strategy, even by those bought into the system but who failed to appreciate their new role as a delivery channel and the implications that sprang from this.

We can draw the fundamental nature of strategic thinking from the case studies. In each case the developing company had to ask itself 'Where do we want to go?'; 'Why (specifically) do we want to go there?'; before it could begin to tackle fundamental questions like 'Should we rebrand?'. They had to identify not only the nature of the existing market place but also the future market place in which they intended to operate.

It is interesting to speculate that we are still in the early days of this new market place. The major companies have established their bridgeheads. Their branch networks and initial management structures are new in place. They are beginning to tackle the mechanical problems of personnel and facilities management. They have had to face the realities of a lack of inherent profitability in 'pure' estate agency. The next phase is the consolidation of market shares and positioning which will ensure their long term survival as profitable operations.

Into the equation now will come the detailed examination of the market place; identification of profitable market sectors or niches followed by the search for and matching of competitive advantage against the opposition.

There is a long way to go. The avowed strategy of each of the majors at the time of writing is the achievement of competitive advantage through superior service. If they all compete head on then, assuming that each has broadly equivalent management competence, none will achieve a significant advantage, leaving them more or less in equilibrium, none with sufficient share or positioning to cushion them against the fluctuations of a market which has been uncomfortably volatile over the past few years.

In Chapter 1 we reviewed the fundamental bases of strategy – cost, differentiation and focus. In this chapter we change the emphasis to the search for, and achievement of competitive advantage and explore some areas in which competitive advantage can be found or generated by both estate agents and by surveyors and other professionals.

What is strategy about?

Management can be defined as 'the art of getting from A to B profitably'. The fun is in identifying A – i.e. where you are now – and B – where you want to be. Defining B involves consideration of a wide range of issues; profit, relative profitability, turnover, unit turnover, staffing and materials implications, financial needs and planning. At the heart of the equation, however, having chosen a product and market in which to compete (major tasks in themselves outside the aims of this book) is marketing strategy. Perhaps the best definition to emerge comes from D. A. Aakers in 1984: 'The development of a sustainable competitive advantage with which to compete in a chosen product/market'.

From this definition come several key words.

'development' – an ongoing process which must be managed. It does not happen on its own.

'sustainable competitive advantage' – anyone can achieve short term competitive advantage, price cutting to buy market share is an obvious tactic. The problem with short term advantage is that as the advantage is eroded by your competitors you have to start all over again – often from a position of relative weakness.

'chosen product/market' – a specific combination of a product – or subset of a generic product – aimed to a specific market or subset of a market.

So the questions to be answered are:

How do you choose your product/market?
How do you derive competitive advantage?
How can you manage the development of advantage?

How do you derive competitive advantage?

In Chapter 6 we introduced the notion that the customer pays the wages. The customer can only pay the wages from profit and only derives profit from added value. The logical deduction, therefore, is that competitive advantage derives from unique ability to add value to a customer. A producer's ability to exist derives entirely from his ability to add value to the operations or lifestyle of his customers.

Competitive advantage derives uniquely from his ability to add value in ways that competitors are unable to match. The Heineken advertisements are quite explicit about this. 'Heineken reaches the parts that other beers can't reach' – competitive advantage in a nutshell!

In what ways can a supplier achieve advantage? Michael Porter, as we have seen, analyses the bases of strategy – alternatively stated as the bases of competitive advantage in terms of cost, focus and differentiation, each base providing pointers as to where advantage can be gained. In his book *Competitive Advantage* he refines the arguments further, identifying the activities of a business as a value chain.

Seen as a value chain, the activities of a company can be analysed into;

Inbound logistics – purchasing ability, raw materials supply, expertise, track record, contact circles;

Operations – the mechanics of production, technical facilities available, quality control, financial and cost control;

Outbound logistics – delivery systems, service management and quality criteria;

Marketing and sales – product design and research, sales management, promotional activity, corporate image, distribution networks;

Service – after sales service, customer satisfaction management, on-going relationship management.

These factors are all conditioned by:

– the firm's infrastructure – the chief executive officer's image of the firm and its markets, his overt management style, the corporate ethos, its perceived status (with all that this implies);

– human resource management – perception of the growth potential of the people available;

– technological development – the ability to buy and use state of the art technology productively (tanks are useless without drivers!);

– procurement – relationship with supplies, control of raw materials, friendly links with universities highlighting emergent talent.

This gives a list of factors all interacting to produce the corporate whole. It is the result of these interactions, expressed as a function of their combined ability to add value, that provides the operating margin in financial terms – the profit.

From the variables already discussed come clues to added value to the customer. The customer also has a value chain and the alert supplier should always try to identify not only the total added value to the customer but also the specific areas in which value can be added uniquely.

For example: the rent review surveyor can add value to his client not just through his ability to agree a favourable rental but also through his ability to simplify the client's procurement process, either through acting on a regular basis in an 'institutionalised' format or through his ease of access to the client when the client needs reassurance or a progress report. In a new purchase situation he can add value through a self-evident track record or through his ability to provide 'instant mini-delivery'. Each of these activities adds value in a way that, with difficulty, can be quantified – even where the quantification must, of necessity, be based in subjective assessments.

Difficulties of assessment should not mean that assessment is shirked as it is from seemingly unimportant areas that critical value is often added.

The procedure, then, in assessing competitive advantage, is logically simple. Assess the client's value chain, that is, the areas in which he can experience added value. Then compare the firm's ability to add value with those of the firm's competitors. The areas in which the firm differs from its competitors are the keys to competitive advantage.

The fact that this process is logically simple is, unfortunately, of little help to the practitioner. There is still considerable hard work needed to translate the simple statement into a usable reality!

Assessing added value

It cannot be said too often that the concept of added value must always be assessed from the viewpoint of the receiver – the client. A moment's reflection demonstrates the link from this idea to the problems experienced by firms that operate from a product or sales orientation. In either case consideration of added value is from the wrong perspective and comes up with answers that are only 'right' by accident. A product orientation results in products full of technical excellence which fail to meet customer criteria – perhaps because they are 'too dear' – i.e. they cost more than the value that they add, or because they provide a potential to add value which the customer cannot use. A sales orientation results in products being 'sold', using structured openings and closes but no regard for customer needs (and hence limited results in the long term).

'added value relates to customer needs!'

In order to assess added value potential it is necessary to gain a detailed understanding of the customer's activities into which the product is fitted. Valuers considering retail warehousing failed, at first, to appreciate the customer's earning potential (and hence his ability to pay rent) through not paying attention to the customer's reasons for buying in the first place (his need to make money through retailing). In the surveying world public house valuers are perhaps the closest to this ideal – where their valuation is based almost entirely upon the valuer's understanding of the trading potential of the pub.

A checklist approach to the problem will help to structure assessment.

Inbound logistics

Can the client's purchasing costs be reduced, either directly or indirectly, in a way that does not detract from his end product? The cost of purchasing arises from initial investigation, discussion and ranking of alternatives plus the physical costs of interview time, paperwork etc. It is heavily affected by the client's perception of risk in the purchase.

Is there some means whereby risk can be reduced to the client? Is there some way that direct costs can be reduced? A reduction in cost is added value.

Operations
Can the product be tailored to fit easily into the client's use control system? Could the client participate in quality control at an earlier stage? Are there areas where supplier activities or warranties could reduce quality control activities? Can parameters be fed directly into the client's financial and cost control systems? Linked computer systems are a possible example – the banks' use of direct debiting is an example of adding value to a client by reducing direct costs. Beware, however: this particular saving is achieved at the expense of an increase in the client's perceived purchase risk, particularly to unsophisticated clients. Such cross-effects need to be carefully examined for an overall benefit to be identified.

Outbound logistics
Can the product assist in end-product delivery, quality testing or service control? For example, a building society commissions a valuation from a valuer. The valuation is passed, via the building society to its client – the home buyer. If user-friendliness of the valuation is improved – perhaps by avoiding technical jargon or by improving service turnround – value is added to the building society by reducing waiting time (and therefore administration) and by reducing time spent on unnecessary explanations to its clients.

Marketing and sales
How can value be added in these areas? Again the building society valuation explains. Valuations are normally provided on a form supplied by the building society and are passed on direct. At one time valuers supplied valuations in their own 'in-house' format which then needed processing/translation before submission to the client. The valuer now participates directly in providing the building society's product. There is considerable scope within this area for client-supportive marketing, promotion and involvement in the client company's image activities, all of which potentially add value and can be quantified.

Service
Any provider is concerned with after-sales service and customer satisfaction. There is great scope for property professionals, in particular, to contribute to a client's customer care. The valuer that avoids contact with an end-product user, often on the grounds that it might be unprofessional, does no service either to himself or to the client. His unhelpful attitude reduces end-user satisfaction to the detriment of the client. A helpful attitude adds value directly by increasing the client's customer satisfaction.

   In the preceding paragraphs we have explored the bases in which value can be added. Every provider is different and every customer is unique. There exists, therefore, an infinite opportunity for adding value, often uniquely. It is not always easy to identify these opportunities but unless the effort is made the advantage shifts to the more caring and observant opposition.

Competitive advantage

It is not sufficient just to be aware of the implications and intricacies of the client's value chain (although the exercise of evaluating the chain itself gives an important insight into marketing advantage); the service provider still has to identify competitive advantage.

It is a reasonable assumption that within the chosen product/market there will be alternative providers, i.e. there will be competition. The firm has, therefore, to establish clearly where it is at an advantage against the competition – and where it is potentially at a disadvantage – if its product is to be successfully marketed in the longer term.

Porter, as we have seen, identifies generic advantage in terms of cost, differentiation and focus. This analysis is sound but should be further considered in terms of the specific value chains to which the product potentially relates. It is possible that, at different phases of the value chain, advantage can be derived from different strategic bases.

The proposition is, fundamentally, that advantage derives from a unique ability to add value and that this ability must be sustainable.

Cost advantage is easily addressable as it derives directly from a firm's internal management and resourcing facilities. If it derives internally from company activities then it is capable of being managed and repays careful management. As we have already seen, a cost advantage, once gained, is potentially self-perpetuating (although if it goes unrecognised it can be easily diverted into short term profit-taking to long term strategic disadvantage).

Focus and differentiation are different expressions of a similar concept. Even within a focused strategy competitive advantage is achieved through differentiation. Differentiation can be defined as 'adding value through being different'.

A word of warning is immediately in order. Being different does not necessarily add value. A red car is not necessarily more 'valuable' than a blue car, if the purchaser's purpose is simply to have a conveyance. Colour could, however, add value if the purchaser's need is to have a conveyance instantly recognisable as a post office van or a fire engine.

The question is, therefore, 'Can differences be identified which can be exploited as uniquely adding value to a purchaser?'

Some obvious examples spring to mind. As between two firms of surveyors competing for business the personalities of the individual surveyors are different and will add value to the client in different ways. One may be blunt and abrasive but complete his task very quickly and efficiently. Another may be charming and approachable but operate to a longer timescale. Each adds value uniquely to different elements of the client's value chain; the first is oriented towards the 'production' element, the second towards procurement and customer service. These two examples are, perhaps, extremes but illustrate the principles.

It is worth considering differentiation in more detail as it is in this area that competitive advantage can often lie, unrecognised and unremarked, but the key to significantly increased revenue and profitability.

How can a product be differentiated?

Make it more unique. Within any product there is an almost infinite series of events or perceptions. Each of these is unique although it will be mirrored in the 'generic' product (as supplied by competitors). The trick is to identify the product as adding value uniquely across a range of readily identifiable factors. This makes it more difficult for competitors to duplicate and makes the product, itself, stand out from the crowd.

For example, a surveyor can be differentiated by his personality, experience, the car he drives, type of clothes, writing/reporting style, availability to clients, quality of secretary, track record, perceived track record, breadth of services offered, service reputation, contacts network, local citizen profile, and in numerous other ways. He will be different from every other surveyor in all of these respects. Each respect, however, adds value in a different way. Some contribute in some circumstances; others contribute in others. The greater the sources of value-adding differentiation, the more unique the value of the surveyor to a client.

Signal the sources of value. It is all very well for the surveyor to be unique – and to uniquely add value – but does the potential client perceive the benefits? Unless the potential to add value is clearly signalled to the client misinterpretations are likely to creep in. For example, the estate agent with a Ferrari signals success to one client, 'flash' to another. Success adds value by association. 'Flash' does quite the opposite. The benefits of uniqueness must be clearly identified.

Match the product to the use. If the estate agency client is looking primarily for reassurance then differentiation which adds up to reassurance will add most value. There may be other elements available but in this situation they will not constructively add value. The 'flash' agent in this circumstance will differentiate to his own disadvantage.

Turn cost to advantage. Benefits to a client are often inexpensive to a provider. A smile and a sympathetic ear cost very little yet can add significant value to a stressed or distressed client. Similarly, a brochure which demonstrates a verifiable track record in a particular area costs little to produce but significantly reduces a client's perception of risk – thus adding considerable value.

Ensure that the costs of differentiation are known. For example, a daily telephone call to a client informing him of progress may seem to have a trivial cost. The same telephone call repeated over a period of weeks may seriously erode product margins without providing significant advantage over a weekly or even fortnightly call – as long as the client perceives that he is being kept informed. The client experiences added value from being informed, not from the daily telephone call.

Highlight differentiation which can be sustained. Personal experience is unique and cannot be duplicated. If it adds value significantly it is therefore an important and sustainable element of advantage which should be strongly signalled.

Cut out non-value-adding activities. In the 1960s management consultants made fortunes from a simple question 'why?'. Question activities. If they do not add value to the client look for ways of getting rid of them. How much research activity quantifiably adds value to the product offerings of its sponsors? How much business really comes from the pub/civic lunches?

Change the rules. The commercial property industry operates, traditionally, largely between professional agents acting as intermediaries. Could a new value chain be identified by shifting activity directly to the real buyers – the corporate decision makers? Some people think so, hence recent attempts by firms to involve corporate decision makers through targeted promotional activity.

New criteria can often be uncovered, or even generated, by which product offerings can be judged. The management consultants are currently doing this by identifying property advice as consultancy in corporate assets, thus changing the rules of selection and engagement in their favour.

Reflect changing times. If the rules are changing, reposition the product offering to anticipate the changes so that they change in your favour. As times change, so do perceptions of added value. Your product's differentiation must continue to signal added value or it will cease to be bought.

Reconfigure the value chain Consideration of a firm's value chain often starts from what is there. Consider it in reverse. What adds value to the client? How can we identify an offering specifically to add this value. Which parts add most value? How can they be identified and signalled directly to the client?

Sustainability in differentiation

We have already touched upon the importance of highlighting sustainability of differentiation. But if sustainability is so crucial to long term success, where can we find it and how can we engineer it?

Sustainability arises from two sources. First the client's perception of advantage from a factor must remain unchanged – for example, he must continue to believe that your specific experience adds significant value to him. Second there must be a lack of imitation by the competition. If a surveyor's experience in the district valuer's office, dealing with rating and compensation in a particular district, is a key value-adding factor to his clients then he is always potentially vulnerable to another surveyor with similar experience attacking his markets. His experience factor will no longer be as unique and his advantage from that source ceases to be sustainable.

Uniqueness can be derived from entry barriers. Building societies are, for example, reluctant to instruct valuers who are not members of the RICS or the ISVA. This reluctance (not a legal constraint) provides a measure of protection to such valuers against potential competitors in this market. Similarly experience can be an entry barrier. Few arbitrators are appointed without considerable experience of rent review. Uniqueness derived in this way is sustainable against competitors who cannot pass the barriers but does not provide competitive advantage against others with similar basic qualifications.

As we have already seen a cost advantage can be self-sustaining if it is recognised and managed. Differentiation deriving from cost advantage is therefore relatively sustainable and is often a critical component of competitive advantage overall.

Differentiation from multiple sources is difficult to duplicate and therefore is relatively sustainable although it should be recognised that individual advantage may be eroded so that the balance of relative advantage is changed.

Advantage tends to be sustainable if there are substantial costs involved in changing suppliers. If, for example, a supplier provides significant advantage through its differentiation and a purchaser modifies his behaviour to take that advantage then, unless another supplier can duplicate the specific differentiation the behaviour changes needed to switch suppliers will work against the second supplier thus enhancing sustainability. For example, a firm of surveyors with specific expertise, offering a rigorous and standardised reporting and contact format will tend to lock its purchasers into that format to the point where they will modify their operating procedures to match as closely as possible with the supplier.

Danger in differentiations

Not all differentiation adds value. There is no premium in being different for its own sake. Indeed, in some cases, being different can be a positive disadvantage. It is vitally important, therefore, to review a product regularly, *from the client's viewpoint*, in order to ensure that advantage is being maintained. It is easy to spend large amounts of money on 'being different' without adding anything at all to the value-adding potential of a product.

Too much differentiation confuses the issue and makes added value difficult to perceive. In this circumstance the potential for misleading and even contradicting signals is very high – and contradictory signals lead to an increased perception of risk.

Differentiation, even if potentially adding considerable value, is of no practical use unless that added value is clearly signalled to a potential purchaser. For example, a surveyor's specific experience of rating valuations in a particular area is of no value to a potential client unless that client is aware of both the experience itself and the ability that this experience gives the surveyor to achieve significantly improved results in rent review/ dilapidations or whatever.

Differentiation, even if it adds value, and even if that added value is fully perceived by the client, is of little use to a supplier unless it can be provided at an economic cost. For example, the estate agent who uses a Ferrari as a 'me too' success symbol should look carefully at the cost/benefit equation. The Ferrari certainly adds value – at a cost – but does it add sufficient perceived value (as measured by increased instructions and profitability directly attributable to the Ferrari) to justify the differentiation. This type of questioning leads naturally into the consideration of lower cost alternatives as a means of providing similar benefits – for example, a second hand Porsche with a personal number plate may achieve almost the same result. This, of course leads to the question 'Is it the car or the number plate?'

The questions are easily posed but less easily answered!   A major danger in considering differentiation is focusing attention upon the product rather than upon the client. We have already considered quality perception in Chapter 6 and have clearly identified the subjective nature of quality from the client's viewpoint. How many firms, nevertheless, still concentrate on managing internal quality control (i.e. a product orientation) rather than on managing the client's perception – the contact point between the product and the client's value chain?

At this point we should have a pretty clear idea of what the client thinks is important – that is, his perception of the value chain – and of the special potential of our product to satisfy the value chain in specific ways. This gives us a powerful starting point in considering competitive advantage. There are, nevertheless, two important areas which still need careful analysis. These are the key factors which make the difference between success and failure in the market and our balance of specific advantage in these keys areas against our competition. Again we shall investigate these areas in some detail.

Key success factors

In any product/market business area it is readily apparent to even the casual observer that there are clear winners and equally clear losers. What is not so obvious is that there is usually a much higher number of partial winners and partial losers who bumble along, never quite achieving the heights but never quite descending into penury either. Although they are not consistent they must be doing something right – usually by accident.

Further examination suggests that, in any product/market, there are key factors which must be satisfied before success can follow. For example, a surveyor may be highly intelligent, articulate, experienced, well thought of yet still remain a 'small-time local surveyor', dealing with local matters and never quite earning the fees attaching to the mega-developments which less competent people in other circumstances are handling to their considerable financial advantage. What's wrong? The local surveyor simply does not know the right people – he does not move in the right circles to generate the right instructions. The key factor here – know the right people. The expertise, experience and intelligence – whilst being important to the continuing prosperity of an operator – are not the key factors in obtaining instructions in the first place.

Similarly, in the 1970s and into the 1980s, many chartered surveyor estate agents found it difficult to understand why, despite their professionalism, knowledge and experience, vendors went to the 'flash' newcomer. Their expertise was not the key factor; perceived ability to find buyers (probably) was.

The lesson from all this – competitive advantage must be targeted first and foremost to the key areas which affect success. Kenichi Ohmae in 'The Mind of the Strategist' (1987) calls them KFS – key factors for success – and we follow his convention.

In any situation, business or domestic, however complex the problem, there will almost certainly be one or two factors which overwhelm the others. In considering private education, for instance, the availability of finance is, for most people, the overwhelming key to whether or not a child can be given its benefits. In a household where finance is not a problem the aptitude of the child – secondary where there is no money available, may become the key factor. The trick for the business strategist is to strip away all the misconceptions, prejudice and accumulated 'conventional wisdom' from the equation and examine it in the spotlight of the simple question 'why?' – and through the eyes of the potential client.

Some examples might help to clarify the situation.

It is easy for the professional educator to think that his clients wish to receive the benefits of his accumulated wisdom and research; when the client wishes only to pass an examination – and will pay greatest attention to the educator's track record in attaining examination passes for his students.

Estate agents beaver away at customer service programs (vitally important as base levels for their activities) – while the customer, first and foremost looks at the agent's ability to provide a buyer – PDQ!

BMW Motors achieve a price premium for their cars (based on their established reputation (or customer perception) for high quality engineering and solidity), but well aware that their price premium provides what most of their customers want – a status symbol! (Quality over a long period may be a key factor in establishing the premium but the key factor in the market place – now – is the price premium and all that it implies about the purchaser.)

Look at the competition – how does the firm rate against its existing and potential competitors? At the heart of this comparison is our old friend the SWOT analysis where we analyse our operation, and that of our competitors, in terms of strengths, weaknesses, opportunities and threats. The conventional expression of the SWOT analysis is simple to say but difficult to do in practice. Strengths can arise under so many headings – as can weaknesses, opportunities and threats. For the product/market analysis, however, the road should now be clear. We have already considered relationships with the market place in terms of contribution to a value chain. Using this same concept strengths etc. can be clearly examined with reference to the value chain as the reference point.

Once again, some examples will help to clarify the point. Returning to our friend the local surveyor, his SWOT analysis would probably look like this:

Strengths	**Opportunities**
local connection	larger contracts
local expertise	larger fees
intelligence	more jobs
local track record	National firm relocating
low costs	

Weaknesses	**Threats**
lack of national connections	National firms have
lack of breadth in experience	instructions
little economy of scale	competition from
no access to technology	breadth of Nationals
lack of management expertise	fee pressure from local
	competition
	new firms opening

This analysis immediately gives pointers to competitive advantage and disadvantage. For example – local experience is listed as a strength. But to what market specifically? To a local market local experience adds value – they know that there are specific local problems. This local experience is bolstered by local connection.

To a national market local experience could potentially add value – if they were aware that there might be local problems – but they probably aren't! In any event the key factor in the national market is likely to be national connections (see Chapter 5 for the importance of institutional relationships).

The potential to add value in a non-key area in the national market is submerged by other constraints so reliance on its providing competitive advantage would be misplaced.

Similarly, consider a threat; 'Fee pressure from local competition'.

Fees (or rather reducing levels of fee) add value at the procurement stage of the value chain. The surveyor is potentially at a disadvantage. But does the value of a reduced fee outweigh the added value of local experience plus track record, plus connections? Practical experience suggests that it does not – witness the problems of starting a new local business against established competition – and this experience supports the insight gained from matching perceived strengths and so on, against potential in the value chain.

Summary

In order to establish a base for competitive advantage it is necessary to consider a firm's activities:

a) with a focus to a specific product/market;
b) within the context of the key factors for success in that market;
c) with a clear understanding of the way in which customers perceive value being added to their operation at specific points within their value chains;
d) with comparative reference to the activities or potential activities of competitors or potential competitors within the product market.

It should be remembered that, whilst analysis of competitive advantage is an integral part of strategic development, it should not be seen as a 'one-off' activity. The prudent firm – the one identifiable as a winner in any market – is continually engaged in competitive analysis. This enables it not only to plan its activities but to react quickly to competitors' moves – and often to pre-empt those moves before they become a threat.

Tom Peters identifies 'winning' companies as being oriented fundamentally towards customers (the customer-based value chain) and fundamentally innovative. You can only innovate successfully through on-going critical analysis of the key areas in which value can be added through innovation.

Strategic development

As we said earlier, strategy is about getting from A to B profitably. In the preceding section we have considered the bases within which competitive advantage, the key to any kind of strategic planning, can be identified. In this section we turn to the objective 'B' and the planning which goes into its achievement.

'B' – where do we want to be?

A product/market is, potentially, a big place. There may be large amounts of money at stake, there may be many 'players'. There is an infinite variety of specific positions within the market that the firm could wish to occupy. The first question, therefore, must be 'Exactly which of these positions do we wish to achieve?'

The simplistic answer to such a question is often 'We want to make as much money as we can!'. Yet, when analysed, this is often not the objective of many firms, particularly professional partnerships. Their objectives are often couched in quite different terms with an emphasis upon personal quality of life – spare time, cash to enjoy it, interesting work, freedom from undue stress – all the things that professional partnerships have traditionally enjoyed. The product/market situation that such a firm would aim for is simply one that gives an adequate return – given the amount of resources committed to it.

To this definition add the word 'sustainable' and the equation becomes clearer and more transferable – but it does not get any easier to define. It is a truism that nothing stays the same. A business gets bigger – or it gets smaller – over time. The market share that is not managed will manage itself – or be managed out of existence by a competitor.

It is a corporate decision, either taken on corporate asset terms within a company or in personal aspiration terms by a sole trader or partnership, to define the amount of resources which it wishes to commit to a particular market and the return which is required upon those resources.

Product/market strategy comes into play after this fundamental decision has been made.

Once this decision has been made, however, strategy comes into its own. In order to achieve the corporate objective a revenue level must be achieved from the market which meets the defined constraints. This revenue level, in itself, defines the quantity of money which must be taken out of the market – the market share required by the company. It also leads to further considerations – the sales/profit relationships needed, the unit volume of sale activity etc. These constraints combine to produce a preferred market profile.

The activity of subdividing the market to a preferred profile – that is, selling 30 units that make a contribution of £5 rather than 5 units at a contribution of £30 – tends to impose operational limits on the product offering. It positions the company as a high or low added-value provider and management must obviously ensure that its product offering is in accord with this positioning. What it also does is indicate more clearly the target market in which the product must compete.

Unfortunately, it is seldom that a firm will have this target market all to itself; there will normally be competitors with competitive aspirations. The firm then has to decide how much of this target market it needs in order to fulfil its defined aspirations. The relationship between this statement and the total market available is its market share – of the specific target market.

The extent of market share required by the firm has considerable bearing upon the strategies which it can employ in achieving and maintaining it. The problems of remaining a market leader, for example, are quite different from those of a small-scale follower and from those of a market challenger.

Let us examine these positions more closely.

There are four situations in which a firm can find itself when it looks at the market share that it wants. It can

– expand an existing market share
– reduce an existing market share
– maintain an existing market share
– carve out a new market share.

At the same time it can be in several positions within the market; that is, it can be

– market leader
– a major follower
– a low share operator
– a new competitor.

Within its chosen market there are further subdivisions, namely

– niche leader
– niche follower.

Each of these situations imposes different constraints upon the strategic thinking and the strategic options available to the firm.

Expand existing market share

A firm which wants to expand market share has only one option available. Any expansion in market share must be at the expense of other players. It must take market share away from others. This does not, of course, mean that the firm wishing to grow has only this option. It can maintain relative market share whilst simultaneously expanding the total market place – at the cost of others expanding likewise.

How can this be achieved?

We have debated at length the nature and origins of competitive advantage. Growth is achieved through the exploitation of this advantage. Strategies to achieve this exploitation will be highly dependent upon the relative market share of the firm and the resources available to it.

Reduce market share

The danger with reducing market share in any market is that unless such a reduction is carefully controlled it can spin off with unpleasant consequences into other, related markets. For example, the estate agent that consciously chooses to reduce its market penetration in the first time buyer market will necessarily reduce its board coverage. This could be perceived by potential customers as a reduction in overall attractiveness and could react badly on schemes to increase penetration in the adjoining middle market.

At the same time its share reduction will provide an opportunity to a competitor to increase share – and thence credibility – to the very market approached by the agent.

Timing of the two strategies is therefore very important and the related effects of any strategic approaches must be carefully examined before they are adopted.

Maintain market share

It is a truism to say that a firm either grows or gets smaller, but this is generally what happens in a competitive market place. Maintaining a market share implies both defensive strategies against predators and aggressive strategies against weaker competitors – strategic approaches which can easily work against each other. In many ways maintaining a market share is the highest risk strategic situation of all and should be avoided if possible!

Carve out a new market share

In this situation there is all to win and little to lose. Strategies available will depend upon the size of the firm and relative size of competitors coupled with associative synergy available from diversification. Any strategy will be, necessarily, aggressive and success will often depend upon speed of execution and lack of defensive ability amongst the existing competitors.

Clearly the strategic options to market share, then, depend on more than a simple statement of what the firm would like to achieve. Its existing position, both within the particular product market and outside it, will have considerable bearing upon its strategic options.

Market leader

A market leader holds a position of some dominance within a product market. If it holds a sufficiently dominant position it may be able to exercise price leadership, it may control a significant proportion of distribution channels, it may hold barriers to entry – perhaps through patents or proprietary knowledge. It will almost certainly owe its leadership to the possession of competitive advantage in one or more areas.

In the case study example at the start of Chapter 3 we saw how a young firm achieved market leadership very rapidly through its exploitation of superior marketing capability in a small town. This superior capability gave it a significant competitive advantage where it mattered.

In the same way IBM has achieved its market dominance through superior marketing capability, backed up by achieving a cost advantage through economies of scale which was then used to mutually strengthen its marketing and production management capabilities (a positive growth circle).

Encyclopaedia Britannica maintains its market leadership similarly through perceived excellence of its product range (duplication of which by a competitor being, in itself, a high entry barrier), which is maintained and strengthened through judicious reinvestment of the high profitability achieved through high profile and effective direct selling. If any of these factors were to slip then other predators would quickly seize their opportunity.

A market leader, then, is likely to have considerable weapons at its disposal. High entry barriers, maintained and strengthened through re-application of cost advantage all combine against competitors.

Any market leader, however, is vulnerable at certain points, and it is through these points that determined competitors will squeeze and generate market share of their own. The problem for the market leader, of course, is that in order to gain more market share it has to remove share from those who have only achieved it through the leader's weakness! The market leader can also be assured that any moves that it makes, or considers making, will be the subject of intense scrutiny by its competitors who will probe even deeper for the new weaknesses inevitably exposed as the leader changes tack.

IBM, for all its strength, found itself outmanoeuvred in the personal computer market place by the smaller guerilla competitors who grew through their niche markets and exploited their superior specialist knowledge – often learnt within IBM – to the giant's disadvantage.

Market follower

The market follower is usually a fair sized player in a market but, for many reasons, does not control the operation of the market in any way. A follower may, as far as the leader is concerned, be either a good or a bad competitor, and may be tolerated, attacked, or even encouraged in the same circumstances.

It faces similar challenges, in many ways, to a market leader; its market place is the same, its product will be broadly similar. It may have inferior resources available but is content to maintain its relative share without attracting retaliation from the market leader. As such, of course, it is always vulnerable to aggressive pursuit of market share by the market leader but often avoids this, as a 'good' competitor, by taking the brunt of attack from smaller players, effectively 'guarding the leader's back'.

In maintaining its position, of course, the follower needs some elements of competitive advantage, often in areas which are barely profitable for the leader to develop, and these advantages sustain it against emergent competition.

The 'bad' competitor – as a market follower – is less helpful to the market leader. It does not necessarily follow price movements, it innovates aggressively, picking off the leader's prime business, normally just short of the point at which it attracts retaliation. From this position it is likely to develop, given the right conditions, into a market challenger.

Market challenger

In many markets will be found a clear market leader together with a principal challenger. The Cola Wars broke out – and continue – between Coke and Pepsi, both of whom perceived competitive advantage in the greater profitability available from a market leadership position. Similar battles take place in the washing powder markets between Unilever and Proctor and Gamble, with each achieving elements of leadership at different times. The danger in a market leader/challenger situation is that one wins – and the winner takes all – as did IBM when it eventually entered the personal computer market, to the particular detriment of Apple and Commodore. A secondary danger, of course, is that neither wins but overall industry profitability is severely diminished.

It is interesting at this point to speculate upon the likely structure of the UK residential market over the next few years. Despite the institutional takeover of a sizeable market share overall, no clear market leader has emerged. This may have been only delayed by the market turndown or it may be a result of the very different strategic entry reasons for the major players. It may also be the result of incomplete strategic thinking applied to potential sources of competitive advantage to these players. It is hardly conceivable, however, that, given the perceived losses in 1989–90 sustained by these players, that there will not be parent pressure upon them to rectify the situation.

Each player has readily identifiable potential advantage. The banks have a residual perception of financial expertise, building societies have inbuilt trust and goodwill, insurance companies may have positional perception which enables them to take dominant positions – and nationally dominant positions could quickly arise for successful players.

At the present time (1991), however, all overtly target the same key to advantage, therefore providing significant advantage to none. Perhaps barking at a different tree might help!

Niche positions

Even within an identified product/market, market segments lurk, in which players and key success factors differ from the market as a whole. We have seen how markets relate to many facets of a product, from core to intangibles and have identified many bases for segmentation of property markets. Within the residential market there are clear examples of niche activity, often by quite major players. Knight, Frank & Rutley and Savills are two examples of clear niche players in very specific sectors where, interestingly, access is virtually impossible to the institutional majors through the interaction of product intangibles (reassurance and club membership).

At the other end of the market is the 'Seekers' franchise chain which segments directly to the low cost/low perceived value buyers.

On a larger scale we saw in the introductory example how Black Horse Agencies has settled into a large market niche between the low value and 'top provider' markets and how they consciously and assiduously reinforce this market positioning through their promotional and product design activities.

Strategic operations

The scope for alternative strategic operations is virtually limitless. In a finite world most would have already been tried. This is, therefore, a very fruitful area for creative thought.

At the forefront of every thinker's mind, however, should be the military analogy. Corporate and marketing strategy is almost warfare. The war is for profitability – and profitability comes from customers. Small wonder that marketing strategists talk about guerrilla actions, encirclement, head-on attack, flanking movements and all the other jargon from military manuals.

It is as well to remember, at this point, that the analogy stretches further than strategy. Strategy can also be defined as the effective implementation of tactical advantage. In the battlefield tactics concern guns, tanks, cavalry, infantry. In marketing our weapons are product design, packaging, advertising, public relations, selling – the elements of the marketing mix.

We should rub home the analogy. 'You cannot fight a tank battle without tanks. Even if you have the tanks you need drivers, and you still need to be able to talk to the drivers.' It's no good fighting IBM head-on in the market place without a competent sales force – with the specific ability to fight on their home ground.

Strategy deals with the implementation of competitive advantage to the sustainable benefit of the company's bank balance. If that is forgotten then strategy is just talk – no action.

Strategic defence

'The secret of making money is not to lose it.' Put another way 'Always buy at a price where you can get your money back – most of the time you'll make a profit as well.' These words from Cardiff businessman Alex Gaba echo from the early 1960s where, after retiring through ill health, Alex built a highly profitable small warehousing business 'just to keep his hand in'. Similar phrases come down the years.

'Always sell too early.'
'Don't gamble what you can't afford to lose.'

We all know of situations where people gamble their last penny and win. Lord Davies, the builder of Barry Docks, survived on a wing and a prayer – and won. But he might have just as easily lost. That is the way of the gambler. Business fortunes have been made – and lost – on a gamble. But marketing is about management, not gambling. And the first rule of strategy is 'protect yourself at all times.'

All strategy is concerned with making gains at someone else's expense. The strategist must therefore remain aware that whilst attacking someone else he remains vulnerable to attack, either from the attacked or from another competitor taking advantage of his temporary preoccupations!

There are a variety of 'generic' strategic approaches available to the strategist. Scope for specific applications of these generic approaches is virtually unlimited but must be closely tailored to the specific circumstances which apply to the market place and the firm.

Some of these generics are:

Frontal attack
Flank attack
Encirclement
Bypass
Guerilla activity

In a defensive mode we find:

Positional defence
Flank defence
Pre-emptive defence
Counter attack
Mobile defence
Contraction

Most strategic issues revolve around combinations of these positions or approaches and we will review their essentials whilst referring them to practical applications.

Frontal attack

In this situation a direct attack is mounted upon a competitor, pouring resources into direct competition at the competitor's strong points. Such a strategy is almost inevitably resolved on the basis of superior resources or superior ability to deploy these resources tactically.

The Cola Wars, where Pepsi attempted to win market leadership of the Cola market from Coke, through the use of high profile 'role model' advertising was finally resolved through the superior resources and staying power of CocaCola which weathered the storms (after some horrendous errors) and retained its predominant market share. In the property market it would be difficult for a competitor to make severe inroads into Knight, Frank & Rutley's market position as that firm has significantly greater key resources (track record, club membership, reassurance) than could be marshalled by a competitor in a head-on attack.

Flank attack

In this situation a competitor looks, rather than at the strong mainstream product area, to the weaker aspects of a firm's product offering. For example, the British motorcycle industry foundered not against a head-on attack against its high profile superbikes but against a quality perception built up by its Japanese competitors in the undeveloped (and undefended) market for smaller, more economical motorcycles designed for and used by the younger, inexperienced rider. They then used their perceptual strengths (of quality and innovation) as their tactical weapons in a direct attack on a market place where the established British competitors had no effective weaponry. They used their tactical tanks (quality and innovation) against the British Infantry (beautiful but out-of-date engineering plus fading track glories) with predictable results.

The case study in Chapter 3 is, in effect, the chronicle of a similar flank attack, aiming initially at an emerging market place then using the success symbolism derived from this as a superior weapon in the head-on storming of the 'professional' barricades.

Encirclement

The benefits of encirclement as a strategy have been well documented in military terms since ancient times. The seige was a recognised weapon of warfare in the Middle Ages and was even attempted against Berlin in the period since the Second World War. It works effectively, by cutting off sources of supply and translates into corporate terms by cutting off sources of revenue.

This strategy was played effectively by Seiko in the 1970s where the breadth of their product range, coupled with the value for money image which they carefully engineered, effectively 'surrounded' competitors, ruining their revenue inputs to an uneconomic level.

Few players in the property world are yet able to adopt such a strategy but the majors are clearly aware of its potential and are actively involved in product range extension to avoid such entrapment.

This is a relatively high risk strategy as it implies a heavy concentration of resources and relies upon capitulation of the target competitor without undue delay. The more protracted the campaign, the more difficult it becomes to sustain and the greater the risk of long term market damage to the aggressor in the event of failure.

Bypass

The classical bypass strategy was the Maginot Line. A heavily defended 'strategic barrier' was erected which was perceived by both forces to be invulnerable for all practical purposes. The aggressor in this case simply ignored it, developed an advantage in a nearby undefended territory, then walked around the defensive strip with minimal losses.

In a similar way the market for 'home movie' cameras was sunk without trace by manufacturers who developed the video camera, through a radically different technology, and expanded laterally through their dominance in consumer electronic markets. Major players here, of course, are Sony who were never 'in' cameras let alone in moving pictures but perceived and capitalised upon the synergy with home entertainment in audio and TV systems.

This may be a strategic area for the future in both residential and commercial. As computerisation spreads to the Land Registry the door is opened to on-line computer shopping for landed property – if a commercial advantage can be identified!

Guerilla warfare

One of the interesting facets of guerilla warfare is that it is often seen as 'cheating' or uncivilised by military (or establishment) thinkers.

The 'Red Indians' of North America were perceived as savages, un-trustworthy and sub-human because they preferred to attack undefended rather than defended positions – that is, fight and run away. So were the hillmen of Afghanistan against the British, the Zulus in South Africa and the bushmen of Burma and Malaya. What they actually were, of course, was skilled and careful guerilla forces content to wear down the enemy through harassment designed to cause the maximum trouble for the minimum risk and exposure.

Similar epithets would, I am sure, be applied to an estate agent who, recognising the importance of a telephone on Monday morning to another estate agent and that a telephone engaged from a call box (in particular) could not disengage itself, ensured that as many agents in town as possible received call box enquiries on Monday morning and that these call box enquirers left the phones off the hook, thus effectively disabling the competition.

Illegal?	Yes
Bad manners?	Yes
Unprofessional?	Yes
Uncivilised?	Yes
Effective guerilla warfare?	Yes!

In similar vein a competitor in the Computer industry spread guarded rumours about the adequacy of a new IBM product release – thus effectively tying up significant proportions of the opposition's sales force on spurious defence whilst the competition concentrates its sales force on effective competitive selling – effective guerilla warfare!

Defence

What about defensive strategy? How can these approaches be effectively rebuffed?

Fortifications

If attack is anticipated, build some fortifications. Increase entry barriers, tie up supply lines, tie in distribution networks. Ensure that you have the tactical ability to control your battleground. This is what happened with the Maginot Line. Unfortunately the enemy didn't come that way – and the fortifications were useless.

It is worth reiterating here that, particularly in the property industry, the key factors which relate to market success are often intangibles rather than specific product features. This makes it even more important that the product should be the subject of careful analysis to ensure that the 'right' features are being protected.

Over history, direct fortification, whilst it may have some short term – or even medium term – benefits, rarely succeeds as a long term strategy. The Normans built castles – hugely powerful and influential against infantry and archers, but virtually useless against sustained attack by cannon. The French built the Maginot Line. The British motorcycle manufacturers jealously guarded their home markets. All succumbed to changed rules – technological, territorial or perceptual. Fixed fortifications are dangerous, because they

a) become redundant;
b) breed a sense of false security.

Flank defence

A dog is a pretty formidable animal. Against most other animals of similar size it can give a good account of itself in battle. A wasp's nest is only a fraction of the size of a dog. A wasp is even smaller. Yet in a contest between a dog and a wasp's nest the outcome is quite predictable. The dog is attacked from directions it doesn't expect, in quantities it doesn't expect and with weapons it not only doesn't understand but has no idea how to counter. After a few seconds painful bewilderment the dog runs blindly from the scene leaving the wasp's nest somewhat irritated but quite capable of fighting another day.

A company or firm is like the dog – often good at dealing with direct threats but intensely vulnerable to attacks from unconsidered sources with weapons that it does not understand. The problem for firms in the 1990s is that advanced market thinkers are increasing their understanding of products and buyer behaviour to a point where they are increasingly able to mount not simply the traditional flank attack – where they attack through an undefended market sector – but also more sophisticated flank attacks – where the attack is based on flanking product attributes, perceived benefits, behavioural aspects or any of the plethora of areas which we have addressed elsewhere in the book.

Flanks are multi-dimensional rather than simple, as might be inferred from cursory reading!

How then do you protect your flank? It is easier to recognise after the event that your flank has been attacked – even breached – than it is to build fortifications or move in tactical troops in advance. The problem for the business is recognising that

a) the flank exists
b) deciding, or even planning, its protection.

Recognition of the flank

Strategic appraisal, as already discussed, should indicate potential areas of vulnerability. Each of these areas is likely to be a 'flank', particularly if you perceive it as relatively unimportant to the main stream of the business. The more detailed the level of analysis, the more areas of potential vulnerability are likely to emerge, some of them defensible, many of them not!

For property professionals this has been of little concern in the past. The business has provided a comfortable living for most. It could proceed along 'comfortable', 'professional' lines – and professionalism generally militates against competitive activity (where professionalism = membership of a professional body = protectionism, as opposed to being excellent at what you do).

The situation now, however, is somewhat different. Both the residential and commercial sectors contain significant elements of 'external' ownership

– in the form of banks, building societies and other financial institutions – and these new owners, in particular the financial institutions, are renowned for the quality and breadth of their research into markets and behaviour. Many employ professional strategists whose job it is to identify and capitalise upon 'flank' weaknesses in their competition. Those who have never looked, or are not currently looking, at their vulnerabilities should start – now – others are already looking.

So, the best defence to a flank attack is intelligence:

'Where am I vulnerable?'
'Who might know about it?'
'Are there technological or other developments which might increase/decrease my vulnerability?'
'What kind of tactical defences might I wish to use?'
'Do I have or can I develop the necessary tactical ability?'
'What are the potential costs of not doing anything?'

If you are the subject of a well planned flank attack – it's probably too late to do anything about it. Like the dog, yelp and head for cover while you think out your next move.

Pre-emptive defence

A careful evaluation of potential weaknesses in your defensive armoury is also likely to provide pointers as to the sources of potential attacks at these weak points. If a potentially serious competitor can be identified before his strength grows sufficiently for an attack can be launched then it may be possible to attack the source of his strength and thus avoid being attacked at all. Conventional strategists often use the adage that 'the best form of defence is attack' and, as long as the attack is carefully targeted, this probably holds true in a commercial situation.

Such attacks generally need only to be partially disabling, sufficient to keep the competitor from achieving a 'critical mass' in his competitive strengths. Against a major competitor, of roughly equal strengths, there will be continual attack and counter-attack as each strives for relative ascendancy.

The moves of several major commercial players in targeting their promotional activity to decision makers rather than the traditional property influencers in recent months can be seen in this light. By changing the rules the major player hopes to avoid the smaller players building up sufficient 'channel strength' to shut them out of new markets. Such strategy can be countered through:

Counter-offensive defence

In this scenario a firm counter-attacks rather than leads an offensive action. The counter-attack may be head-on or, more profitably, aimed at a temporarily vulnerable flank. In the previous example, if the major player were perceived to be 'light' on local knowledge, a determined local competitor might both withhold local assistance itself and organise a resistance movement amongst other smaller players which could 'starve' the major player out of local markets.

In anticipation of such local retaliatory strategies, of course, the major player will be devoting considerable resources to building a local database, if possible using external data sources, solicitors and the Land Registry!

Whilst the UK property market remains influencer-oriented major players tread a tightrope between internal growth and retention of goodwill from smaller competitors.

Other defensive strategies

The firm should not look simply at its obvious competitors but also at external threats.

For example, building societies, faced with external threats to their core mortgage markets from secondary lenders, diversified into estate agency as a prime channel for capturing their market at the point of sale.

The new major estate agents (majors) quickly became aware of the potential within their new portfolios for width in their product mix – commercial supports residential and is in turn supported by agricultural or plant and machinery specialist operations.

A market under severe pressure can be bolstered by overall market growth or by diversification into other products. The tobacco industry is an interesting case in point where a major firm faced with a potentially declining tobacco market, whilst protesting the 'innocence' of tobacco products as health risks, nevertheless hedged their bets through the purchase of an insurance company – who apply a loading to life insurance taken out by smokers!

Contraction

The ability of firms to maintain its competitive edge across a wide variety of product/markets is limited by a number of factors, not least the quality and capacity of management talent available to it. Even within a single market there will be a variety of market segments and the firm may not be able to service all of these sectors adequately against determined niche players.

In such a circumstance a firm may defend itself best by withdrawing, even if temporarily, into segments where it has relative strength and conceding other segments, hopefully less profitable segments, to locally stronger players.

As stated earlier, such a strategy must be carefully managed, as the synergy from a contraction strategy, particularly in local markets, can rebound destructively.

There is, then, a variety of strategic positions, a variety of offensive formations and a variety of defensive formations available to a firm. Permutations of these positions are almost endless and will apply across product portfolios, individual product/markets and niches within product markets. Different 'balances' are likely to be of use to different positions and we will examine a few as illustration.

Options

Market leader

A market leader, if it wishes to grow, needs more customers. It can get these customers either from competitors' market shares or by expanding the total market place. New customers, whether from within the existing market or from an expansion of the market, are won through the provisions of superior benefits to their value chains. In the residential market the majors are attempting to win market share from the independents and from each other through the provision of an extended product range (benefits range) which is, effectively a head-on attack against their large competitors and, simultaneously, an encirclement attack against the smaller independents.

To date, the majors appear to have been content with winning share from the independents and have not competed aggressively against each other. In doing this they are conceding some market share to the independents, who are having to compete on lower commission rates, presumably in the hope that they can use superior financial resources to 'see them through the storm' whilst the independents will run out of cash, thus increasing the effective divisible pool.

Unfortunately for the majors, many of the independents have infinitely superior resources available in terms of quality of staff (ex pre-buyout partners doing the job they were trained to do), local knowledge and contacts, freedom of movement and reaction to local conditions and often sheer bloody-mindedness as an incentive. Their strategy, therefore, whilst tenable as diversifications, channel building or product defence – assuming that these things are inherently profitable – is unlikely to secure any of them as market leader (in usable strategic terms although there may well be a 'largest' player) and will leave them continually vulnerable to local – and maybe national – niche players to the continuing detriment of their profitability.

As we have seen there are no identifiable clear market leaders in the world of property as a whole. Most players at a national level behave as if they were market followers in the main market place. Their strategies seem to find virtue in their lack of dominance like the car hire firm – 'We're No.2 so we try harder'.

In this position each will generally strive to achieve market share at the expense of other players, at both a local and national level. At a local level a firm will tend to use strategies which relate to local relative market share, sometimes market leader, sometimes follower, sometimes niche player. Strengths and weaknesses will tend to revolve around local tactical constraints, sale management, relationships management, local advertising, supported where appropriate by national initiatives in product design and background promotional or channel activity. In this scenario there is little strategic advantage in 'being national'. In fact, if a perception should develop that being national means low commitment, poor quality of local management, hidebound by bureaucracy, then 'being national' could become an important weakness in local strategic balance.

Commercial firms, once within a 'corporate' banner, often find that they are unable to retain key players against the lure of the entrepreneurial image of the commercial niche player – and all that this implies financially and socially, carrying within them on incorporation, therefore, the seeds of their own competitive disadvantage.

Perhaps the key competitive advantage for firms is a working knowledge of strategy and a killer instinct in its local management forces – an impossible dream?

Niche players

Most property-related firms are, to a greater or lesser extent, niche players in that their expertise at local levels relates to niche markets rather than to the full market range. Even where a firm does adopt a broad stance it will be competing, in the main, against specialised niche players across its markets and, in the absence of a heavy-handed centralised market growth strategy, will have to compete as if it were a niche player.

A few firms, of course, have established themselves in almost unassailable niches. Certainly the Knight, Frank & Rutley's, the Savills and the Humberts are unlikely to be concerned about competition from the majors who are, as we have seen, disbarred from the 'club membership' which is a key success factor in their chosen markets.

The key to success, of course, in a niche market, is specialisation. Stern Studios in London specialise in studio flats within the Greater London area and their whole market operation caters for buyers and sellers in this market exclusively. Knight, Frank & Rutley specialises – with all that this entails – in the 'top end' of the 'country market'. In Chapter 3 we saw how Parkhurst penetrated the market initially through a niche strategy aimed at a sector of the buying public who had grown up prepared for doing business in a supermarket.

Attempts are being made by the estate agency majors to sub-brand niche players in 'executive and country homes' with varying degrees of success.

McCarthy & Stone have built a multi-million pound business in catering to the specific needs of the elderly for private, sheltered, housing – and have designed their product offering very carefully to include the intangible needs which are a clear key factor in the buying decision for this sector.

There is still scope for imagination in considering niche strategies for property professionals. The obvious niches are well catered for – yet there is no national chain dedicated to first time sellers and buyers! The commercial world thrives upon niche specialists – rent review, dilapidations, retail, rating, licensed trade, leisure – and there is endless scope for subdivisions of these niches. The key again is specialisation – and the expertise (invaluable) that specialisation can develop.

Summary

Marketing strategy is directed towards the development of sustainable competitive advantage. This may be found in three generic areas – cost, focus and differentiation.

Sustainable competitive advantage derives from an ability to add value to customers. Customers derive value throughout their value chains and the astute producer will analyse carefully the impact of his product upon the value chains of potential customers.

There is considerable scope for the development of competitive advantage, even where a producer does not have an inbuilt cost advantage, through creative consideration of differentiation within a product offering. A product may be differentiated from its competitors on a wide variety of factors but strategists must avoid the pitfalls of over-differentiation and differentiation which fails to add value.

Within a market different firms occupy different strategic positions – and they may occupy various positions simultaneously in various markets. There are a number of offensive and defensive strategies available. The task of the strategist is to identify a permutation which best fits the specific strategic circumstances of the firm at a specific time.

References and further reading

D.A. Aaker (1984), *Strategic Market Management*, John Wiley & Sons, New York, p. 6

K. Ohmae (1987), *The Mind of the Strategist*, Penguin Business Library, London p. 39

T. Peters (1990), (Seminar) *In Search of Excellence*, Bristol

M.E. Porter (1980), *Competitive Strategy*, The Free Press, Macmillan Inc., New York

M.E. Porter (1985), *Competitive Advantage*, The Free Press, Macmillan Inc., New York

A. Ries and J. Trout (1986), *Marketing Warfare*, McGraw-Hill Inc., New York.

8 Marketing Tactics

These are the areas of marketing tactics – advertising, public relations, sales promotion, direct marketing, packaging, selling and sales management, distribution and channel management, pricing. In strategic terms these are the infantry, tanks and air cover of the marketing professional. Strategy, as we have seen, is concerned with the implementation of tactical advantage. The marketer can turn his tactical advantage into sustainable profit.

Within this chapter we shall review the essential features of these tactical weapons with a view to turning them to advantage, both in the sale of property and in the sale of professional services.

Advertising

The principal tactical weapon available to the marketer or business strategist is advertising. Advertising is the propaganda of the military strategist, seeking to condition its recipients into acceptance of product claims thus smoothing the way of the product in the market place. Advertising is ubiquitous in developed countries and we are all subject to sophisticated images exhorting us to 'be like a role model', 'keep up with the Jones's', 'make sure our children don't suffer by comparison', 'follow the opinion leaders' and the whole panoply of the adman's trade.

So all-pervasive is the power of advertising that most of us experience between 200 and 400 advertising messages from various sources every day of our adult lives. No wonder that our minds have developed powerful strategies for ignoring most of them.

Advertising works on many levels. It can influence attitudes, it can arouse interest in product ideas, it can reinforce brand images, it can turn us right off! Its very power can work against it unless the benefits which it is capable of providing are clearly thought out and its powers harnessed to produce the desired effect.

As a tactical weapon advertising is used to generate a desired effect on a specific target market. If it is not used deliberately and carefully then its results may be equally unexpected and careless.

Myths

There are some unfortunate myths surrounding advertising.

'The only bad publicity is no publicity'– Not true for advertising. Advertising that creates dissonant or non-supportive images simply confuses potential purchasers, adding to the risk factor interest in any buying decision, thereby reducing any likelihood of changing buyer behaviour for the better.

'Subliminal advertising persuades people effectively against their will' – Almost certainly untrue. The idea came from research in the 1950s immortalised by Vance Packard in 'The Hidden Persuaders', but subsequently found to have been a hoax. More recent research suggests that there may be minimal effects, but nothing to make a song and dance about.

'Advertising can force consumers to buy my product' – Misleading advertising may help in generating product trial. As we have seen, however, quality reflects the perceived difference between expectation and actual performance. Failure to perform creates a perception of poor quality, or even a sense of having been cheated in the customer. In neither case does this give a sound foundation for future purchasing behaviour.

'The more media we use the better' – Very doubtful – our perceptual screens work against noticing advertising anyway, so it is much better to concentrate on media which will be read by people already interested. Advertising video editing machines in *Camcorder User* is much more likely to reach an interested customer than it would in *Radio Times* or in the *Estates Gazette*. (Except, perhaps, in an issue which features the use of video as a promotional tool.)

What is advertising about?

The purpose of advertising is to change behaviour in some way.
Advertising may:

- increase awareness of needs which might lead to the purchase of a product;
- increase awareness of us as a producer;
- generate inclusion of our brand in a choice set;
- generate acute desire to purchase our product.

If it does not generate some kind of behavioural change, it is not worth doing at all. In their book *Marketing Warfare*, Al Ries and Jack Trout say 'Marketing Battles are fought in the mind. Inside your own mind and the mind of your prospects, every day of the week.' Advertising is a primary path to the mind of a prospect – not the only one by any means – but a direct road which is well signposted.

Within these paragraphs is the key to effective advertising, whether it be product advertising, say for a client's home or office block, or whether it be image advertising; for example, Jones Lang Wootton's series of advertisements aimed at decision makers rather than influencers.

The key is that unless you know precisely what effect you wish to have on the minds of your readers/listeners/prospects, then the chances of your succeeding are minimal.

What do you want to happen

The first question, therefore, is, what do you want to happen? What behavioural change do you want your advertising to produce? As we have seen this can vary across a wide spectrum. You may be able to achieve several changes in one hit. But you must identify clearly which ones or your efforts will stand as much chance as throwing a lump of coal blindfold over your left shoulder into the heart of an active volcano and hoping that it will be ejected as a diamond and land at your feet.

How can you make it happen?

If you know what you want to happen then your chances of making it happen improve dramatically – but the story is by no means over.

Let us take an example. You would like someone, who might possibly turn out to be a purchaser, to telephone your office to ask for information regarding a property on your books (whether residential or commercial, the principle is the same).

Note here, however, that the objective is to get someone to enquire. Setting the objective as selling something would be unachievable in practical terms, so why waste money?

At this point the fried and toasted 'AIDA' formula comes into effect. AIDA means:

- Attention
- Interest
- Desire
- Action

The required behavioural change is to get some action – that is, telephone the office and ask for more information.

First of all, though, you have to attract attention. Even assuming that your likely prospect is already in the stage of heightened awareness or, even better, active information search, you are likely to be in competition with other advertisements, both those of other providers and those for other properties within your own advertisement.

Note that attracting attention is not easy. How many of you noticed the words 'fried and toasted' in the preceding paragraph? It should, of course, read 'tried and tested' but the typist could not read my writing so made the best sense she could. The chances are that you did too!

What do most of us do? Read any regular property advertisement and you find that most of the information that a purchaser might want is already given – except the detailed address. For example:

> DURHAM ROAD
> 3 Bed Terrace, Super condition
> forecourt, gas c/heating, 2
> living rooms, small garden, garage space. Fitted kitchen
> Suit first time buyer.
> £53,750

Super advert – tells you everything. The sort of ad we see every day and that we would be quite happy with.

But what does it tell your prospect?

DURHAM ROAD – 'I don't want to live there for a start. They play tag with hatchets in Durham Road.'

Next advert! No chance of changing perception. No telephone call. It failed totally to meet your advertising objective. Let's move on further:

'3 bed terrace' – 'I only need 2 bedrooms, this is too big, it'll cost too much to heat and, anyway, it's terraced.'

Next advert! – same comments. Try this one:

> FIRST HOME FOR GROWING FAMILY
> Close to schools and shopping.
> Easy access to motorway.
> Space to grow but easy to
> live in.
> £53,750.

The first question is, where is it? And they have to ring you to find out. Once they are on the phone you can deal, directly, with objections and you have achieved your objective.

You could, of course, argue that your real objective was to find someone who specifically wanted to live in Durham Road. Fine, if your targeting is that close, but this lets out all the people who might have been persuaded into substitution.

The advertisement relates to needs – now and future – and creates a desire to know more – hence achieving the stated objectives.

Let's be a bit more adventurous in our aims. Let's try to change behaviour so that you are included in choice sets – as an agent.

1) | CHARTERED SURVEYORS & AUCTIONEERS & ESTATE AGENTS
> • ACCOMPANIED VIEWINGS   • 7 DAY OPENING
> • REGULAR MAILING LIST   • NATIONAL COVERAGE
> • MODERN OFFICES   • EXPERIENCED, HELPFUL STAFF
> NO SALE – NO FEE

2)

> ESTATE AGENTS & AUCTIONEERS AND SURVEYORS
> WE HAVE AGREED SALES ON
> £35M WORTH OF PROPERTY
> SINCE JAN 1ST 1990
> ***Can we do the same for you?***

Compare advert 1) with advert 2). What are the differences? Which one changes behaviour?

1) tells you all the interesting things that most estate agents' adverts tell you. There is no impact, no novelty and nothing for a potential vendor to get excited about. It does not even make a trial suggestion and close – 'Can we help you?' etc. It deserves the effect that it usually gets – not a lot!

2) on the other hand, says 'we're successful', 'we get the job done', 'we can give you a real benefit' – and asks you to consider it in the future. The chances are that you will, and that you will remember the invitation. It changes behaviour – the object of the exercise.

Many will find the second advertisement a little off-putting. Perhaps 'it is not really professional' or 'we could all say something like that'. Many will prefer the safer first advert. After all this is what we actually do isn't it?

The problem with 1) is that the benefits are those perceived by property people – not those understood by customers (except for the 7-day opening). The second advert says 'Never mind how we do it, you can take it for granted that we do anything anybody else does. The fact is – we get results and we are proud of it.'

Background/foreground

As we have seen many times within this book, people's perceptions work on many levels, often at the same time. This means that it is possible to include cues in adverts that work on different people in different ways in different circumstances.

For example, the full page residential advert with its chessboard of smudgy photographs says:

'What an unimaginative lot estate agents are'.
'These must be good, look at all the property on the market'.
'Why does my £100 000 house get only the same space as this £50 000 one?'
'Those lovely people 'gave' me a photo listing of my £40 000 house – for nothing'

You can't win!

At the same time, people considering a move may be influenced by the total size of the advertisement, matching it with their 'knowledge' base of the number of boards which they see around, general profile of agency staff, prominence of the office and so on.

In this situation it is clear that the advertiser must give very careful thought not only to the detailed content of his advert but also to the layout, balance, 'sales messages', logo style and all the 'background' images that it contains.

Again, it is of paramount importance that the specific objectives of both factors in the advert be defined clearly and that the finished result is critically examined to make sure that these objectives are met.

If the image conflicts are great it will be more cost-effective in terms of effective behavioural change to split the advertising so that conflicting messages are neither given nor received. If mutually supportive images can be sent the power of the advert is significantly improved.

Attention

Let's go back and consider some areas which might help in attracting attention. As you might expect there has been considerable research within this area – which means that some of your competitors will be using some or all of these ideas in their advertising.

Size

Following the general principle that strength usually wins, it does not come as any surprise that the bigger the message, the more it will attract attention – but bear in mind that it is relative size, not actual size, that is the attention-getter. This also applies to space allocation within an advertisement. The property with a large photograph (or large type) attracts attention more than its neighbour with a small photograph.

Colour

The use of colour, even spot colour, in an advert increases its chances of attracting attention. In one study a single colour advertisement in a black and white periodical stimulated 41 per cent more sales than equivalent black and white. It is dearer, however, and the benefits must be carefully balanced against costs.

A black and white advert in a predominantly colour-based medium – for example, TV – carefully used, can have similar effects because of the contrast effect.

Contrast

If some degree of conflict can be created with the surroundings attention is likely to be stimulated. TV ads which fade from colour to black and white than back tend to have this conflict effect.

Intensity

In the natural world many species use intense images to 'sell' their wares. Brilliant colour, overpowering aromas are used by plants, animals, fish and reptiles to warn off predators, attract mates or attract pollinators. People do the same thing – just look at some of the creations on the fashion show catwalk, male and female!

Position

In the Property Centre walk-round showroom people were for ever complaining if their property was not displayed in what they considered to be a prominent position – that is, at eye level and away from direct competition! There is an instinctive awareness of what catches the eye.

Research suggests some interesting ideas: newspaper advertisements attract greater attention if they are

- at the front rather than the back
- on the right hand page rather than the left hand page
- inside front cover
- inside back cover
- outside back cover

Direction

If you include pointers in an advert the reader's eye is likely to follow. The illustration of the Weatherall's advert (p. 164) shows this clearly – the eye is drawn directly to the main feature – Bristol. Contrast this with the Harlow advert (p. 165) where the diagonals in the upper photograph take you nowhere – and add nothing to the effect.

Movement

Movement in an advertisement, even where it is only implied, adds interest and is likely to attract attention.

Isolation

Here the Harlow advert scores. The four squares are surrounded by white space and arrest the eye sufficiently to generate a search for more information.

Novelty

Perhaps the most famous property advertisements of all time were the Roy Brookes series which were so different from conventional advertising that they become a cult in themselves.

Any effect used for attention-grabbing must be used with care to ensure

19 20 **(21)** 22

BRISTOL

WEATHERALL GREEN & SMITH

On the 21st May 1990
Weatherall Green & Smith
opened their Bristol office at
62 Queen Square, Bristol BS1 4JZ
Telephone: 0272 255918

For further information contact
Hugh Savage BSc ARICS or Robert Orrett BSc ARICS

OFFICES IN LONDON · CITY OF LONDON · BRISTOL
EDINBURGH · LEEDS · PARIS · FRANKFURT · DUSSELDORF
HAMBURG · MUNICH · NEW YORK · TOKYO

Weatherall
Green & Smith

(Reproduced with permission from Watherall Green & Smith,
and by courtesy of *Chartered Surveyor Weekly*.)

Located to the north-west of the town centre, Harlow

Business Park enjoys the best of both worlds: whilst

being situated minutes from the M11, Stansted Airport

and Harlow Town railway station, it is set within a 50

acre green field site, adjoining green belt.

that the attention effect does not override the message. Everybody recognises Snoopy as an attention-grabber, but how many recognised the link with Nationwide Anglia? Similarly the Dron and Wright minefield TV advertisement catches attention – but does it add anything to the image of Dron and Wright?

Interest, desire and action

We return to influencing behaviour. Persuasion. What makes an advert persuasive?

- First – and foremost – does the message relate to needs? If the message does not relate to needs the mind will suppress it – and no persuasion can take place.
- Second – is the message believable? Here we can look at the message from two angles, its source and its content.

Source

A credible source generally enhances persuasion, hence words like 'scientific tests show'; 'your family doctor recommends'; 'readers recommend'. Hence also Michael Jackson and Kylie Minogue being associated with Pepsi-Cola. The 'Pepsi Generation' receives increased persuasive credibility from role models at this level. The barrister figure portrayed by Leo McKern in the Black Horse series of adverts (1989/90), even whilst directly associating with the humorous Rumpole, adds credibility through the self-mocking, anti-establishment imagery which makes the endorsement all the stronger.

Many products receive credibility on TV advertising through the use of recognisable voice-overs. Richard Briers is a star performer in the genre together with Penelope Keith, Simon Cadell and many others.

'Thank you' letters in an estate agent's window add credibility to the whole operation – unless the names are blanked out or turned into 'Mr B', 'Mr W' etc., at which point they become mere puffery.

Message

The content of the message itself, relating to previous perceptions within the product area, contributes to credibility. Claims of 'Experienced, professional service', backed up by 22-year-olds in white socks (or a perception of this) are not credible.

The nature of claims made within the message is important. How strong are the claims? A strong claim is likely to enhance persuasion particularly if it is relevant to perceived needs and if it can be seen to be objective. This is why the 'we have sold £42 million worth of property since January 1st' is strong. The claim is direct and can be interpreted as objective. Contrast this with 'our professional staff put you – the customer – first – every time'. The second claim, whilst laudable and even possibly true, is subjective. It cannot be tested directly or audited in any simple manner. It is neither a strong nor a persuasive claim.

To be persuasive a claim must be strong, objective and verifiable in some way.

The Advertising Standards Association also imposes a duty upon advertisers to be 'legal, decent, honest and truthful'. Any statement of fact must be verifiable.

The number of claims within the message can affect persuasion, particularly where purchasing is relatively low risk – therefore involving less commitment on the part of a purchaser. It is worth remembering that as house vendors – and commercial vendors – become more experienced and sophisticated in their purchase decisions (choice of agents) so their potential perceived risk and involvement is also likely to be reduced. In this situation they are less likely to be influenced by multiple claims in a message.

There is also research which suggests that unsophisticated purchasers, at their first involvement, are unable to distinguish between the relative quality of different claims and are therefore likely to favour multiple claims as a first step in decision making.

Bias

Consumers are likely to perceive bias in messages and are likely to be influenced favourably by balancing features. For example, an advert that says 'We're number 2 – so we try harder', is likely to be more believable than 'we try harder' (unless the reader can be 'trained' to imply the first statement as in the 'Pure Gold' Benson & Hedges series). In this context there is evidence that comparative advertising is likely to yield, in general, better results than direct product advertising.

Having looked at some of the factors which affect credibility in the message, how can we achieve the next stage – action?

Action

There are some basic techniques in common use, not just within advertising but also within the selling field. They are generic techniques and have a wide range of potential applications but some understanding here is possibly helpful.

Prompting

'How can we help you?'; 'Ring us now for a detailed quotation'; 'Ring now for full details'. This is the old technique of asking for the sale. If you do not ask you seldom get. All the 'How to get super sales' textbooks right back to Dale Carnegie stress the importance of asking for the sale. Yet many sales people still don't ask!

Neither do adverts! Look again at the Weatherall's advert. It asks you to do something. The chances are that if Bristol interested you, you might contact them. At least the firm will probably enter your choice set. The Harlow advert, on the other hand, having attracted your attention, just tells you interesting things. It does not even give you a phone number or a person to ring. Not even an address. (To be fair it is part of a series advert occupying several interleaved pages, but that does not excuse it.)

Foot in the door

People take big steps more easily if they can take a small step first. This is the basis of the sales technique of proceeding by agreement.

'You agree, Mr Prospect, that if you died your family would be worse off?' 'Yes'.
'Doesn't it make sense, then, to take steps to protect them?'. 'Yes'.

And the policy is sold – subject to dealing with objections etc.

In advertising you want something positive to happen – a telephone call maybe. Would the Weatherall's advert be stronger if it asked you to do something small before telephoning for further information? Maybe if it asked you to write down their phone number, **then** telephone for further information?

If you can persuade someone to take a small step they become much more likely to take the big step that you are looking for.

Readers Digest mail shots use this technique very effectively by asking you

a) Not to throw the envelope away
b) To take part in their prize draw
c) Buy the product offered.

Door in the face

In selling, though perhaps not so often in advertising, we find the reverse technique where, by asking initially for the impossible – and being refused – you can scale down demands to the acceptable (which is perceived as being even more acceptable by reference to the first demand).

Property people do this all the time.

'Asking Price? £250 000' – 'Too much? Well try £220 000'.

A much more sensible basis for negotiation made even more sensible by the earlier high demand level.

Some interesting research in this area suggests that where the salesman offers his top-of-the-range model first he is likely to achieve significantly higher value sales than where he starts at the bottom and works up (John

Collbrecht). Perhaps the advertising use of this technique would be to invert the conventional 'prices from £69 000 to £413 000' and quote 'prices from £413 000 to £69 000'.

'You scratch my back'

If you give something to another person you put them under an obligation to give you something back. An extreme example of this is the 'puppy dog close' in selling where your prospect takes the puppy home to 'try over the weekend'. How many come back? A similar case occurs with the motor salesman who says 'there are the keys, take it out for the afternoon'. (He's not stupid, your existing car and house keys are safe in his pocket).

It is not the trial that makes the difference, it is the generous gesture which now demands reciprocation.

In advertising terms it pays to highlight the 'giving' activity. Don't 'offer' free valuations. Tell the prospect 'we give free valuations'. It is a small point but it makes a difference by generating an obligation.

Labels

People are very keen on labels. Our professional communities reply on subtle labels and badges as symbols of membership. We have already seen how consumers are influenced by membership groups. In advertising prospects are included into reference sets, particularly if product ownership can, itself, be a label. At the height of the Docklands boom, ownership of Docklands residential property achieved that status. The labels spun off even as far as recruitment advertising which extolled the 'Waterside living and working concept'.

Labelling can also be more subtle. Motor manufacturers, brewers, distillers, couturiers, perfumeries all strive to attach lifestyle labels to their products. The Lotus advertisement (p. 170) subconsciously labels its owner as well-to-do, well connected and stylish by the juxtaposition of the car and its country house background. At the same time it overtly labels its owner as British upper class, a high achiever (the sporty image) and environmentally aware (green). Powerful appeals in a single advertisement.

Little advertising for property or property advisors uses labelling images in a sophisticated manner. There is a world of scope available to the creative advertiser.

These are just some of the areas that affect the impact of advertising upon consumers. For many of us common sense is a good guide to successful results. In more sophisticated campaigns it may pay to seek the services of specialist advertising consultants who should be able to advise you on layout, content, typestyle, column mix, message design and all the other interactive factors which make up a good advertisement. In addition to design they should be able to advise on effective use of different media.

British racing and green.

Britain's new chargecooled Lotus Esprit Turbo SE produces 264 bhp and reaches 60mph in 4.7 seconds, on the way to a possible 163 mph, where conditions and regulations allow.

Speed, however, should never be the ultimate goal.

Racing experience, gained over 40 years on the circuits of the world, has enabled us to develop still further our celebrated chassis, suspension and brakes.

And in keeping with the times, the Lotus engine in this latest addition to the Esprit range employs unique new technology and a catalytic converter for a cleaner, quieter environment. The engine accepts only unleaded fuel and comfortably meets the toughest noise regulations in the world.

This brings a whole new meaning to British Racing Green.

Handling performance and style.

The Lotus range includes the mid-engined Esprit from £34,900 to around £47,000, the Elan and the Elan SE from under £20,000 and the four seater Excel SE from £27,800.
For a test drive with your nearest dealer or for a brochure call the Lotus Brochureline on 071-253 7073 (24 hours).
Lotus Cars Limited, part of Group Lotus PLC, Hethel, Norwich, Norfolk.

(Reproduced with permission from Lotus Cars Ltd,
and by courtesy of Monitor Advertising Limited.)

Media

We began the discussion of advertising by stressing the importance of knowing what you want to happen, that is, what behavioural change you wish to take place.

We have not yet discussed just who you wanted to influence, although our previous discussions within marketing have indicated very clearly the importance of targeting. Targeting implies aiming very specifically at a clear target.

Having once decided upon the target, however, there is more than one way of hitting it. It is often true that the more specific and elusive the target, the broader the scatter of ammunition that is needed to hit it.

Carrying the shooting analogy further, the sportsman uses a rifle to shoot at fixed targets on the rifle range but a shotgun for clay pigeons. Advertising is subject to similar constraints. The more elusive the target, the broader needs to be the network of images that catches it. The tighter the focus group of potential prospects, the tighter can be the imagery and media used to reach it adequately.

What media are available?

Mass media
Television
Radio
Newspapers
Hoardings

Focused media
Cinema
Specialist magazines and manuals

Throughout the 1980s there was a shift of emphasis away from the press towards TV and radio advertising, reflecting the increasing importance of advertising in commodity markets.

Property – and property people – are still not traded as commodities – and this is reflected in the relatively low level of usage of impermanent media as a means of prime communication. The property world operates predominantly through trade journals and personal contact, particularly in the commercial arena where a large proportion of business tends to operate through intermediaries acting, as we have seen, as gatekeepers and influencers.

In the residential market there have already been some changes in that the Prudential, GA, Nationwide Anglia and BHA have all, to some extent, dipped their toes in the television market. There has similarly been tentative use of local radio as a background medium.

Let us examine the various media and some of the factors which are appropriate to media choice and usage.

Television

As a medium television has much to offer. It allows an advertiser to use moving pictures, stills, voice, background sound and music in an almost infinite series of combinations. Skilled use of the medium can create mood, imagery, relationships and provide behavioural cues; it can be used for demonstration of a product, it can carry both direct and indirect messages both as foreground information and as background information simultaneously.

Unfortunately, the medium itself is not selective in that audiences are either casual (just switched on, watch anything) or derived from the content of related programming. Audience response can be influenced by carry-over from related programming. For example, an audience for a 'heavy' programme like War & Remembrance is unlikely to be in a mood to respond positively to holiday adverts either during or immediately following the programme.

It can also be an expensive medium to use in that advertisements must be carefully designed, scripted, acted and filmed – preferably by professionals. Even a simple 30 second advertisement can cost over £30 000 to make. The complexities of creating successful TV advertising contribute to an inherent inflexibility which makes it difficult to respond to rapid changes in environment, particularly the fluid British economy.

For property people, therefore, TV is a difficult medium. It is expensive to use and, except in very specific circumstances, difficult to ensure that the message will be seen by, never mind penetrate the cognitive screens of, a tightly targeted audience.

There are exceptions to this. In the early 1980s a husband and wife team of estate agents in Chepstow (Archer & Co.) made very effective use of TV 'snapshots' over the Christmas period to promote their telephone number – Chepstow 2468 – using the obvious '2–4–6–8' catchphrase. Few are lucky enough to obtain such a direct marketing hook – and even fewer sharp enough to use it.

An interesting development in TV advertising may be approaching. ITV covered the 1990 World Cup 'In association with National Power' – and National Power advertising liberally interspersed the action in the 'commercial breaks'. Presumably this was designed to enhance the image of National Power! Whatever its purpose, if joint productions are to be the way of the future there must be considerable scope for larger players in many industries to cooperate in suitable programming – and related advertising – in this way. This is a logical and potentially profitable development of sponsorship and product placement.

There is similar creative scope in cooperative advertising. The Newport Property Centre cooperated with a furniture retailer in an advertising scenario which showed a house for sale, then sold, then the satisfied buyer furnishing their home from the showrooms of the retailer. This was relatively low cost local advertising with a restricted 'lead-in' commitment, but succeeded in raising consciousness of the Property Centre logo and contributed to its inclusion in potential vendors' choice sets.

Further possibilities exist for product placement – not strictly advertising but a useful diversification within the medium. Inclusion of fascia displays, 'For Sale' boards, logo-carrying cases etc. in 'crowd scenes' seldom does any harm!

Use of a complex medium such as TV probably implies use of professionals and, if best results are to be obtained, the services of an advertising agency should be considered. Advertising agencies generally work on a commission basis, the commission being, effectively, allowed at source to the agency by the media provider: The agency then charges the client at the full 'rate card' rate as applied by the producer. This may not cover all costs and it is usual for agencies to apply additional charges for specialist services. It should be noted, however, that like most agents, advertising agencies can sometimes be persuaded to operate on the basis of a fixed fee.

Some of the choices involved are:

– When are our targets (individuals within the targeted market with all that this implies for perceptual processing) likely to be watching television? For example, Saturday morning television tends to be dominated by product messages to children;
– What types of programming might attract a target audience?
– Is there likely to be programme content which could add to or detract from our messages?
– What types of appeal might facilitate message penetration and/or acceptances? Will our targets respond to fear/humour/comparative vehicles?
Is there scope for aspirational or associative messages?
– How can the advert be designed to ensure that the message creates the desired behavioural change? Can it be assisted by colour choices, musical backgrounds etc?

Clearly this is not an arena for the amateur, considering the size of budgets required if an appropriate impact is to be made.

Radio

Local radio advertising went off with a bang but has never quite lived up to its promise. It suffers by comparison with TV – it lacks the pictures and has to sell its story in sound. On the other hand it reaches parts which TV cannot reach – particularly into motor cars where millions sit each day stuck in traffic jams.

Unfortunately for advertisers, the staple diet of commercial radio is music

– pop music – mobile audio wallpaper – and this tends to restrict the listening audience into bands which may not include those whom the property industry would wish to target.

This, however, is by no means exclusive. In the residential market considerable efforts must be made to attract first time buyers and sellers, many of them in the age groups well targeted by local commercial radio. On a background basis there should be considerable scope for the local advertiser.

In South Wales, Darlow and Co. (case study, Chapter 3) made profitable use of local radio, commissioning a catchy jingle which supported their overall persona. (The jingle was released as a single record and sold well locally thus increasing the 'legend'.)

The Property Centre also used local radio, taking advantage of the potentially short lead times involved to present regular newsflashes throughout the day promoting individual properties.

Once again there are choices to be made as for television. The difficulty here is in establishing credibility for commercial radio as a source and in ensuring that a campaign makes sufficient impact upon consumers to generate behavioural change.

The press – newspapers

By far the largest proportion of total advertising spend in the UK goes to newspapers and journals. Newspaper advertising has the advantage of relative permanence, giving time for readers to digest messages thoroughly – if they can be attracted to read them. More information can be provided, a mixture of images (words and pictures) can be provided to match the message required.

There is a wide range of newspapers available, most of them clearly targeted to a specific readership. Advertisers can therefore start with the advantage of understanding some of the behaviour to be expected from this readership.

This gives the potential for specific types of advertising to be projected to specific market segments, thus hopefully increasing prospects for message acceptance.

The property industry generally makes good and well-established use of newspaper advertising, particularly within the residential sector. There is built-in segmentation through the use of 'local' editions of national news-papers plus 'local' evening and daily papers. The Times has different appeals from the Sun, for example.

Newspaper advertising sales departments will generally be delighted to provide detailed breakdowns of their readership profile for the benefit of advertisers.

There are problems in newspaper advertising.

– The format is well developed and familiar. Most things have already been tried. It is relatively difficult therefore to be creative at a level which will attract special attention.

– Advertising tends to be grouped together. Most evening papers, for example, will carry a special 'property' section one or two evenings in a week. Within this section will be a quantity of advertisers using similar techniques to promote similar products. While the synergy of grouping tends to attract focused attention to the feature section, the level of competition tends to work against the impact of specific advertisers.

– The advertiser is restricted in his use of the medium. The economics of newspaper production tend to result in standardised typefaces, grey and grainy photographs, restricted use of colour (unless a high surcharge is to be paid).

– Advertisers are often restricted as to placement of their copy. Where less than a full page is taken the newspaper will set to their convenience – not to the needs of the advertiser.

Perhaps some of these factors – not just the actual copy supplied – contribute to the perception of property advertising as being drab, un-interesting and lacking in creativity.

There are, nevertheless, some advantages.

Newspapers, particularly evening and Sunday papers, tend to be read slowly, thus providing advertisers with scope to include expanded infor-mational messages rather than the concise 'image' appeal required by the less permanent media. Newspapers, particularly local ones, tend to have a regular readership making them ideal vehicles for advertisements that rely on a cumulative learning effort for their full impact. Where grouping of advertisements takes place size of advert can be made synonymous with the effectiveness of the organisation – and relative size of the advertisers can be perceived by the reader. Experience in the Property Centre and other agencies showed a clear direct link between size of advertisements and number of instruction leads received.

Newspaper advertising is relatively inexpensive (compared with TV and radio). It has a short lead time from submission of copy to publication which allows adverts to be topical and relate to current events. Special effects – logo blocks, shading and overlays can be readily incorporated. Most newspapers are able to accept specialist copy if submitted in an appropriate format.

The property industry makes extensive use of newspapers as an advertising medium, in particular at a local level within the residential sector. News-papers have, in the past, been the principal image building vehicle for estate agents (who operated primarily on a local basis) and has provided valuable supportive advertising for the more sophisticated campaigns of the larger house builders (Wimpey, Barratt etc). In addition we have recently seen increasing sophistication in the use of selected newspapers by the larger commercial firms.

It will be interesting to see over the next few years whether the new residential groupings will attempt to change the balance of advertising in any serious way. Clearly the potential now exists for image and awareness advertising to be shifted into the wider media – in particular to television thus reducing traditional dependence upon local newspapers. Some have already tried, notably the Prudential who stopped local newspapers advertising completely for a while, preferring to rely upon their own in-house property journal.

The probability is that there will be a shift but that the message 'come to our local shop' will need to be clearly communicated, together with the benefits of such a behavioural change, before consumers are convinced that their home can be adequately sold without local advertising.

The press – magazines

Magazines, almost by their very nature, cater for specialist readerships. They are, therefore, closely targeted to the needs of their readers and provide a powerful vehicle for the sophisticated advertiser.

A specialist readership is, by definition, specialised which implies that readers will probably have a relatively sophisticated understanding of technical terms and, more importantly for the marketer, will have probably passed already through the barriers of the extended problem solving decision (EPS) into the realms of limited problem solving (LPS).

An illustration of what is happening here may help understanding. In February 1990 the author purchased (in Hong Kong) a video camcorder. This was, to an extent, a 'spur of the moment' decision which sprang from a recognition of need triggered by special circumstances. The decision process was accelerated and concentrated by time constraints resulting in a decision which satisfied rather than optimised product benefits and features.

The five hours or so of video tape which resulted from the Far East trip led to a recognition of the need for editing facilities which would enhance use of the (very expensive) camcorder; and the need for knowledge about such matters triggered the purchase of specialist magazines such as *Camcorder User.*

A few months' regular reading of such journals develops a reasonable familiarity with specialist terms and technical jargon. Such terms as 'insert edit' and 'audio dub' generate meaningful concepts to the reader.

At this point the basic product is now familiar; basic brands are also familiar. What remains of the purchase decision is the specific brand and model of the particular piece of kit that services my needs best – limited problem solving.

It is irksome to the reader, therefore, if an advertiser

– uses (by now) familiar terms in an unfamiliar way;
– leaves out specific technical data which might influence brand choice;
– refuses to quote prices;

and so on.

Once a purchaser moves into limited problem solving some interesting effects occur which advertisers should be aware of:

– alternatives are perceived as essentially similar;
– beliefs tend not to be strongly held (that is, the purchaser is likely to develop an open mind);
– advertising exposure becomes passive, with only superficial information processing.

There are some important factors here for property people in the commercial sector.

Commercial property, and commercial property services, tend to be advertised in specialist journals. The commercial property world revolves largely around property people as intermediaries; that is, they advertise to each other. The *Estates Gazette* is reputed to be the most profitable magazine in the UK – reflecting its pre-eminence as the 'house journal' of the property profession.

The majority of people reading the *Estates Gazette* or *Chartered Surveyor Weekly* are likely to be experienced property people well versed in the terminology and the arcanities of the profession. They are likely to be undertaking routine purchase assignments which, while they may appear externally to involve extensive problem solving, are in reality processed as if they involved only limited problem solving; so readers remain unimpressed, involved only at a limited level and retain a healthy scepticism.

They are, therefore, unlikely to respond to 'hidden messages' or to over-enthusiastic descriptions and will focus only on what are to them at the time, the salient facts.

What are salient facts to property people?

Users –   where is it?
                what sort of footfall (retailers)?
                local competition?
                local economic trends?
                demographic shifts?

Investors –   current returns
                projected growth potential
                time yields (income and capital growth)
                reversion potential
                quality of tenants
                quality of leases

Developers –   unidentified potential demand characteristics
                timescales
                yield sector growth
                sensitivities

The fundamental question is 'How can this property produce money' – and yet these factors are seldom addressed directly. Nature deals with LPS situations directly. A menaced snake (even a non-poisonous one) threatens to bite. An angry bull paws the ground, snorts and bellows. The message is clear and direct.

Do not annoy your readers by making them guess when they are in an LPS mode. They do not perceive you – or your products – as being fundamentally different from anyone else's – unless you convince them otherwise.

This interesting diversion into the world of magazines is, perhaps, particularly relevant to the professional press but applies, to a greater or lesser degree, to readers of other types of specialist magazines. For example, readers of The Caterer will know more about catering than the average property professional and, whilst the magazine is a first rate vehicle for reaching these readers, the effect will be spoiled if an effort is not made to talk to them in their own language.

For example, a front page sample of a 'Daltons Weekly' showed that of 22 businesses advertised only 10 referred to gross profit – and three of these referred only to a percentage. None referred to staff levels. What sort of bases do they think potential purchasers apply? In the leisure section one advertisement referred to 'Excellent t/o last season with equally healthy net profit' – what on earth does that mean? And to whom? The sophisticated LPS purchaser (at £525 000) is going to be singularly irritated rather than intrigued.

Other media advertising

External and the cinema
Within this area we are principally concerned with fixed point advertising, posters, estate agents boards, moving vehicles etc. Cinema at one time was well used among estate agents but tends not to be a regularly used modern medium.

Posters
Posters provide an ideal medium for large scale messages, often at strategically placed entry or exit points from towns or cities. Over the years extensive use has been made of this type of medium as background advertising, notably by Guiness and other brewers who have engineered a series of eye-catching, often humorous, adverts that reinforce often subtle points made in other media. The problem with the poster advert is that, generally, it is visible to its audience for a limited period during which it must make its impact, attract attention, and deliver a message, perhaps in

the space of only 2 or 3 seconds. Images must therefore be bold, direct and immediately accessible if they are to make an impact.

There has been little use of regular poster advertising by the property profession in the past but perhaps the time is rapidly approaching, with the birth of the estate agency majors, when the use of this medium may become more appropriate.

A variation on the 'maxi poster' can be seen at many railway stations, particularly those strategically placed on InterCity lines where commercial agents have not been slow to see the advantages of catching the attention of the immobile passenger waiting for a train. It is interesting that South Wales, Swindon, Bristol and Reading are all represented on posters at Paddington Station.

A further variant on the poster theme is to be found in the London Underground and, often in taxis, where Stern Studios in particular, have clearly gained benefit from their highly focused niche advertising.

A variant on poster advertising is the mobile poster, for example, a delivery bus or furniture van. Vehicles such as this often provide substantial opportunities for colour-themed background advertising which is likely to considerably heighten awareness of brand names, in particular, in localised areas. It is worth mentioning, of course, that if care is not taken to ensure that the vehicle carrying the poster is kept clean and tidy, and does not create traffic jams, the effect of the advert might be counterproductive.

The difficulty with this kind of background advertising is, of course, in monitoring its effect and comparing benefits with costs. Little direct research is available but many property people have a gut feeling that perhaps the benefits are not as great as spending the same portion of the promotional budget on an office refurbishment or increased press advertising.

Summary

We return to our theme. The test of good advertising is 'does it create the desired behavioural change?'. It is worth remembering that any advertising will create behavioural change, but unless that change is carefully planned and the advertising images and media correctly matched, the change may well be unexpected.

PR – public and press relations

'A column of editorial is worth a page of advertising'.

In some circumstances the ratios are probably considerably greater than this. The kind of banner headlines which attacked the Halifax and other major estate agents during 1990 did little good to the image of the property profession. As we have already seen when we looked at consumer behaviour, people are likely to be influenced, particularly during periods of heightened awareness and information search, by messages which they perceive to derive from an authoritative source. The more authoritative the source, the more likely they are to be influenced – either for good or ill. The alert organisation therefore maintains policy guidelines which allow managers to react positively to potentially damaging situations and, hopefully, turn these situations, if not to advantage, into channels which limit damage as far as possible.

Perhaps the leading example of damage limitation is the tale of Tylenol (a pain relieving drug made by Johnson & Johnson which is a market leader in the United States) which came under attack from a maniac who laced a number of Tylenol capsules with cyanide. Inevitably some deaths ensued but the manufacturers reacted quickly and immediately withdrew all stocks nationwide from the market place. They responded positively to the threat, without apparently counting short term cost, and were then able to relaunch with a tamper-proof capsule and container; within 12 months they had recaptured their market share.

Less fortunate were Townsend Thorensen who, at the time of the Zeebrugge disaster, were still rationalising their management structures following corporate takeover and whose reactions immediately following the disaster were therefore unprepared and appeared less sympathetic than they undoubtedly felt.

The message is clear to property people. The property industry is perceived fair game by the press. An industry which appears to earn high fees for little apparent effort is always going to make interesting copy and, unless images are carefully managed, will find itself presented in a consistently bad light.

All is not gloom and doom however. Newspaper editors have to fill space as well as providing banner headlines to sell their newspapers. This means that they are always on the lookout for stories which will interest their particular clientele.

There is the key. 'Their particular clientele.' In exactly the same way that the marketer targets a specific market segment, the newspaper proprietor/ editor targets specific readership segments. In the same way that different market segments have different perceived needs for product benefits so readership segments have different informational needs. The Times has little use for salacious titbits about the stars of Coronation Street, whereas the Sun or the Sunday Sport feed their readers on the detailed activities of the denizens of Albert Square and Brookside. The natural effects of this are that a press release sent generally to a variety of newspapers will be written up, if at all, in vastly different styles by the respective journals and the author of the press release can sometimes wonder whether the journalist even read the same documents to start with.

What sort of things interest journalists and editors to result in their being printed? As usual the answer is 'different tales for different readers'. A financial magazine will be interested in a financial angle. A local evening newspaper will be interested in stories with a local angle, particularly if those stories relate to local people or local issues.

In the property business there is a core of information that is of fairly general interest. For instance, most people are interested in the progress of the housing market. Whether prices are rising or falling is a perennial topic in many gatherings and is perceived as an attention grabber by local editors. The commercial market, similarly, is now becoming perceived as being germane to the financial health of business organisations. Property is a strategic asset in that corporate finance is often inextricably bound to property valuations. The vagaries of the commercial market, particularly in flagship units, are therefore of considerable interest to financial and business editors.

How can you identify story opportunities? In a word, through practice. The first requirement is an awareness that property is, intrinsically, interesting and that it is worth looking for the special interest to push to the journalists. It is very easy to miss the obvious. On one occasion the writer advertised a property as 'the highest house in Newport' and was quite startled when the local newspaper took this up and ran a half page feature which was very helpful in leading to a sale!

Don't ignore the obvious.

Many properties have been sold because of the legends about the ghost, the sale of a cat with a house thrown in, the illegal lottery for a house, etc.

Look for any historical associations – however tenuous. A sixteenth century property near Cardiff gained some very handy publicity through its associations with Captain Morgan, the pirate. A house at Caerleon gained interesting publicity through an alleged association – a painting contained in the house – with Garibaldi.

Creative opportunities are all around us. Look for them creatively and they can be found.

Getting the message through

It is all very well to find interesting stories; it is quite a different matter to actually get them published. A journalist's perception of interest relates to many factors, not least of which is the availability of space in a particular issue of his journal. Cultivate the journalists, find out what sort of things they think their readership finds interesting. Encourage the journalist to telephone and always be ready with potential copy when there is a space to fill. Many otherwise uninteresting stories have found favour simply because there was nothing else about that week!

Don't overdo the copy

Journalists pride themselves on their being able to write good copy. Give them the facts and let them add the frills. If you add frills journalists will either ignore the story completely or go through it with a heavy blue pencil.

Make sure that any copy submitted makes its points and its 'hooks' quickly and concisely so that the journalist or sub-editor's attention is caught and stimulated.

Observe the courtesies

Make sure the journalist or the sub-editor is aware of your appreciation when interesting articles appear and that you are aware of their problems when they are not able to use your scintillating copy. A long term cooperative relationship achieves much better results than occasional contact. Always remember that this exchange of information is as much a selling function as any other.

Informed comment

Make yourself a source of informed comment if this is at all possible. The professional bodies appoint press contacts in most of their regions, often with difficulty. Few people seem to want to spare the time for what can be a pivotal role in gaining media access for raising background levels of awareness of the firm and its members. Be aware of what is happening both within your local community and within the wider professional world and be available for quotes, even on the difficult subjects. Regular press exposure of individuals increases their credibility to the buying public and, as we have seen elsewhere, the greater the credibility of the source, the greater its ability to change behaviour.

Be a contributor. Most journals, particularly the smaller, localised ones, appreciate well-written articles which deal with matters of general or local interest. Think up some topics, compile the articles, and submit them for publication under your own name. Do not be upset when the sub-editor uses his blue pencil, it usually improves the finished result. The regular or even the occasional article increases credibility and with it your ability to influence buyer behaviour.

Media events

In the absence of intrinsic interest in your properties or services it is worth considering the use of media events as a promotional tool. We have a considerable track record within the property industry in this area. Chartered Surveyor Weekly, in particular, carries regular reportage of such events as topping out ceremonies, 'finishing the steelwork' ceremonies, rugby or soccer tournaments, five-a-side cricket matches etc. It has now become almost traditional to launch new enterprises through promotional parties to which are invited potentially important clients, members of the professional community, any dignitaries that we can lay our hands on and, of course, the press. From the press' point of view these events are often spoilt by their very sameness or by the use of gimmicks which, whilst highly entertaining to those close to the action, hardly translate to the more general audience sought by the press. If the basic questions of who is going to be interested and why, are posed before the event is organised, then a more satisfactory outcome can probably be engineered.

Sales and sales management

The property industry is bedevilled, as is the motor trade, by the image of the slick 'real estate salesman' serving up dodgy deals to unsuspecting purchasers. The implication here of course is that people are persuaded against their better judgement to buy what they do not want, do not need, and at prices that they cannot afford, to the financial benefit of the sales person and with no regard for ongoing relationships.

The residential sector is particularly prone to such images although the commercial area is by no means free of them. Well within the knowledge and perception of most property people is the image of the high powered (highly rich) commercial property specialist who has prospered on putting together dubious consortia that have achieved high profits through the realisation of marriage or breakup values in property transactions.

But is this the true image of selling within the property profession? Is it that easy to deceive people and is that what selling is all about? The realities are rather different. Property in the UK, for good or ill, comes with a built-in cooling off period and virtually everybody involved with the sale of property knows the trauma that this causes in terms of drop-out rates, particularly in a difficult market. Equally, every sales person trained in other markets, quickly comes across the realisation that it is relatively easy to persuade people that they would like to buy a property but that if this is done too quickly the almost inevitable consequence is a telephone call the following day (or even worse no telephone call at all) to say that they have thought it over and the deal is now off.

And what about the professional people? The surveyors, the valuers, the auctioneers, the architects, the engineers, all of whom have property related products to sell. Do they fit the stereotype of the slick salesman? Many professional people would be very hurt to think that such a label were to be applied to them. Yet without selling, in some dimension, they would quickly run short of clients.

Clearly, we need to look rather deeper to identify just what forms of selling are applicable to the property industry. Perhaps a look at some conventional definitions of types and levels of selling would help. And what about this curious character that exists in the property world, the negotiator?

Levels of selling are conventionally broken down into order takers, order getters, problem solvers, and relationships managers.

The order taker is the sales representative who visits the corner shop or the supermarket and simply picks up orders to maintain stock levels. A slightly more refined version of this is found with the van salesman who carries the stock around and takes orders for what is on the van.

The next level is the order getter – a rather more purposeful form of sales representative who helps with general merchandising, suggests alternative product ranges and introduces or insinuates new product lines into the retailer's consciousness.

Then we move to the problem solver – the typical IBM representative who, as we saw in Chapter 1, concentrates on the infrastructure into which his products are designed to fit. At this level a considerable degree of technical knowledge is required as the ability to influence his sophisticated buyers is heavily dependent upon both his general and specific credibility.

At the top end of the scale is the relationships manager who tends to deal with established clients and manages the institutional relationships which evolve, hopefully to the benefit of both parties, but particularly to the benefit of his own company.

We have readily seen that the edges between these levels of activity are hard to define and become very blurred in practice. It is nevertheless clear that each level of activity involves different skills; different skills demand different levels of training, and different styles and approaches to sales management.

What of the property negotiator? In the UK, property salespeople (excluding new homes) tend to operate as agents. Their operation as agents implies a client/agent relationship which imposes duties upon the agent vis-à-vis the needs of his client. In particular it imposes a duty to use their best efforts in the client's interests and to make the client's interests paramount. Property people therefore tend to act as a rather special kind of intermediary, with the brokerage objective of bringing two parties together but with tight constraints on the amount of persuasion that can be utilised in the direction of his client. A complex animal indeed. The principles involved are the same in both residential and commercial but are probably easier to clarify by taking residential examples. The commercial reader should not switch off at this point, however, as the messages are the same and need relatively little translation to be equally appropriate.

Let us construct a model of a typical residential sale.

A potential purchaser comes in to the office and is 'qualified' by a negotiator. The qualification process involves finding out what kind of property the prospect might be looking for, how much money is available to spend, what sort of area they would like, when they would like to move, and whether they have a house to sell.

On the strength of this qualification the negotiator will present a short list of perhaps half a dozen properties and steer the client through the pros and cons of each in the hope of generating an even shorter short list which he can then demonstrate to the client by showing him around.

This he duly does and, if the negotiator is reasonably skilled, he can probably close the prospect on one of the properties. (Note that this is a simplification; we all know that it is a little more complex than this in practice.)

The negotiator then qualifies the prospect further and, if possible, introduces him to a financial services specialist who sorts out the money. A mortgage application is put in train together with instructions to solicitors for both vendor and potential purchaser so that the mechanics of the transaction can start rolling.

Inevitably, problems occur and the negotiator is called back into play to sort some of the problems out, for example, dry rot in the skirting boards, a leaning chimney, or a lack of foundations in the garage.

The negotiator now has to manage these problems to his client's best advantage and may be called upon to manage renegotiations of price and other matters to allow for the new factors in the equation. Finally, after much prompting from the negotiator, contracts will be exchanged and hopefully all then proceeds satisfactorily.

Within this train of events several potential moral dilemmas occur for the negotiator. First of all he showed the client six properties initially then reduced to a short list of three or four. In doing this these two properties were discarded. The negotiator is now concentrating on the three or four. Fine in practice, but what about his duty to the vendors of the properties which he discarded? Does acting simultaneously for a number of vendors constitute a conflict of interest? Or is this covered by the principle of 'taking the rough with the smooth'?

Quite a dilemma, and one that is dealt with by most people by the time-honoured method of displacement behaviour which simply ignores the problem.

At the time of agreeing the sale to the purchaser there were almost certainly differences of opinion about price or other matters. The negotiator is under a duty to act in the best interest of his client. At the same time he or his company is almost certainly paid a commission by the vendor for the introduction of said client. There is, therefore, considerable pressure upon the negotiator to get a 'sale agreed'. In such circumstances there is inevitably conflict between the negotiator's desire to agree a sale and his desire to do the best he can for his client.

There is of course always the rationalisation that it is in the client's best interest to get a sale agreed anyway 'particularly in this very difficult market which we are currently experiencing'.

The same problems keep coming up. We mentioned potential problems with the valuation and/or survey. By this time of course the negotiator has a considerable investment of time and probably money – or at least future expectation of money – in the sale and will not want it to fall through. There must be, therefore, some temptation to use the 'client's best interests' argument to allow persuasion to be used in order to bring about a mutually satisfactory conclusion. It should also be remembered that at this point the client has also made a considerable investment in the sale and will consequently be vulnerable to such persuasion. The ethical dilemma increases.

It would appear from the foregoing illustration that the first qualification for a property sales negotiator, given the legal and moral dimensions of the UK property system, is that the negotiator should be a candidate for canonisation.

Having mentioned the apparent dilemma within the negotiating situation, however, we will take the standard route out and indulge in displacement behaviour rather than tackle problems too intractable for a general text. Displacement behaviour in this case involves analysing some of the selling functions which took place within the illustration.

Initial qualification

All selling is about relating benefits to needs. This is further complicated as we saw in Chapter 3, by the translation of needs into wants thus often disguising their essential nature. The task of the negotiator in the qualification interview is to try to strip away the behavioural layers so that the underlying needs can be exposed. If the needs can be exposed then product features can be turned into benefits which can then be related to satisfaction of the buyer's need.

The next step is the identification of a range of products which goes some way towards satisfying those needs. We saw in Chapter 3 how, at this stage, the negotiator can modify the buyer's behaviour by influencing attitudes and even beliefs about the subject properties and their competitors.

The scene moves to property inspections. At this point the task of the negotiator is to reinforce the match between needs and satisfactions to the point where the prospect can satisfy as many as possible of his needs and wants, hopefully persuading himself that he did it all off his own back. (A useful tip for sales negotiators in this situation is that if the client catches you selling, you're dead, and so is the sale.)

The most difficult part of any sale, and the part where most sales fall apart or fall down, is the act of asking for the sale. The simple fact of the matter is that most salespeople – in any environment – do not ask for a sale – then they wonder why they did not get one. In property matters the equation is further complicated by timing. The negotiator is dealing with a potentially volatile situation in that the purchaser may be engaged in extended problem solving and will need time to work through his or her decision process thoroughly. If the negotiator asks for the sale at the wrong time in that sequence he is likely to induce cognitive overload. If this happens, as we have seen, buyers are likely to make decisions – but make them badly. The effect of this is that when they have further time to consider the matter they are likely to perceive that they have been 'caught'. The inevitable outcome of feeling caught is that the sale is cancelled and they never darken your door again. The negotiator, therefore, must pick his moment very carefully. Too soon and the sale gets cancelled, too late and somebody else has got there before you.

Post commitment

The act of agreeing the sale, in property, is fundamentally a preliminary commitment only. Buyers commit themselves subject to contract and are normally aware that they can pull out if they so wish. In a 'buyers market' there is ample evidence that they do this, in many cases, as a matter of buying policy – which does not make the negotiator's job any easier. The negotiator therefore must carefully manage the sale from the point of preliminary commitment right through to the point of full commitment or there is a 30–40 per cent chance that he will lose it.

There are many reasons that a sale can fall through in this area, some of them technical (dpc, foundations problems, etc.), some of them personal (somebody else has influenced their perceptions or beliefs to the detriment of this particular property). The negotiator must be sufficiently skilled to recognise the underlying behavioural change and to take steps to make sure that any unfortunate events (like cancellation) are averted before they become irrevocable in the mind of the purchaser.

Finally, assuming that the job has been thoroughly done, the contracts are exchanged and the negotiator breathes a sigh of relief.

The scenario outlined above suggests two things. First of all the job of a property negotiator is highly involved and involves personal and technical skills of a high order. Second, there are very few property negotiators who are even aware of the complexities of what they are actually doing, let alone skilled or competent in managing the activity successfully.

Selling property – even residential property – is a highly skilled activity with elements of the order taker, the order getter, the problem solver, and the relationships manager, all mixed up together.

This has serious implications for the tactical management of property sales. The sales manager must take a view as to what is an acceptable level of performance, recognising that in the absence of other beneficial factors performance is likely to be relatively poor.

Fortunately, in the residential market, purchasers tend to buy rather than be sold, thus cushioning sales negotiators (and their managers) against the worst effects of their lack of ability.

Sales management

The function of sales management is to ensure that the sales function is capable of achieving and achieves its technical objectives. There is little point in providing an effective marketing structure which provides a range of sales leads if these leads then cannot be converted by the individuals concerned. The sales manager therefore needs to concentrate on some fundamental questions.

a) What are the specific objectives of the sales function?
b) What are the key factors for successful selling?
c) What are the appropriate indicators for success in the various areas in which the sales function operates?

Selling objectives

What are the specific objectives of the sales function? Does it concentrate predominantly upon getting offers? Is it more important to concentrate on holding sales together, or does the function involve high level relationships management? Who are the people involved? Are they known as sales people? Negotiators? Or are they professional people who see selling as a sideline?

How does the sales function integrate with the overall marketing strategy? Does strategic thinking imply relationships management when the sales force is targeted to achieving initial offers?

Key factors

In order to manage the sales function effectively the sales manager must be aware of the key factors which make the difference between effective and ineffective selling. These factors will vary in detail depending on the technical objectors but can be summarised under generic headings.

a) Do sales people understand thoroughly the nature of their selling activity?
b) Are they adequately trained to achieve these specific objectives?
c) Does the firm's infrastructure and their reward structure in particular contribute to or detract from their achievement of these key objectives?

Awareness

One of the big problems with sales people is that, by their nature, they tend to be oriented towards the next deal. In the residential world too many young sales negotiators seem to be unable to distinguish between agreeing a sale and bringing it to completion. They are surprised, and often somewhat aggrieved, when their sales experience a high drop-out rate. Many perceive a drop-out rate of 25 per cent as being normal for the industry and therefore acceptable to them. Clearly such a presumption makes a less-than-positive contribution to an organisation which exists on commissions derived from completions.

The sales manager therefore has a tricky choice. He can either accept the situation and adjust his sales targets to allow for the effective drop-out rate or he can attempt to change the perspective of the sales people. Alternatively, he could set up sales control systems which allow negotiators to agree sales (however well qualified) and then attempt to manage the sales through to completion after the event.

Similarly, many professional people find it difficult to accept that their professional role is actually an integral part of the selling function and that they should consciously manage client relationships to ensure the continuance of their instructions.

It should be noted that in the property business, which has not traditionally been closely managed, the inherent conflicts referred to above tend to stem directly from failings in the sales management role not from failings in the personnel involved.

Training

Do relevant personnel undergo sales training which reflects the technical requirements of the organisation? Many sales people undergo sales training but much of this is skills related and makes little contribution to overall understanding.

Do all relevant sales people undergo sales training of any kind? Few professional people within the industry have had any significant sales training – indeed many would react adversely to skills training as undertaken by sales negotiators. At more senior professional levels it becomes perhaps even more important that sales training relates to and underpins specific organisational objectives.

Organisational support

In Chapter 1 we saw how organisations can display different orientations towards the nature of their business. The sales manager must look precisely at how the sales effort is affected by the many overt and covert messages received from within the organisation. For example the young negotiator is unlikely to be motivated towards sales completions if the friendly managing director calls at a local office and, searching for something useful to say, asks 'how many sales have you agreed this month then?'. Similarly professional people are unlikely to adopt a relationships management orientation if the chief surveyor makes it obvious that his orientation is towards product excellence (and to hell with the customers).

Other questions should also be addressed. How flexible is the sales effort to changes in strategy? Can resources be quickly redeployed and at what cost? Are people locked into particular theatres of operation by the complexities or perceived complexities of their jobs and relationships? How closely is future profitability of the firm linked to specific individuals whose departure would inevitably deplete the client base?

There is, therefore, a wide variety of factors to be considered by the sales manager who must ensure that he has access to reliable indicators of performance, most particularly in areas which are perceived as being key or crucial to the overall performance of the business.

Performance indicators

The function of performance indicators is to help the sales manager to identify standards of performance in areas which he perceives to be important to achieving the company's sales objectives. Note again the use of the word 'perceives' in the introductory sentence. Perception varies from person to person. An indicator that is meaningful to one sales manager will be meaningless to another. Surrounding the indicator and its use will be a variety of influencing factors, each of which is closely linked to the previous experiences and breadth of outlook of the sales manager. It is important therefore to consider the implications of indicators – and the inferences that might be drawn from them – as well as the absolute format in which they might be provided.

What types of indicators are available? As in quality, indicators can be hard or soft. Hard indicators are fairly obvious: number of sales, total value of sales, average value of sales, sales per negotiator, number of completions, ratio of sales to completions, etc. Hard indicators, by their nature, will be, generally, readily measurable.

Soft indicators. Customer satisfaction, lost opportunities, friendliness, helpfulness etc. These are much more difficult to measure, but are often critical to the effective sales operation; so they should be the subject of serious consideration.

Hard indicators. What is being measured? The fundamental questions should be 'Are we achieving our objectives?' and 'Is our selling activity as effective as it might be?'

In the final analysis sales objectives are likely to be financial in that a given financial value of sales is required in order to provide the basis for the overall financial objectives of the business. A purely financial statement of activity, however, can be misleading, particularly where there is a highly variable contribution from sales to fixed and variable costs. For example, in the residential world the variable costs of a sale tends to be pretty much the same whether the property sells for £50 000 or for £200 000. The contribution to fixed costs in those two situations however is vastly different. (Assuming a 2 per cent commission where variable costs are £100, the contribution to fixed costs in the £50 000 sale is £900 and the contribution to fixed costs in the £200 000 sale is £3 900.) Clearly, in this scenario the number of sales agreed, without qualification, would not be a particularly useful indicator of potential profitability. Similarly the total number of completions in the period is an incomplete guide.

The sales manager needs indicators which reflect key variables that influence profitability. In this case that means figures which show total sales agreed, probable contribution level, fall-out ratio in each sector, and finally the ratio of completions related to sales agreed.

These figures, however, give no grasp of how the sales force as a whole is performing. The sales manager now needs to look at the ratio between instructions received and sales agreed. In order to measure the quality of 'instruction performance' the sales manager also needs an indicator of timescale between instructions received and sale agreed. This combined fallout rate gives some measure of the competence of the lister in the first place.

In the commercial world similar constraints apply. In this environment contribution levels may be higher and timescales may be considerably longer than in the residential environment and may extend across several individuals. This makes it more difficult to design appropriate indicators but probably makes them even more important (perhaps this is one of the reasons why the function has seldom been managed effectively in either environment).

Soft indicators

This area is notoriously difficult to tackle. Our general approach is to indulge in displacement behaviour and to concentrate on something else rather than tackle the problem. It is nevertheless an area which, as we have already seen, is a potentially critical source of differentiation and requires systematic evaluation.

The key to progress is a regular and routine telephone canvass of customers chosen at random across representative and recognisable segments of the customer base.

Management at this level is not easy. It is time consuming and involving. But the best companies do it – as a matter of policy. That probably means at least one of your competitors – probably the effective one.

Such a telephone canvass should be structured and designed to provide information about the company's performance – the good points and the bad points. These customer responses can then be built into a more reliable model of performance and can be used as a basis for decision making. In larger companies a larger sample is required. Some companies maintain an ongoing customer survey department which routinely questions a wide range of customers on a wide range of topics and use these results as a trigger for product and service innovation. Tom Peters recounts in 'In Search of Excellence' how Domino Pizza Company in the USA use their service survey to generate a service index which then becomes part of staff reward packages. That's really showing interest in customers!

Having got the indicators right – or at least meaningful – the sales manager can now turn to the use which he might make of the information provided. Some of the questions which the sales manager will wish to ask are :

Is the sales effort concentrated on areas which are key to meeting business objectives?

Can the sales effort be readily redirected to meet changing conditions?

Is the sales force adequately motivated and does the reward system contribute to motivation?

Is the sales force adequately trained for the jobs required of it?

Technical appreciation – Are we asking the right questions?

Innovation – Is there anything else that we should or could be doing to improve effectiveness of the sales force?

Concentration on essentials

Back to basics once again for the sales manager. Some of the complexities associated with indicators were illustrated above when we looked at the difference in contribution between low value properties and high value properties. This was further complicated by the relationship of the quality of the original listing to the contribution of the final sale. The sales manager must think carefully about these relationships and define clearly the essential factors that make the difference in the final balance sheet. The natural motivations of staff with a sales role may work against the sales manager's objectives. For example, many sales people are naturally motivated towards the next deal rather than looking after those that they already have. A professional operator may be more interested in practising his profession than in managing the relationships that surround his work and which lead to future business. The sales manager must identify the key areas and ensure that all the imagery at his disposal, corporate and individual, is directed towards excellence in key areas.

Deployment of sales force

As we saw in Chapter 7, corporate strategy relates not only to internal activities but also to the activities and depredations of competitors. In a competitive market a firm must be able to take different kinds of action depending on the threats and opportunities perceived in strategic analysis, particularly as related to competitors. The sales manager must be constantly aware of the potential use of his function as a tactical weapon and must therefore ensure that his sales activity can be redirected in order to meet revised strategic constraints. The organisational and motivational constraints upon redeployment can be extremely complex and need substantial pre-thinking if expensive mistakes are to be avoided.

Motivation and reward

People in any environment only perform well if they are adequately motivated. We have already shown how different people's motivations can lead them into different styles of performance and that motivation which is not correctly harnessed can lead to work which can detract from achievement in key areas. Motivation, as we touched upon in Chapter 3, is an enormously complex area and has been the subject of probably thousands of hours of research. In this chapter we do not propose to go into great detail on the subject but a limited consideration of some of its aspects is relevant.

In a workplace setting an integral aspect of motivation is the concept of reward. Reward involves much more than the simple idea of pay structures; it includes status, recognition and other factors that contribute to an individual's sense of well being and achievement.

One of the few things that management, writers and pundits seem to be agreed upon is that motivation derives from striving to achieve goals rather than from achieving them. That is once a goal is achieved it ceases to be a motivating factor. Theory also suggests that a wide range of factors, often perceived as being motivators, are in fact only demotivating in their absence rather than motivating by their presence. For example, money, in itself, is not a motivating factor (generally) although its absence or perceived lack of adequate compensation can be a strong demotivating factor. Of course for some people the achievement of money, for its own sake, can be a motivating factor in that it can become a goal.

To many people, once a reward in money terms which is perceived as being reasonable has been achieved, other factors achieve greater importance and can be powerful demotivators if they are absent. For example, status, and all the symbolism that surrounds it, can be very important factors. A variant on status which is often underplayed because it may be perceived as being 'not quite British' is overt recognition of achievement. The Americans go in, in a big way, for office league tables, competitions, open praisings, shared experiences, shared triumphs etc., which many British people would superficially reject. Their importance however should not be overlooked as overt recognition contributes greatly to status within and without an organisation and, as long as clear guidelines are set through which recognition can be achieved, can easily be turned into motivating goals.

Training

We have seen elsewhere how source credibility is of considerable importance in persuading buyers into a behavioural change. Source credibility is greatly enhanced by demonstrable product knowledge, experience and gravitas.

Gravitas comes, like experience, with experience. Other aspects of sales performance however can be imparted through training. There is an old saying that 'Strength comes from the use of knowledge – not from its acquisition'. Too often sales training is directed at imparting knowledge rather than in its end use. The serious sales manager will be concerned to see that staff not only develop a knowledge base but also are closely monitored in the way that they put this knowledge to use.

We touched on training earlier in the chapter. It should by now be abundantly clear that training, particularly for people involved in any kind of selling role, is not simply a matter of imparting technique but is an integral part of ensuring that corporate objectives in terms of targeting and flexibility can be achieved.

Before any training is undertaken therefore, the sales manager should clearly identify the nature of the sales activity to be undertaken by people and ensure that the person being trained is fully aware of the organisational constraints which surround the training.

For example, a professional surveyor may well be dismissive of technical sales training as being for 'salespeople', the implication being that he does not perceive himself now and has no wish to perceive himself in the future as being a 'sales person'. His perception is likely to have been shaped by exposure to such lurid titles as 'How to become a super power salesman in three easy lessons', or even 'How to win friends and influence people!'. If his perception can be changed to incorporate the idea of relationships management, emphasising the crucial role that he, as a professional, plays in maintaining the present and future customer base, he may well be persuaded to take an active and productive part in meaningful sales training.

This is not to say that training in basic sales technique is unimportant. To the contrary it is essential foundation knowledge to more complex sales activities.

This area of motivation is perhaps the most important aspect of a sales manager's task. In the Chapter 3 case study we saw how a young surveyor transformed the estate agency business in a South Wales town in the space of only 2 or 3 years. What was omitted from that case study is the understanding that the young surveyor had one key asset possessed by no other estate agent in that town. Every single person that worked for him believed that they (in some cases after a period of only 2 or 3 days) 'walked on water'. He was a first class man-manager as must be any manager.

Technical appreciation

The sales manager's job is by no means finished at this point. As we have seen elsewhere the maintenance of strategic advantage depends not just upon the internal activities of the firm, but probably to a much greater extent, upon the activities of competitors. The sales manager must therefore be continually vigilant in appraising the competition and appraising his own activities relevant to them. The basic questions are again the following.

Are the indicators relevant? The indicators in current use may well have been relevant when they were first put in to use but are they still relevant. Have conditions changed in any way that might change the balance of importance between particular indicators. For instance in a buoyant market where sales easily convert into listings, where listings easily convert into sales and sales tend to stay together through the activities of competitive buyers, it may be adequate simply to use a net quantity of listings as a reasonable day-to-day indicator. In a more difficult market it may be necessary to look much more deeply into the indicators and direct management activities into more productive areas. For example the fall through rate becomes critical in a difficult market and demands maximum management input if it is to be kept to a minimum. In the absence of competitive buyers every sale saved could be the same as a sale earned.

Could other indicators give a useful insight? Is there some means of providing ongoing comparison with competitors? For example, in residential again, it is fairly easy to cross-check the number of first advertisements or new listings advertised each week against those of competitors. This gives a useful (but by no means definitive), cross comparison of sales and advertising effectiveness. In the commercial world the number of clients gained from or lost to other competitors could be a useful indicator of ongoing client quality perception and could direct efforts towards remedial action.

In a similar way regular calculation of market place potential and comparison of actual penetration both for the company and major competitors can be of great assistance, particularly if they direct effort to trouble spots or opportunity areas in time for remedial action to be taken.

Qualitative assessment can be undertaken; for example, regular and routine comparative assessments of report quality between professionals within the department. Again this kind of work is time consuming and difficult to do. But, as we have said before, management is a difficult task, so that should not stop anybody.

Innovation – is there anything that can be done better? Interestingly, the answer to that question is always Yes. There is always something that can be done better. The sales manager must ensure that within his area, everything that can be done to encourage innovation is actually done. Innovation is difficult enough without forcing people to fight against a culture that discriminates against it.

What are the sources of innovation?
The people doing the job are also the experts in how to do it. Ask the leading question 'In a perfect world how would you do this job?'. You might be surprised at the answers.

Look at competitors. What do they do? Is there anything that can be learnt? Is there anybody with specific specialist expertise and knowledge that might be bought?

Attend conferences. Listen to other people's perspectives – you may not agree with them but you may gain insights which can be translated into your own organisation.

Share experiences within the selling group. Most innovation comes from applying lessons learnt in one area into what may, at first sight, appear to be an unrelated area. This was the principle behind the operational research groups set up during the Second World War to deal with the knotty problems of the day. They brought together multi-disciplined groups where ideas from across the frontiers of different sciences could be brought to bear in common problem solving. On a smaller scale regular meetings of direct sales people with professional people in a well-structured environment can often generate immense dividends in terms of shared cross-cultural experiences.

Market and marketing research

Why does a house buyer, given the choice between two identical houses, both the left-hand partner in adjoining parts of semis, choose one rather than the other? Why does an investor, given two properties with similar rents, tenant mix, leases and yields, pay more for one that he will for the other? How many total transactions are there in a given market place over a specific period? What are the relative market shares of companies X, Y and Z in that market? In what terms should we identify the market place? How strong is company X compared with us in its ability to attack the market place?

These questions are the equivalent of military intelligence to the military strategist. What is the terrain of the battlefield? What are the benefits from winning it? What are the implications of losing it? How many tanks, infantry, machine gun nests do the opposition have. Without such answers, or reasonable approximations, any strategic or tactical decision making is, at best, suspect and, at worst, terminal. So it is with the business strategist and tactician.

The military refer to 'intelligence', 'reconnaissance' and 'espionage'. We call it market research and marketing research. The end product is the same thing – the 'stuff' of tactical and strategic decision making.

What is the difference between the two descriptions?

Market research
Market research looks at the size and nature of the market place. How many transactions are there? What is their total value? What is their average value? Is there any grouping of value effects?

Other questions, such as: What competitors are there? What are they good at? What are they bad at? What type of market exists? Is it static, expanding or contracting? Are there obvious substitutes? Is technological change in the offing which will change the rules in any significant way?

Or again: What is the pattern of purchasing? Is it seasonal, regional, cyclic, repeating or one-off? Is there any synergy with other products that we may already supply or may be prepared to supply in the future?

Marketing research
This looks at the reasons behind demand. What is the behavioural infra-structure underlying the market? Is behaviour based in society's attitudes or is it based in more localised reference groups? Does purchase behaviour change through social groupings, economic groupings or both.

Is there a demographic or economic bias to the market place which allows prediction of future behaviour? Does general purchasing behaviour show significant trends which can be turned to marketing advantage? Do particular purchase groupings behave in a way which could identify them as a sub-market (or market segment)? Does a market segment have behavioural characteristics that might limit the effectiveness of an advertising or other promotional initiative?

Market research examines the physical aspects of a market place, whereas marketing research examines the behavioural aspects of a market place.

Research is not confined to predicting behaviour in a market place. It is also used effectively in identifying change within a market, particularly relating to marketing initiatives taken by an organisation.

Research is not the answer to every maiden's prayer. Research does not take decisions, it simply provides data which can then be interpreted and interpolated into a decision-making process. Not least important in the decision-making process is the question 'How accurate/representative/reliable is the research data?'.

It is not the aim of this chapter to examine market and marketing research methods in detail. Such a task lies outside the scope of a basic text and a number of more expansive texts are listed in the references and further reading. Within the chapter we will try to identify areas where research can be relevant and indicate varying levels and types of research, some of which will be within the purview of organisations and some of which require specialist assistance.

It should be stressed at this point that much usable and meaningful data can be collected very simply and is well within the scope of the smallest firm. There may be a perception that 'market research is only for large companies'. Nothing could be further from the truth.

Market research

We are concerned here with the physical attributes of a market place. Where is it? How big is it? Is it growing or shrinking? How much is it worth?

Who else is in it?

Data is available from two sources, primary and secondary.

Primary data is collected directly from the market place, secondary data collected from the results of other researchers.

Primary data may be further subdivided into that available from within the organisation and that for which the organisation has to look outside. There is often far more of the former available than is generally realised – a good thing because external data collection can start to get expensive.

What kind of data exists within the organisation?

Sales data

Sales records provide

- Record of actual market share
- Record of actual transaction sizes
- Record of transactions by price band/industry sector/property type/vendor type/purchaser type/geographic area
- Record of actual fluctuations in market profile over a period
- Record of product market 'balance' (that is, the proportion of sales value contributed by different product variants over a period)

From this raw data it is possible to compute some interesting information:

- Sales growth profile
- Shifts in product contribution
- Shifts in product/resource allocation
- Possible shifts in segmentation
- Possible relative shifts in market segment penetration
- Trends in relative product contribution and profitability

At this point, of course, some of the projections will be highly subjective as the internal subset of data may be too small to be meaningful. They may, however, provide pointers to further research into potentially interesting areas.

Enquiries data

If a comprehensive record of enquiries data is maintained (and not every-body keeps one), some further analyses may be made:

- Enquiries volume
- Average enquiry size
- Enquiry volume through price/industry etc.
- Fluctuations in enquiry problems over segments.

These data sets lead to similar further analyses but add the further dimension of comparison. Comparison of results from the two sets of analyses provide an interesting indication as to the 'match' between enquiry patterns and actual sales results. Such matches are often valuable pointers to discrepancies between actual and potential performance and can help to highlight early trends towards changes in market perception both inbound and outbound.

Subjective data

In any organisation a number of people will be in regular touch with segments of the market. Direct sales people, professional staff, receptionists, secretaries, all interact from time to time with customers and potential customers. These interactions provide a useful source of subjective opinion on market trends, product quality and quality perception and can be a fruitful source of productive information and ideas.

The very subjectivity of the source, however, makes it essential that information is gathered in an objective fashion and that it is used as a pointer to further research rather than as an authoritative source in its own right. Tom Peters says 'the guy doing the job is the expert' and this source of expertise should never be overlooked.

Internal data from external sources

Every organisation is bombarded with external data, much of which can form the basis for fruitful research. Trade and professional magazines carry articles, letters and advertising which can indicate market trends and perceptions. Local newspapers feature planning applications and approvals, recruitment news and advertising plus more general news of local people and events, any of which can be indicators of business opportunities.

An interesting example of local news research is found in the ranks of the 'coffin followers' – residential, commercial and agricultural, with a pedigree to the highest in the land – who use reports in the 'hatched, matched and despatched' as a trigger for their attendance at the funerals which provide leads to a significant portion of their business.

Incoming direct marketing, in its various formats, can often indicate competitor activity. New product releases, office movements and relocations, changes in consumer profiles and trends can be deduced from informed scrutiny of what may appear to be 'junk' mail.

External data

Much of the data produced and available internally is likely to be, to a greater or lesser extent, relatively subjective. Even hard data such as sales or customers' records reveals only the world from the viewpoint of the company. It may point to tentative conclusions but can only represent a limited subset of the total picture.

In order to see a broader picture it is necessary to look outside the

organisation. Obviously, the broader the view required, the greater the task of data collection and, by inference, the higher the cost is likely to be. This, however, does not mean that all external data is costly.
Much indeed may be available for little or no cost.

We can subdivide external data into three areas:

- data from public sources;
- data from research organisations;
- specific research – either personal or commissioned.

Data from public sources

There is a plethora of data available from public sources to those who wish to look for it. Much of it is available free, or at very low cost. Much is available through public libraries.

The Marketing Research Society publishes a yearbook which lists a representative sample of public source information – for example the Welsh Office is able to provide economic statistics, demographic statistics, planning statistics and a host of others. The Board of Inland Revenue can provide data on corporate and personal incomes, personal wealth, conveyancing and direct taxes – with obvious interest for the property industry.

Local authorities provide access to planning data, demographics, rating data and so on. Also in the public domain, at relatively low cost, is data (normally in a processed form) from bodies such as the Consumer Association.

Universities thrive on research, much of it published in the form of PhD and MPhil theses and can often point to specific research if the right department can be located.

Professional bodies sponsor research, for example the MAC (Management Analysis Centre) report on Management in the Surveying Profession, which was sponsored by the RICS, was published in 1985.

Commercial databases

Since the advent of the microcomputer enormous strides have been taken in the ability to access, at a price, nationwide and even worldwide databases. Several already operate specifically in the property industry but there is a wealth of consumer data available in the specialist networks waiting to be tapped by innovative marketers.

The principle, in brief, is that a research organisation creates the database – building in a variety of 'tags' or search keys – then makes it available to fee-paying users. These users can either connect direct to the database or, more usually, connect via a 'gateway' in a more localised network, for example Telecom Gold or Prestel.

These databases hold phenomenal amounts of data and access charges are relatively low. The major 'local' networks publish directories to their associated databases and are well worth cultivating.

An example of this type of database use might be in selecting a target list of potential lessees in a business park by identifying hi-tech companies that have shown significant growth in a recent period and who may, therefore, be 'running out of space' in their present location.

A further use, for a developer, may be in identifying relative growth, or shrinkage rates in selected industries to assist in positioning his development to best advantage.

The list of possibilities is huge and limited only by the imagination of the marketer.

Data from specialist research organisations

Not all researchers make their data freely available. Some use it as a 'hook' for potential and existing clients on whose behalf, sometimes speculatively, they research specific markets or aspects of markets. The strength of many marketing and advertising consultancies lies in the content and quality of their research databases. Specific information can often be available at a fee (supported, of course, by 'tailored' research to the specific needs of the client).

Sponsored research

An organisation may buy specific research from commercial research organisations or, alternatively, from universities and polytechnics. The College of Estate Management, for example, provides a research facility to clients and has looked at topics as diverse as 'the World Property Market' (for an international conference) and 'The economic re-use of redundant farm buildings'.

What to research

External research, generally, involves looking at the size and nature of markets (market research) and/or the nature of behaviour within these markets.

Run on a large scale, research of this type can be specialised in content and therefore costly. It is essential, therefore, that before commissioning such research the marketer should be absolutely clear as to exactly what information he needs. In few other fields does asking the wrong question – and therefore getting a wrong or misleading answer – have such potentially dire consequences for the financial health of the organisation.

For example, asking the question 'Would you rather buy a house from a building society rather than an estate agent?' is likely to produce the answer 'Yes' – after all building societies are 'known' (perception again) to be honest, caring and concerned with serving the interests of the client; as opposed to estate agents who are 'known' to be 'shifty', 'overpaid', 'unprofessional' – and all the other epithets we have heard so often – and with so little foundation in fact.

Try the question 'If this building society became an estate agent would you prefer to buy from us?' Once again, for similar reasons the answer would probably be 'Yes'. And look how misleading that might be.

Try the question 'Would you rather buy a house from a well-established estate agency where the principals are well known in the professional community or from a national chain where the manager has no professional qualifications?' You might get – and might have got if anyone had asked the question – a very different answer.

Note that this is easy to do in hindsight. At the time most of us would have asked the first two questions rather than the third. How many of us could or would have thought through the organisational implications of institutional takeover.

Similar constraints apply to sampling attitudes following advertising campaigns. The question 'Do you recall this advert' is very different from 'Following the advert would you buy the product?'

Yet people still ask the wrong questions on occasion.

How to research

There are two distinct dimensions to market research. There is the 'simple' desk research that looks at existing data and uses it to form or shape conclusions or opinions. Even at this level the question of confidence – in the accuracy of the data or the validity of potential conclusions – has to be faced. Some data can be processed simply. Other data can be subjected to varying levels of statistical testing. If you are not – or do not feel – competent to apply statistical tests, use a statistician to do them for you. It pays in the long run.

Then there is the more complex data collection and analysis function which involves asking for other people's opinions. Here there is a wide degree of potential inaccuracy. Interpretation of personal responses, even framing questions to avoid bias in results, is a skilled function. The simplest questionnaire, wrongly framed, can 'lead' to the conclusion that you held all along. More complex data collection, through focus groups or extended interview are likely, in unskilled hands, to produce invalid answers. If you need answers to complex motivational or behavioural questions you need a skilled behaviourist to find them. This is definitely a case where 'DIY' is to be avoided.

That is not to say you should not ask people for their opinions. You should – it is part of your role as a manager – listening to people and assessing their comments is an essential part of a manager's skill set. But the skilled manager is aware of his own potential for bias in interpretation – and makes his own internal allowances. This is part of what constitutes 'flair' in a manager.

But the manager who stakes large amounts of the organisation's future profitability on flair and hunches takes an inordinately high risk. Even the best 'flair' managers get it wrong sufficiently often to be a danger to themselves and their companies.

Good managers – and marketers – get paid for managing risk.

Summary

Within this chapter we have examined the principal tactical weapons available to the marketer. Advertising, public relations, selling, direct marketing and finally market research.

In each phase the message is 'get the objectives clear then design the activity to achieve these objectives – and test the results'.

We saw in the previous chapter that strategy is, in effect, the implementation of tactical advantage. You can only achieve tactical advantage – and sustain it – if you are aware of how these tactics can be managed. This, in itself, implies a need for understanding of the nature and deployment of the tactical weapon.

Rommel lost at Alamein because he was unable to maintain his use of the tank as a viable tactical weapon – his support lines became too stretched. Marketers 'lose' because they do not manage their tactics; they do not use the 'right' form of motivation with their sales force, they do not ensure that their front-end marketing is supported by their back-end marketing.

Underlying the use of any of these weapons is the concept of 'intelligence' – knowing the battlefield, knowing the characteristics of the terrain and knowing the strengths and weaknesses of the opposition. The key to market intelligence is market and marketing research.

Market research is concerned with the physical shape of the arena. Marketing research concentrates on behaviour.

Successful research relies on asking the right person the right question in the right way at the right time.

Direct marketing

We have discussed at length elsewhere the relevance of targeting specific buyers, or buyer types, to marketers. Direct marketing takes the philosophy of the rifle shot rather than the scattergun to its extremes. At its most simple the equation says, 'Find the most likely buyer, or group of buyers, for this product, then tell them about it – directly'.

Within the property industry the agency function, in particular, has made considerable use of direct marketing techniques. In recent years there are signs that the direct marketing philosophy is extending to professional services as well as the more traditional property products.

In this section we look at the basics of direct marketing and consider how some of its practices may be extended to more profitable usage in both spheres.

Targeting

The fundamental principle of direct marketing is that it tries to reach 'the most likely buyers' for a product. We have already examined the principles of market segmentation in some detail so will not repeat them here. Suffice it to say that successful targeting relies on an understanding of market segmentation if its benefits are to be fully realised.

What are the sources of information for targeting? There is a variety of trade sources available. RICS membership list, ISVA membership list and the lists of other professional and trade bodies are normally available in a variety of media – published books or electronic tapes or discs are obvious examples. The Institute of Marketing publishes a list of useful trade sources for 'mailing' or 'contact' lists in a variety of alternative segmentations which can be put to use.

Every business, however, has its own personal source of customer data. Records of enquiries, previous sales, trade contacts, seminar attendees, job advertisements all provide fruitful sources.

Electronic computers are available with an enormous range of software (programs) specifically designed for the swift extraction of relevant data which can transform 'raw' lists into powerful marketing weapons.

In the property industry both residential and commercial agencies maintain mailing lists which are used to a varying degree of success.

The key, then, is a range of contact lists which provide sufficient detail for meaningful selection against specific product or benefit-oriented criteria.

Use

Having found some data we must consider the use to which it may be put. There are two prime media for using contact list data for direct marketing, namely:

the telephone
mailings.

In addition to the prime media there are possibilities in electronic mail, facsimile transmission (fax) and, probably somewhat in the future, cable communication systems. We will examine first the two prime media then suggest some possible avenues for the future.

Telephones

In any marketing medium it is probably true to say that the closer the physical link with the buyer, the greater the potential for behavioural change – positive or negative. In the absence of a direct sales call – by a representative in person – the telephone is probably the most powerful medium available. It is relatively cheap to use and can generate disproportionate benefits in revenue achieved.

There are problems, however. The telephone is probably one of the most misused pieces of office equipment. It can as easily generate adverse behavioural change as positive change. Its use is often delegated to untrained personnel whose status is markedly lower than that of the more glamorous 'personal sales person'. In many organisations its use as a marketing tool is undervalued and undermanaged. Neither is its potential range of uses fully understood and appreciated.

For successful direct marketing telephone use must be planned – to extract maximum benefit from minimum use – and it must be carefully managed – to ensure that planned benefits are being fully achieved.

Telephone marketing can be utilised in two, distinct modes, outbound and inbound messages. Telesales is generally perceived as being an outbound activity only – i.e. a negotiator or receptionist or 'tele-salesperson' both individually and in concert with other tactical initiatives.

The objective, therefore, of a specific initiative may be simply to generate a behavioural change that moves the prospect to a point where a further initiative actually completes the transaction. For example: the 'sales call' which tells the prospect that a particular property is on the market may be designed simply to arouse interest. Alternatively, it may be designed to persuade the prospect to view the property so that he will become the subject of a sales initiative designed to generate commitment to purchase.

The whole chain can come apart if the original caller tries to achieve the second objective at a point where the prospect is not 'ready' to move that quickly.

It is vital, therefore, before any calls are made at all, to specify clearly the objective – thus allowing the call to be planned so that the objective is likely to be achieved – and so that feedback can be obtained as to the success of the initiative. Many marketing initiatives have been adjudged failures – and successes – because they were the subject of incorrect judgement criteria. The incorrectly judged 'successes', of course, lead to future failure when principles 'learned' in the previous situation are found to be inappropriate in the next.

Scripting
Having established a clear objective – for example 'generate an appointment to view property' – it is possible to plan the method by which this objective can be achieved.

Any sales call has the following main features in common:

– Open the sale;
– Qualify;
– Trial close;
– Answer objections;
– Close.

It follows, therefore, that the person making the call should be aware of the stages and have some mechanism which ensures that each is adequately followed through.

At this point many readers will wish to switch off with the thought that 'Property isn't like any other form of commodity and, anyway, I know how to sell on the phone and, anyway, I certainly don't need any kind of scripting or fancy sales training to tell me what to do'.

We sympathise with that view. The experienced property professional dealing regularly with clients and potential clients by telephone, will have instinctively absorbed a working knowledge of telephone sales technique and will have evolved a 'script' that works for him.

Please don't switch off, however. Think about your more junior staff making sales calls, for example your secretary telephoning a business contact to ask whether he would like to see the super new retail shed on which you have just been instructed and which you 'know' is ideal for his needs.

Ask yourself how often this occurs and how many times you have been forced to make the 'close' call yourself when, after three or four attempts she has been unable to pin him down to an appointment. (Once again, if you think this never happens in your organisation keep a log of your own activities for a few weeks. You will be amazed.)

Telephone selling is a relatively expensive activity. It can be highly cost-effective (indeed it is the lifeblood of commercial and residential agencies), but to be fully effective it needs to be managed – and this means planning and monitoring.

Effective telephone selling is a complex and highly skilled activity. Ineffective telephone selling is expensive at both a direct level – failure to convert 'obvious' leads- and at an indirect level – damage to established relationships through inappropriate 'selling' activity; for example, telephoning at the wrong time of day, using poor imagery or simply failing to adapt to the listener's needs and thereby putting his back up.

Management of complex activities implies training – training for the manager and training for the managed. If you and your staff have not received such training, invest in some, now. You first.

Inbound marketing

The telephone is one of the two principal means of communication between the firm and the outside world. As such its use should be maximised wherever possible. Incoming calls provide an important potential source of new business to the firm, not only when they form an obvious direct enquiry but also when unrelated calls can be diverted.

An extreme example of call diversion is in complaints management where a complaint, handled in a sensitive and positive manner, can often be turned into new business.

The underlying principle is that any incoming call represents a source of potential new business, although it must be remembered that the new business may not arise immediately. Selling in the wrong way at the wrong time is a major turn-off to many potential clients.

Conversion of incoming calls is not easy. It involves recognition of the context of the call, recognition of the purchasing power of the call and the ability to recognise business potential.

Most firms recognise the importance of initial telephone reception in reflecting the image of the firm to the caller and many pay considerable attention to managing this initial contact. The real potential, however, exists further down the chain – where the call is processed. And at this point few firms show any understanding of the call as a source of business.

Having said this, agencies have long been aware of the potential for cross-selling services. Property enquiries are a prime source of new instructions; property purchasers are a prime target for financial services; property vendors are a prime target for professional services and so on. The rise of the 'majors' in residential markets have brought these issues to the fore and identification and conversion of such cross-selling opportunities form an important part of staff training.

There is similar potential within the commercial world but many firms identify organisational difficulties in transferring leads across internal boundaries. For example, established rent review relationships can be a source of development or investment appraisal opportunities. Increasingly, however, firms are organising along functional lines which make transfer of specialised knowledge (often crucial in the specialist sales arena) increasingly difficult.

For such leads to be maximised, therefore, there must be

a) clear identification of potential at senior levels;
b) internal commitment to maximise growth through internal transfer;
c) intensive and ongoing training for all contact staff in the recognition and processing of sale potential.

All this from a simple telephone call!
In the professional services area there may be resistance on professional

grounds to the transfer of information which can assist the selling function. Many professional people resist the concept that they are involved in a sales function as we saw earlier in our discussion on sales management. In the increasingly competitive commercial world, however, such a 'commercial' orientation is essential for future success and broad-based ongoing selling is crucial for this success to be achieved.

Summary

The telephone is a crucial tactical weapon in the battle for customers and their future business. It can be used as both an active and a reactive weapon. Each mode of use has different constraints but both involve

> awareness of objectives
> operational training

if these objectives are to be fully achieved.

Mailing

The power of mailing systems lies in its flexibility – it is able to pass messages in a variety of formats – written word, graphic images, video and audio. The drawbacks are:

> – the increasing use – and therefore the increased competition – of direct mail in both private and commercial capacities;
> – one-way communication.

We have already encountered both problems in other guises in other sections of the book, notably when looking at consumer behaviour and at advertising in general and have discussed some of the basic techniques which can overcome some of the difficulties. Direct mailing, however, has some specific factors which should be addressed.

Flexibility
The message need not be constrained by a single medium. Early direct mail involved solely the printed word and pictures. More recent mailings have included the Heinz Beans tin (with a reprinted label identifying that the factory producing the beans was for sale), executive toys, 45 rpm records (with a jingle or recorded message); video cassettes with specific presentations.

The ability to mix media – if the prospect can be persuaded to follow through and process the whole message – adds considerably to the selling power of the mailing – if the message is apt and well designed.

Once again, the key phrases keep reappearing 'if the prospect can be persuaded'; and 'if the message is apt and well designed.'

At the risk of being repetitious the basis of design must be:

– What is the specific objective to be achieved?
– What factors are likely to work against achieving this objective?
– How can I get past problems and achieve the objective?

In the property industry considerable use has already been made, for example, of video in mailing. An example is the video circulated in 1989/90 by The College of Estate Management which, regardless of whether many people watched it, stimulated an element of interest through its relative novelty. For the active step to be taken – namely, watch the video – some specific benefit (however intangible) needs to be provided which prompts the receiver to take the next step.

Time availability

Television or press advertising suffers, like posters, from the attention span normally available to it. TV adverts are, by their nature, limited in duration and often occur when the watcher's attention would prefer to be elsewhere. Press advertising competes for time, in the tube, taxi, bus or lavatory, with the reader's greater interest in sport, page 3 or the stock market.

Mailing shots, if opened at all, tend to become part of a more structured information gathering activity – learning the worst from the telephone company, checking the minutes of recent meetings or relaxing with a post card from Auntie Mary in Majorca. If the attention can be caught, a relatively large tranche of time can be made available to deal with message content. This means that advertisements can be more informative and can therefore seek to take the purchaser further through the mechanics of the buying decision.

An example of this use of the medium are book company mailings which provides a 'hook' to get attention – then use that hook to lead into the extensive (and well-planned) sales presentation culminating in a request to purchase – coupled with a direct incentive for an early decision.

The preceding example, of course, takes us back to the basic principles – clear objectives:

a) read me
b) move to stage 2 (sales pitch)
c) move to stage 3 (fill in purchase order).

It hardly needs to be said that successful design at this level is a highly skilled function – nor that most people get it wrong. Even one of the market leaders in its early days addressed its letters to Mr Owen Bevan ... and followed up in its 'letter' with 'Dear Mr Owen Bevan' – a tactic hardly likely to endear them to anyone!

Property mailing

In the property world, despite considerable experience of mailing property details to potential purchasers, we are still relatively unsophisticated. We continually hear the cry, 'I gave them specific details of the type of property I wanted yet they still send me things which are of no conceivable use'. There is no real excuse for this. One of two things has happened. Either the client has misunderstood what you can do for him (your fault for not making things clear; the client does not know what he expected so you, by definition, are a low quality provider); or you failed to find out his real needs. Either way it's down to you. It all comes back to objectives. What is the objective of mailing property details to a potential purchaser? What do you want them to do?

In both residential and commercial the objective is clear. You want them to telephone you so that you can make an appointment for a real, live demonstration.

(Note that commercial auction mailing may be rather different, particularly for investment property. Here people are buying money – an investment – so you may wish to provide sufficient information to allow people to decide on whether they may be able to come and buy their investment at the auction. The property itself, may be no more than marginally relevant to the buying decision!)

Normally, then, the objective is to set up a demonstration. So what do we do? We provide so much information that the prospect can decide not to proceed – without our even speaking to him.

The Newport Property Centre ran into both of these problems – plus the complaint that people were being inundated with 'useless bumf'. Accepting that they neither had the technology for perfect targeting, nor the manpower available for adequate (at this level) qualification (like most estate agents), they switched to the provision of weekly lists of new instructions, grouped in price bands, providing minimal but potentially intriguing information – effectively the week's newspaper advertising a day early. The result was an increase in telephone enquiries, an increase in demonstrations (with a concomitant increase in sales) and a considerable increase in customer satisfaction.

A little thinking goes a long way!

This, of course, is routine mailing, designed to fulfil a specific objective in a specific environment. Other forms of mailing may be more or less sophisticated but they have in common the fundamental need for clarity in objectives, message and design. Without such clarity mailing is, at best, an expensive luxury; at worst a disincentive to potential clients.

Other direct marketing media and approaches

In this section we review a few direct marketing approaches which may be appropriate for use in specific circumstances. There are many others and the reader is directed to the references and further reading which lists a number of books covering direct marketing in more detail.

Catalogues

Auction houses (chattels and property) make considerable use of catalogue mailing, in most cases so successfully that they can make a charge for their catalogue. A variant of the catalogue approach is the 'property newspaper' tried by most estate agents, particularly the majors, but dropped, in most cases, just as quickly. (Why? Because the copy objectives are wrong; they tend not to generate inspection leads – although research suggests that people like to read them.)

Commercial agency firms use an element of the catalogue approach in their corporate brochures which set out, often in glorious technicolour, the services which they provide and the potential benefit to the client in using those services. Unfortunately, this type of catalogue often fails to ask for a sale, or any other behavioural change – although they may help to add the originator's name to a choice set. This is doubtful, however, given the potential for institutionalisation of commercial buying relationships and such catalogues or brochures are likely to result in only marginal sales benefit.

Back-end marketing

We have referred throughout our discussions on direct marketing to the importance of defining objectives in the marketing initiative. We now distinguish between two aspects of the marketing initiative; front-end marketing, which is concerned with the generation of leads and back-end marketing, which is the next stage in converting the lead into a sale. We have identified some of the problems and opportunities in the 'front-end'. Now we look at the 'back-end'.

Many marketing campaigns are made or marred by the effectiveness of back-end marketing. Customers telephone for property details then wait a week to receive them. Customers commission a private valuation or survey then receive a report which does not satisfy their needs because the surveyor (despite professional exhortations) did not discuss the nature of the report with them before he carried out the survey. Customers respond to invitations to apply for mortgages then wait a fortnight for an appointment with the building society manager.

These are all obvious errors – and surely do not happen in your company (Or do they? They happen in everyone else's from time to time).

These 'little errors', like failing to return a telephone call, are the equivalent of the exhaust falling off a brand new car, or the new microwave oven exploding. They are, de facto, poor quality and cost money – often far more than you are aware of, particularly in the closely inbred and mutually aware commercial world.

Solutions are often very simple – a matter of thinking things through. If a special offer is promoted make sure that everyone, from the MD down, is aware of its structure and implications. The caller will always land on the person who knows nothing about it! If a new development is given a high profile direct mailshot make sure that there is an adequate supply of details in all the offices to meet likely demand – unless you plan to 'run out of details' as a sales ploy. Manage your response capability!

Back-end marketing implies more than initial response. Every caller is a potential customer, but his desire and willingness to be a customer starts to diminish from the time he makes the call. Follow up enquiries until they have definitely 'died' and find out why they died. An enquiry indicates potential demand. You have done the expensive bit – creating the call – now make sure you convert it.

Leading direct mail firms normally use some kind of routinised follow-up procedure. A 'no' response on a Reader's Digest mailshot will almost certainly generate a further mailing to qualify the 'no' and suggest further or alternative products.

Make use of routine communication. A sale and invoice is not necessarily the end of a sales relationship. Many organisations use 'ride-along' mailing where the invoice contains further invitations to the use of related products, often with a 'special offer' or limited discounting.

Use 'package stuffers'. A number of firms in the commercial world make use of Chartered Surveyors Weekly (CSW) and Estates Gazette to circulate promotional material. Henry Stewart's and ICC, in the property training industry, make regular use of both journals for initial mailing, then follow up previous responders with personal mailshots, in some cases supported by telephone canvas. Other carriers are available. Professional branches will normally include a limited amount of promotional material with branch communications – for a fee, of course.

Summary

Direct marketing is now endemic to our way of life, both personal and professional, in both the UK and the USA. It has been the subject of considerable practical experience and academic research. There is a variety of media available to the direct marketer all of which have in common the need to set clear objectives for the initiative and the need to design the promotional vehicle to achieve, specifically, the set objectives.

A direct marketing initiative may extend across several boundaries and relate to many aspects of the firm. Careful management is therefore needed if the initiatives are to be fully used to the company's benefit.

Inherent complexity in the direct marketing field is such that professional help may often be needed and should be sought. Mistakes in this area can be catastrophic.

References and further reading

J. Collbrecht (1974), 'To Get Volume up Sell Down', *Sales Management* 22, July

J. F. Engel, R. D. Blackwell and P. W. Miniard (1990), *Consumer Behavior*, ibid. p. 474

V. Packard (1970), *The Hidden Persuaders*

T. Peters and N. Austin, *In Search of Excellence*, p. 88/9

A. Ries and J. Trout (1986), *Marketing Warfare*, McGraw-Hill, New York.

P. Drucker (1985), *Information and Entrepreneurship*, Heinemann, London

9 The Marketing Plan

Case study

In the 1990 Finals examinations for the Royal Institution of Chartered Surveyors candidates were asked to prepare a marketing plan for a 5 ha site which contained a derelict factory. The plan should have included an analysis of the site which explored its potential for alternative uses and identified target markets; from the site analysis an approach to pricing and method of sale should have emerged; this, in turn, should have led to a promotional plan which ensured that the right purchasers were approached in the right way, at the right time and to maximum effect.

Only a handful managed to put all three elements together in their answers. Many made a competent analysis of the potential product. Many more made a competent promotional plan. Most made a reasonable stab at methods of sale. Few identified the whole picture.

The case study highlights, albeit in an artificial format, one of the difficulties that property people – and others involved in marketing – seem to experience in the development of marketing plans. They do not look at all the angles in a systematic way.

What was also demonstrated very clearly in the candidates' responses is that there is no excuse for this. They had the knowledge and skills available. They simply lacked the 'corporate ethos' that led to their thinking the problem right through.

Property people, traditionally entrepreneurial in temperament, are oriented towards results rather than management.

Marketing, however, as we saw in Chapter 1 of this book, is a management function and requires a management-oriented approach if professional marketing advice to clients – or business plans to financial backers – is to remain credible against the growing competition from management consultants, accountants and the like which is becoming so much a part of the property scene.

What is a marketing plan?

First and foremost a marketing plan is a selling document. It is the encapsulation of considerable thought about products, markets, pricing and promotion which communicates our vision to our reader.

Who is the reader? A marketing plan could be produced externally, for a client or a financier or internally to a departmental head, chief Executive officer or the board. But it does not stop there. Once produced, amended and accepted it may become an operational document, referred to for guidance and instruction over an extended period.

Why is it, then, a selling document?

Consider the client. The marketing plan is a synopsis of your advice, set out in whatever detail you consider appropriate. To the client it is concrete evidence of the quality of your service product. In this context it contains both hard and soft quality indicators – the external covers and headings, internal layout, quality of paper, even the typeface used, say something about you and your company. English style, spelling and grammar help to indicate the quality level which the client can expect from your advice. On more detailed acquaintance the style and content of argument, words used, annotations, all make statements which contribute to the client's confidence in your advice. The client has probably paid for this report. If he has, he will certainly read it – and form value judgements as he does so.

Viewed purely from a marketing viewpoint your marketing plan is a document of the highest importance – and it must be treated accordingly.

Consider internal readers. A marketing plan for a new or existing product can have a vital impact upon corporate planning. A marketing plan with all the right advice poorly presented is unlikely to be adopted – to the probable detriment both of the company and of the plan's author. Once adopted it may become the product's 'bible' for most of the planned period. If it fails to provide guidance when guidance is needed, or if that guidance is hidden by elegant but meaningless verbiage, fault will be laid at the door of its author – justifiably.

Management is time consuming and difficult. Its absence, however, is catastrophic. A marketing plan is a vital management document – and its importance must be recognised in its preparation.

External plans

Property people are consultants. They are employed by clients for their specialist expertise, often in the area of marketing property. Increasingly, in the commercial area, property marketing consultants are required to tender for work and to present their proposals in 'beauty contests'. Increasingly, too, commercial buyers (of property marketing services) are marketing aware; that is, they have had some exposure to marketing as a discipline within their business training or experience. They expect, therefore, that marketing proposals will, at least, take account of modern commercial thinking and will be expressed in contemporary language.

There is a growing trend, as part of beauty contest presentations, for property people to be asked to 'prepare a marketing plan for this property'. In the past a promotional plan showing advertising budgets, PR proposals and possibly some advertising designs might have been adequate. For some properties, particularly smaller ones, it might still be. But for a major proportion of presentations a marketing plan which talks only of promotion demonstrates little more than its author's lack of understanding of the wider commercial world and is likely to be viewed (and rejected) in this light.

We will look later in the chapter at the contents of a marketing plan in more detail. For the moment it should suffice to say that the plan should include, at least, discussions of the four 'Ps' of the marketing mix:

Product
– What, precisely, are we selling?
– Who, precisely, might want to buy it?
– Why?

Place
– Where should this product be sold?
– Where might buyers (as already identified) find access to the product most easily?

Price
– What constraints affect product pricing?
– Is there a specific pricing strategy which can be recommended?
– Why?

Promotion
– What mix of promotional tactics should be applied?
– Who will manage the mix?
– Are there any special constraints?
– How much will it all cost?

Clearly, from the simple questioning technique applied above, the preparation of a marketing plan, even for an existing property, can become a complex task and may result in a complex solution.

Internal plans

Here, potentially, the nature of the product is likely to be fundamentally different. The external product is normally a tangible or identifiable interest in land (or a set of interests). Once these interests are disposed of successfully the task is finished and the consultant turns to other matters. The internal product, by contrast, is likely to be an ongoing programme which is of crucial concern to the continuing viability of the firm.

It is likely, essentially, to be a service product with all the marketing implications of service products that were explored in Chapter 6.

Similar constraints apply as with the external product in that the marketing plan looks at the four Ps but now come added complications in the form of, often sophisticated, segmentation decisions, market size and share considerations and the strategic constraints that these imply. From strategic constraints stem tactical constraints – how do we manage the marketing mix? What are the implications for personnel recruitment, training, supervision, targeting, remuneration, promotion, etc.? The list is long but the marketing plan must embrace it if it is to be, and remain, credible.

An internal marketing plan is a crucial document in managing a company. its production is time consuming and often subject to tight deadlines. It is a management function.

Timescale – How long does a marketing plan last?

This is the archetypal 'How long is a piece of string' question. The answer, of course, is 'it depends'; depends on the type of product under consideration, the market environment, the economy, overriding constraints such as the imminent need for a sale; complexity of the market place – a whole range of factors difficult to identify, let alone quantify.

The best answer, probably, would be 'as long as it remains relevant'. If circumstances or constraints change then so must the plan to allow for the new regimen.

The marketing plan, like all plans, is a starting point. It should reflect the best available thinking based upon the knowledge available now. If, as a result of research or other new information received after development and publication of the plan, better options become available, then the plan should be changed – if necessary scrapped and started again. It should always be remembered that many businesses fail because they insist on seeing their position in the light of yesterday's standpoint, rather than seeing the world as it is today.

It follows, therefore, that a marketing plan should not be considered as written in 'tablets of stone'. Rather, it should be considered as a road map, highlighting the important intermediate destinations and indicating local topography together with a probable route. But the route should be kept under continuous review and adjusted if local or overriding conditions change during the journey.

What should the plan cover?

The product:

- What do you wish to sell?
- What needs does it meet?

The market:

- Who needs the product?
- Why?
- How often?
- How many?
- How much will they pay/What is the market worth?
- Is there identifiable segmentation?
- What competition exists?
- Summarise market opportunity.

Strategy:

- How can market opportunities be developed?
- What are the opportunities and pitfalls
- How can competitors and competition be overcome?

Tactical mix:

- Pricing
- Distribution
- Promotion.

Resource allocations:

- Tactical budgets.

Detailed plan (Implementation plan).

Cost/Benefit summary.

How should the plan be presented?

We have already stressed that a marketing plan is, essentially, a selling document, whether written for client or internal consumption. It follows, therefore, that whatever else happens the plan should be presented to a standard that supports the selling objective.

This does not mean that every plan should be expensively printed and contain acres of coloured photographs – although some may need to be produced in this way.

What it does mean is that the needs of the reader in the specific situation should be considered and the plan presented in a way that matches these needs as closely as possible. If the plan is for a high profile client and deals with a high value subject portfolio its presentation should match the importance of the disposal to the client. A plan for internal consumption only should cater to the management needs of those managers responsible for its appraisal and use.

In its most basic form the plan should always be well presented and easily assimilated by the reader.

By now the reader will have identified a startling similarity between the contents of the plan and the general layout of this book. Indeed, the paragraphs that follow are intended as a résumé of the more detailed information already covered and the reader should be able to refer back for additional clarification in a number of the areas covered.

Contents of the marketing plan

Product

Before any consideration can be given to strategy or tactics the report must clarify exactly what is to be sold. In Chapter 1 we identified the three simple product divisions for property as a product – users, investors, developers – and followed this is Chapter 2 with a more detailed consideration of the nature of a product.

The marketing plan should examine the product and identify as clearly as possible its principal attributes at core, tangible and augmented product level. Only by undertaking this level of analysis can attention be directed to analysis of the market place and consumption patterns. For example, it is only by examining the estate agency product in detail that the concept of selling buyers – or, in the case of commercial, consultancy – emerges with all the implications that they entail.

Market

The basic 'market' questions in a marketing plan are fairly simple to ask. Who needs it? Why? In what circumstances? How often? How many? What are the 'value' criteria (how much will they pay? and so on)? They are, however, much more difficult to answer and finding answers may involve considerable research. Research may be directed into needs analysis, consumption patterns, generic competition – a range of areas.

In the case of a client's property much of this needed research may be already available as the 'stock in trade' of the agent/advisor. In simple circumstances this may be entirely adequate for the needs of the client but care should always be taken as no two sets of circumstances are ever exactly equivalent and there is danger in making assumptions based on experience. After all, many readers will have experienced the rebuttal of suggestions on the basis that 'We tried that and it didn't work' (with the implied addition of '20 years ago'). It is upsetting then to see similar suggestions implemented by other firms who thereby steal a march in some way. Experience, whilst a useful indicator, can also be dangerously deceptive.

Comments – and thoughts – along the lines that 'There's no way you'll ever get planning permission to convert that old barn into a dwelling' have been the source of considerable facial egg – in some cases even negligence claims!

For the more complex client property, good market research, targeted directly upon the special product benefits of the specific property, can often be the key to successful disposal. Think around the problem. The obvious is not always the best answer.

When dealing with a client's property a clear identification of the market place, the nature and needs of potential purchasers within it, is the basis for targeting – with considerable impact upon the promotional mix.

Internal marketing plans, as we have seen above, focus on products of a different nature, with different time constraints and with potentially far-reaching effects on the future profitability of the firm. It is essential, therefore that they should fully explore:

the nature of the market
  – customer sizes
  – purchase frequency
  – behaviour patterns

market projections
  – changes in underlying market control factors
  – technological change and potential impact
  – changes in market behaviour

key success factors
  – those factors which affect the ability of a firm to prosper in that market

These factors are at the heart of any consideration of the firm's ability to operate within a market place and may provide useful indicators to market share projections.

From the initial market analysis the plan should consider the market in more detail:

- Segmentation
  – Is there potential for market segmentation? Do different consumers behave in identifiably different ways? Do they place differing weights on elements of the product and are there differences from the basis of a differentiated product which can develop a sustainable competitive advantage?
  – Are the identified segments large enough to justify development of the product and the market place? What level of market share is available within market segments?

- Competition
  – What is the competition likely to be within the market?
  – Who are the principal competitive suppliers? Do they have any weaknesses which can be strategically exploited?

In looking at competition it is important to consider generic competition as well as the more obvious competitors. For example, the buggy whip manufacturers in the USA of the late nineteenth century might have prospered longer had they identified their generic competition in the internal combustion engine rather than their direct competitors in making buggy whips. Similarly, the surveyors of the 1990s would do well to recognise their generic role as management consultants in facing competitive challenges from established – and avariciously growing – consultancy firms rather than from other firms of surveyors. Perhaps even residential agents – still reeling under the onslaught of the major financial institutions – may not recognise the potential generic challenge implied through teleshopping (when linked to computerisation of the Land Registry).

Even more fundamental might be competition at the level of a fundamental attitude shift away from home ownership and back to a rented ethos. Who knows what 1992 may bring in this context?

Strategy

At this point in the plan the reader should have a clear idea of the nature of the product and the parameters of the market place into which it is to be directed. The question to which the next two sections of the plan are directed is 'How?'

As we have seen strategy is concerned with an overview of the campaign. 'Should we attack/defend on a broad front or should we concentrate on attaining a position which we can consolidate and use as a base for future development? Where, overall, are we trying to get?'

In assessing strategic position, it is essential to review, carefully, the present and potential competition in the market place. In most cases market share will be achieved at the expense of competitors either by taking part of their existing shares or by preventing them from taking part of the firm's share, once established.

As we shall see, competitor analysis is particularly important in the context of internal marketing plans but should not be ignored when developing external plans. No matter how unique the product it competes in a finite market for finite funds against other, similar products often in other parts of the UK. In any competitive situation it is essential to understand the competition and consideration should always be given to this aspect within the development of the marketing plan.

Traditional strategic thinking emphasises the analysis of strengths, weaknesses, opportunities and threats. From such an analysis competitive maps can be drawn which indicate openings and should alert the strategist to potential attack from other competitors.

The marketing plan should contain a clear statement of the competitive situation and develop a strategic approach which capitalises upon the product's potential strength whilst attacking competitive offerings at their weakest points.

In looking, in particular, at internal products, the principle that 'strategy is concerned with the successful implementation of tactical advantage' should always be borne in mind. Competitive advantage derives, essentially, from differentiation and the factors which may sustain differentiation (superior local knowledge, unique access to deciders, superior technological management capability) should be searched out diligently and turned to maximum advantage.

The reader may, by now, be thinking that this section contains an awful lot of words which deal with factors which, whilst they may be of crucial import to a multinational cosmetics company, have little to offer the 'Surveyor in the Street'. Perhaps an example would bring us all back to earth.

In Chapter 7 we introduced the vision of the competent local surveyor struggling to earn a living against the institutional competitors. We identified key success factors as 'local knowledge', 'local contacts', and 'local reputation'. Perhaps this surveyor now spots a potential market for golf course development. Additional key factors now arise.

Knowledge of the agricultural community;
Contacts with leisure developers interested in the golf course market;
Understanding of golf and its mythology;
Access to specialised planning expertise;
Creditability in leisure matters.

Assumed competitors for this market place are in the shape of major 'National' surveying firms with 'leisure' departments plus another local surveyor with little experience generally, a limited social connection but direct experience of golf course development with one of the majors and some track record through recent high profile association with one local development.

Our surveyor must analyse his options carefully before he can develop a strategic direction that will stand much chance of success.

Strengths
He has good local knowledge, is well known in the area and has a good reputation – i.e. people trust him. He plays golf and participates regularly in 'trade competitions' so has an understanding of the game and its arcanities. He has acted for and against major firms on many occasions.

Weaknesses
On the other hand he has no direct experience of golf course development and he knows that he is not, at present, the 'first choice' advisor for many potential local vendors in this specialist market. He is also aware that some potential clients might be swayed by the charisma of his youthful local rival.

Opportunities
There is, clearly, an opportunity in this new market in acting for both vendors and purchasers over the next few years. Someone will do it and it might as well be him!

Threats
He is not the only one who can see the opportunities. Both his youthful rival and the major firms are targeting the area. There is an additional threat in that, if he is not seen to be active in this 'modern' area people might get the impression that he is 'out of date' – and that his existing instruction base might suffer as a result.

The situation is clearly complex and he needs to make his moves quickly if he is not to be overtaken.

He considers his competitors. The majors have good professional expertise, both in depth and breadth. On the other hand they have little local track record and are viewed with an element of suspicion by the locals, particularly the smaller farmers.

The youthful rival has an aura of credibility at the moment although his inexperience has already got him in and out of a number of scrapes which cast an element of doubt upon his long term 'stickability'. On the other hand he is well connected in the county and can probably expect some support from the local 'senior establishment'.

What options are available?

He could:

a) decide that the whole thing is too risky and the chances of success so slight that he is better off out of it – a perfectly sensible option but one that does not put much hay in the barn for the winter;
b) join forces with his young rival – a strategy that has much to commend it but which brings in its wake considerable potential change to his working lifestyle and may carry the seeds of an expensive partnership dissolution at some time in the future;
c) operate as a 'runner' for one or other (or even several) of the major firms – he has established contacts with some of them and he would gain many of the benefits in the short term without relinquishing control over his own destiny. Unfortunately, of course, if he does this there is the ever-present risk that he will generate his own redundancy by parting with his contacts (one of his major strengths) for a mess of pottage in the short term.

The reader can no doubt think of other options available to our surveyor, further increasing his difficulties of decision making. This is the point of this exercise. Strategic decision making is difficult and involves considerable heart-searching, analysis and research. It is, however, just as crucial to the small businessman as to the multinational corporation. In its absence the businessman relies upon luck. And Lady Luck is a fickle mistress.

The strategy section should say, in broad terms, 'this is where we want to be and this, generally, is how we want to get there. These are the constraints and we interpret them in this way. That is why we have chosen this route'. The statement should be unequivocal and should enable the reader to follow the decision logic. (What does our surveyor do? No idea – we don't have enough information to advise him sensibly – sorry!)

Tactical management

From strategy we move to tactical management. In the plan we know where we want to go and we know, broadly, how to get there. What are the tactical implications of our decision?

In the area of marketing tactics we start to consider elements of the promotional mix – selling, PR, advertising, direct mail, packaging, pricing – from a management viewpoint (remember that marketing is a management function – not the realm of the 'gifted amateur'). We also need to consider the other 'P' of marketing – 'place' or distribution.

The marketing plan should identify the mix to be used and, from this, specify the resources needed; what, where, when and how they are to be deployed. This tactical deployment forms the basis of the next section – tactical budgets.

In Chapter 8 we explored the nature of marketing tactics in some detail. Here we recap the principles.

Selling

What sales activity is appropriate to the job in hand? For example, in the case of a new housing development, there may be a need for sales activity at several levels. Site operations may involve a sales manager plus a team of 'resident' negotiators covering the site on a 7-day rota basis. This activity may need support from local agency officers both providing direct sales leads and converting leads to resale instructions. On a large site there may be scope for specialist sales personnel dealing specifically with shared ownership schemes. The whole operation will interact with financial services 'consultants' and needs coordination with other activity in the new houses area.

The marketing plan will need to identify these interactions in detail and, in a large scheme, may include job specifications, remuneration packages and recruitment schedules. If the scheme is of finite duration the plan may also need to address policy regarding termination at the end of the contract.

A sales campaign for an office block may involve, similarly, negotiators for a limited period, possibly based on-site. These, in turn, interact with financial or technical consultants and also with institutional sales staff concerned with final (or pre-) sale of the overall investment.

Our local surveyor, assuming that he chooses to develop his golf course niche himself, will need to plan a personal selling campaign – perhaps based on cold calling local landowners and development institutions – if he wishes to pursue his objectives profitably.

Direct marketing

The marketing plan should consider direct marketing initiatives carefully, providing yardsticks against which effectiveness can be judged. It should set the parameters within which direct marketing is undertaken and identify specific approaches which will be used.

For example: the plan for a new homes development may include direct mailing to employees of companies known to be relocating into the area; a different direct mailing to selected personnel officers; local direct mailing to potential first time buyers; reader-response advertising in key newspapers and local interest magazines; catalogue mailing for solicitors' and doctors' waiting rooms together with local hotel lobbies and reception areas and so on.

For the major office block direct marketing might include catalogue mailing to professional advisors, detail mailing to potential occupiers; direct-response advertising in professional journals plus supportive 'informational' mailing to key influencers.

Our surveyor may elect to direct mail personal letters of introduction – outlining his new service – to key local landowners whose land is a potentially attractive target. He may also mail personal letters to developers active in the area of golf course development, supporting this activity with personal tele-sales. He may even solicit further enquiry through limited use of reader-response advertising in the trade press and business sections of the Sunday newspapers.

Public relations

In all of our three on-going examples there are ample opportunities for PR activity and each could gain considerable benefit from well-managed publicity. Again, to be effective, the campaign must be thought through and planned carefully.

The new homes development provides great scope for the PR activity – purchase of the site – even pre-purchase rumours – can be managed to advantage. Photo opportunities of the ex-landowner clutching a cheque can be juxtaposed with angry protestors and balanced with arguments about training needs, new jobs, infrastructure development and so on. Planning applications and appeals are a fruitful source of useful publicity. Photo opportunities of the first new homeowner signing contracts; general interest stories about new staff members, conservation interest with 'badger runs' and 'hedgehog patrols' generate interest and awareness. The list is endless but is more effective if it is pre-planned and managed to an appropriate timetable.

Commercial agents already make good use of PR opportunities with new factories, office blocks etc. Some obvious examples are construction viewing areas, topping out ceremonies, launch parties; more exotic are 'press' trips down (or up) the Thames; seminars in the Channel Islands and so on. Again, opportunities should be pre-identified and pre-planned to ensure that all phases of the promotional mix complement each other.

Our local surveyor can find considerable mileage in PR opportunities. For example, acting as 'Guest Auctioneer' for high profile charitable gatherings can produce good copy. More specifically, becoming a source of informed comment upon specialist topics can often result in considerably increased target market awareness and association with the specialist service. Personal events should not be ignored. We have recounted elsewhere how a young 'up and coming' estate agent chartered a helicopter for his and his young bride's journey from church to reception – and 'won' a front page story with banner headline and photograph to match. These things do not happen by accident!

In Chapter 8 we identified the need for cultivating the press and others responsible for converting our opportunities into tangible results.

When marketing on behalf of clients this pre-cultivation is part of the service for which the client is paying. Where it does not exist firms should examine carefully the benefits of using the services of a full-time PR consultancy who should both have the 'ear' of the media and the technical competence to convert opportunities into 'media friendly' copy which will get used – in the right place at the right time.

Distribution

There is a temptation for property people to think, at this point, that 'OK, I can see the point of selling, PR and direct marketing, but distribution – surely that's only appropriate for things like motor cars, tins of beans and other consumable products?'.

Taking a narrow viewpoint this is probably a valid reaction. After all property and property related products can hardly be stocked in a warehouse awaiting delivery. From a broader view, however, it quickly becomes clearer that extensive, if subtle, distribution networks are involved and these networks can be managed to advantage. They should, therefore, be considered carefully within the marketing plan.

Take the new development, for example. Whilst it exists in one place only and cannot be moved around, potential purchasers can be found through a variety of sale points. Many developments utilise a site sales office; most developers have their own head office with marketing and sales facilities. Many developers use the services of High Street estate agents. Some have their own High Street offices. These are the direct outlets. There is also a potential network of indirect outlets – solicitors' offices, architects' offices, accountants' offices have all been used at one time or another. We referred above to the use of hotel receptions and lobbies. Many tourist authorities publish information packs in which it is possible to include material.

Most of these channels have some potential cost built in. Many are susceptible and sensitive to the use of incentive schemes which can help to maximise their sales potential.

Commercial agents and developers are well used to utilising the services of local development agencies and government departments as potential distribution channels for their products. Overseas agencies are well placed to bring information to the attention of foreign buyers as are airlines whose 'in-flight entertainment' packs are worthy of serious consideration in specific circumstances.

The local agent or surveyor is often dependent upon sophisticated use of distribution channels for his survival. Solicitors, building society managers, accountants (acting in probate, insolvency or Court of Protection matters) can often be fruitful sources of business – and are behaving as distribution channels in that they are an interface between the surveyor and his potential clients.

The role of existing clients as distribution channels for personal service products should not be forgotten and existing clients should always be cultivated for recommendations and personal introductions. Indeed, it may be said that for the sole trader professional person, his distribution channel awareness and management may be the principal key factors to his long term survival.

The marketing plan should consider carefully the available channels and should describe the methods by which these channels should be cultivated. A vital source of business may be otherwise overlooked.

In considering channel management the potentially tricky area of 'quid pro quo' arrangements should be examined. For some professions such arrangement may be outside the spirit, if not the letter, of their codes of professional conduct. Others are less fussy. The marketing plan should consider such arrangements and plan how, if at all, they are to be implemented and managed.

Positioning

Within the body of the book we have paid little attention to product positioning – on the basis that the majority of products handled on behalf of clients already exist and are, therefore, to an extent, self-positioning.

The marketing plan, nevertheless, should define clearly how the subject product is to be positioned in the market place against its competition.

At its broadest level, the discussion of positioning coincides with market segmentation – that is, the product should be aimed at the most likely segment of potential purchasers. Howvever, it goes rather deeper in that, even within a tightly defined segment, product offerings may be perceived as having differing characteristics in terms of quality, customer attraction and so on.

Consider an office in a prestige location. While many potential lessees may want the prestige address, not every lessee will want luxury accommodation within that address. It is possible, therefore, to position the property into the prestige market yet sub-position as a utilitarian version combining high relative visibility with low relative cost.

Similarly, we can readily identify new housing developments at the 'quality' and 'utility' ends of the first time buyer market spectrum. A careful consideration of positioning at this point will help to avoid damagingly dissonant images being developed in the packaging and other promotion stages of the plan and ensure that a cohesive and coherent product image is created.

'If you don't know what you want you are unlikely to get it!'

Return to our golf course-seeking surveyor. He is already positioned, to an extent, by his background as a competent, local surveyor; pillar of the community but lacking in the technological, packaged 'pzazz' of the multinational competition. Similarly, as against his young competitor, he is automatically positioned as being older (but wiser), well known (but staid), steady (but probably unimaginative). Note that you are positioned as well by inactivity as by activity. The problem is here that you are positioned rather than doing the positioning yourself – and the positioning that you get may be very different from that which you would like to get.

As part of his golf course diversification, therefore, the surveyor, within the context of his strategic design, must tactically manage the development of a market position that contributes to his strategic objective.

For example, if he chose to merge with his young rival, he could develop a local positioning which identifies the firm as both youthful in outlook yet steady, broadly experienced and with specific track record – that is, well able to act as local, personal advisors in a complex, high value market – and all of his other promotional activity could be designed to support that positioning.

Packaging

In student tutorials we regularly debate the proposition that 'the package is the product'. Reference to Chapter 2 quickly demonstrates the strength of this proposition yet the idea of packaging either property or professional services as products still sits somewhat ungainly in the mind of property (and other professional) people. Yet if a marketing plan is to succeed considerable attention must be given to packaging.

We saw in Chapter 5 (Service Management) and referred above to the problems generated by dissonant quality indicators in the service product offering. Similar problems can occur with uncoordinated and ill-conceived packaging for property products. The Office of Fair Trading has recently (1990) sponsored legislation which extends the Trades Descriptions Act to property descriptions produced by residential or commercial estate agents. This sponsorship reflects the unending media chorus pointing to misleading property descriptions as a continual source of irritation to potential purchasers. A description in this context is an integral part (perhaps in many cases the only ingredient) in property packaging. That so much ire stems from it is a reflection of the lack of thought given to the importance of adequate packaging by property professionals.

How can we package our products? Again let us follow our examples and consider some possibilities.

- The residential development: Wimpey Homes showed the way in 1989 with their Wimpey Welcome Home TV advertisement campaign. A Wimpey House is not just a house, it is a warm, welcoming place where a harassed young businessman can return to the bosom of his stunning young wife who welcomes him into a warmly lit haven of peace, away from the troubles of the world. That's packaging.

  Of course there are other aspects to the package. Press advertising fills in the details with information on low cost mortgages, part exchange schemes, carefully chosen addresses (Sierra Pines, The Meadows, The Willows, Broadmeadows, The Leas) all add to the image of gracious, easy living.

  Standardised design and use of corporate logos in property descriptions, site boards and notepaper reinforce the corporate image of reliability and expertise. As little as possible is left to chance.

- The new office block: again the product can be 'packaged' by association, initially through artists' impressions of the finished product, then reinforced through press releases identifying completion stages, lettings and appropriate comment.

  An interesting example of product packaging was the use of video to promote the Pacific Place development in Hong Kong which portrayed the development throughout as a market leader in integrated commercial, retail and leisure development.

For the individual surveyor packaging is equally important and, perhaps, the term WYSIWYG might sum up the ideal package. 'What you see is what you get'. Packaging – in terms of office decoration and location, notepaper, telephone reception, advertising style and copy, even home address and type of car driven – should reflect the standard and type of service which he provides. And the actual service delivered should match the packaging. A prime example of this type of packaging is found in the case study which introduces Chapter 3. A significant contributor to this success story is found in the continuity and conformity of the imagery used to package the estate agency – and customers/clients reacted positively.

Pricing

The basic dimensions of pricing as a tactical weapon were spelt out in the previous chapter. Within the marketing plan a considered view should be taken as to the deployment of pricing tactics throughout the campaign, relating these to the overall campaign development. Within the pricing decision can also be considered the rather specific pricing approaches in general use within the property market. Private treaty, auction and tender – any of which may be appropriate in particular circumstances. Again let us consider some examples.

- The residential development. Normally lots within a new development will be sold by private treaty. The use of private treaty here, however, may differ significantly from that in use in a secondhand transaction. A number – often a large number – of units is made available to the market place and pricing constraints become more akin to commodity sales than to the one-off speciality sale. For example, an element of price stimulation may be used in an early release, this being superseded by full market pricing or even premium pricing as the market develops. If the market place were highly competitive at the time of launch – or was forecast to become more competitive during the project life – contingency plans may be laid for penetration pricing at some point during the campaign. In a market forecast to fall an element of top-slicing or even costs-based pricing might be included in the plan.
- The office block. Similar constraints apply as to the residential development, certainly during the initial letting phase to end-user tenants. Pricing tactics for the sale of the development as a whole, however, may relate to relative sensitivities within the scheme. For example, a scheme perceived as highly sensitive to an extended timescale may warrant substantial price discounting if an early sale can be identified. A scheme less sensitive may warrant premium pricing as the basis of better quality achieved over a longer period.
- The surveyor. The sole trader, in developing his product/market plan, will need to balance his need for market penetration with his ability to cope with the business generated, at the same time considering the effects of alternative pricing tactics upon his projected lifestyle. The decision at this level is intensely personal and can retain a considerable degree of flexibility.

Timescales

By this point the plan will have identified in detail the underlying product/ market strategy and the tactical implications which derive from that strategy. Before progress can be made these implications must be rationalised into a timetable which sets key achievement dates and allows operational flesh to be put on the planning bones.

Time constraints may be imposed by both internal and external factors. For example, if a change in knowledge levels amongst operating staff is planned there will be internal constraints on the speed at which staff can be trained and there may be external constraints on the speed at which new staff can be recruited. There may also be external constraints which relate to the activities of potential competitors, technological change and so on.

Without a clear understanding and specification of timescale, however, the planner is working in the dark and the finished plan may neither be achievable nor appropriate.

In complex situations there may be a high level of sophisticated inter- action between elements within the plan and it may be difficult to identify the key controlling factors which affect the speed of implementation. In such circumstances (and often, if only for practice, in much simpler situations) it may be worth using more sophisticated planning techniques – for example critical path analysis – for which there are many 'easy to use' software packages available for use with simple microcomputers.

The plan should identify:

– tasks to be accomplished – for example behavioural change in a specified customer segment;
– physical tasks – for example, changing an office layout;
– tactical change points – for example, a switch from cold calling to 'warm' selling;
– external time constraints – for example, the opening date for a competitor's planned new office;
– internal time constraints – for example, the earliest or latest dates at which a new initiative could be started (perhaps because of holidays, Christmas, wife having a baby or whatever).

Advertising

We have deliberately left advertising until last in this section. This is not because advertising is the least important part of the 'implementation mix'; far from it. Advertising is potentially the most important part of the mix – TV advertising, in particular, has been called 'The Artillery of the Marketing General' and can have a crucial role in the potential success of a product/ market initiative.

It is left until last because this is the point at which it should be considered.

The most common fault and danger in advertising is lack of clarity and understanding of the behavioural change which advertising is designed to achieve. If you do not know precisely what you want and when you want it (whatever it is), you are only likely to get it through luck – not a happy thought for the marketing planner.

The thrust of the marketing plan thus far, therefore, has been to determine what you want (strategy, tactical resourcing) and when you want it (tactical implementation).

The function of advertising within the mix is to facilitate the achievement of these objectives.

As we saw in Chapter 8 the primary purpose of any advertisement is to create behavioural change and it is its ability to create such a change that is the critical test of its effectiveness. Within the currency of a marketing plan, however, different changes are needed at different points in the plan. The advertising that is designed to create a favourable attitude towards possible purchase is different from that which is designed to create actual sales leads and needs to be designed with these differences in mind.

Here is the importance of the timescale plan highlighting key interim objectives. Each objective implies behavioural change of some kind – both amongst customers and often amongst staff. These are the changes to which phased advertising should be directed – they then stand a reasonable chance of success.

Some examples, again, will illustrate – and it should be noted that advertising and PR opportunities should be synchronised as far as possible so that each supports the other and that conflicting imagery is not produced.

- The new residential development. Early advertising copy will be designed to create awareness of the forthcoming development amongst the potential market population. Ideally, a favourable impression should be created of the development as a place to live/invest/speculate depending on the likely motivations of the target group.

  As the development proceeds so can the advertising change its emphasis towards creating desire for involvement in the new development and to encourage site visits to 'look at the show home' where the mix balance is likely to shift towards direct selling, possibly with a direct mail component to those who are not yet at the appropriate point in their buying decision.

  Once the development begins to mature, with new owners already on site, the emphasis can shift again to encourage 'me too' interest and buying behaviour from the later adopters.

- The new office block. This is likely to proceed in a similar way although early marketing efforts are more likely to be direct initiatives to already-known potential occupiers. Advertising initiatives are designed to spread awareness and encourage a positive attitude to the development amongst professional influencers, rather than directly to potential tenants.

Once again, as the development matures, the thrust of advertising can move towards a more direct targeting of potential tenants, building on track record (lettings) and using user-related media as the advertising vehicle. For example, emphasis may shift from the *Estates Gazette* towards the *Investors' Chronicle* and similar specialist trade press which is likely to reach undeclared or uncommitted decision makers.

- The local surveyor. In regenerating his image may find that advertising is of little direct relevance in the early part of his campaign although, as he develops contacts and track record, he may utilise the specialist trade magazines to expand awareness of his specialist services. He is more likely, however, to gain benefit from his direct marketing activities which are likely to result in direct client contact opportunities.

Obviously, the examples used are generalities and should be read as such. They do, however, provide a taste of the changing balance in an advertising campaign and illustrate clearly the relationship between advertising and needs, the advertising campaign changing as needs change.

Many property campaigns already work along these lines. The discussions on behaviour, product design, strategy and tactics within this book should provide increased insight for the property professional to plan his campaigns and to take advantage of the specialist service provided by design consultancies, advertising consultancies and all the other specialist agencies so abundant in the modern world.

Budgets

The preceding sections have identified the operational aspects of the marketing plan. but every operation has cost implications; and for every cost incurred there should be an identifiable benefit, ideally quantifiable in financial terms. In the real world, of course, not every benefit is readily capable of being expressed in money terms but that does not mean that the attempt should not be made.

The budget is, effectively, a profit/loss forecast for the project. It should be drawn at a level of detail that suits the particular project and which satisfies the decision-making curiosity of the reader. That is, if the reader is likely to want the unit cost of each advertisement to be placed in every medium then the marketing plan should give him this information.

Where alternative possible scenarios are considered, alternative budgets which spell out the relative values of the scenarios should be prepared and included.

A typical budget might include the following data:

Market Place	Total Market		Units	Value
	Segment 1			
	Segment 2			
	Segment 3			

Predicted Market Share		Share %	Units	Value
	Segment 1			
	Segment 2			
	Segment 3			

Costs Personnel Training

    Recruitment
    Salaries
    Severance

Costs Direct Marketing

    Mailing –   Material
                        Postages
                        Stuffing
    Catalogues   Preparation
                        Postages
    Telesales   Phone Bills

Advertising

    Medium 1
    Medium 2
    Medium 3

PR

    Press relations
    PR agency fee
    Launch party

Direct selling

    Cost per call
    Number of calls

Product development

    Design
    Packaging

In this form the budget provides an overview: total cost against total potential returns. For financial and general management purposes, however, it may be more appropriate to develop the budget against a timescale so that cash flow may be planned and financial resources made available.

Several spreadsheet computer packages are available (for example, Lotus 1–2–3 or Supercalc IV), which are ideal for this purpose; the reader is referred to *Microcomputers in Property*, by T. Dixon, S. Hargitay and O. Bevan (Spon, 1991), which is an introductory text designed to remove much of the mystique that surrounds computers.

Summary

A marketing plan is a beginning – not an end. It provides a map of an area to be explored, identifying a destination or goal and specifying routes and means of transport by which rivers can be crossed and obstacles overcome.

It is first and foremost a selling document, designed to influence others in their choice of route. It may even be designed to influence its author in a choice of route. It is, in any event, a powerful incentive to think through difficult and potentially costly decisions in detail.

The plan should address all the major dimensions of a product/market; the product itself, potential customers and groups of customers, strategy, tactics, packaging and promotion. If it is to achieve credibility it should include the magic numbers of corporate thinking – budgets – without which it is just a collection of words which cannot be easily related to the needs of the real world.

In the absence of a marketing plan any attempt to launch or develop a product into a market place is, at best, inspired guesswork. In most cases (evidenced by the number of small business failures in their first three years of existence) it is uninspired guesswork.

Professional advisors – and most property people are in the advice business – are unlikely to be highly paid in the future if they base their client advice or their own business development on uninspired guesswork. The days when there was more than enough work to go around and a professional qualification was perceived as a meal ticket for life are long gone. Today's – and tomorrow's – professionals must take a professional approach if they are to survive.

Appendix
Example Marketing Plan

Executive summary

Mr Surveyor proposes to enter the emerging market for golf course development and valuation advice based upon Provincialshire.
The market share available is valued at:

Sales and purchases p.a.	£16 000
Valuations and planning p.a.	3 200
	£19 200

Costs of entry are estimated at:

	Capital	Ongoing
Direct costs	3150	1500
Mr Surveyor's time	6300	15000

If these costs and benefits were applied to a new business they would be difficult to justify. They do, however, contribute directly to Mr Surveyor's continuing profitability as a private practice surveyor and are therefore justifiable, particularly as they augment rather than detract from his core business.

A number of strategic options are currently open to Mr Surveyor in attacking this market. On balance development of his personal contact network allied with an operating agreement with a major provider is preferred.

Marketing Plan for A. Surveyor, Anytown UK. 1991

Introduction

This plan has been prepared for Mr A. Surveyor to cover his proposed diversification into the emergent market for advice on the development of

236

golf courses and related leisure facilities in Provincialshire UK.

The plan considers:

a) the potential market place
b) Mr Surveyor's competitive position
c) Mr Surveyor's product potential
d) a strategic plan for his penetration of this market
e) a tactical implementation plan
f) likely costs and benefits arising from the plan

The market place

Provincialshire, like many other UK counties, has seen, throughout the late 1980s, farmers and other landowners being faced with potential reduction in their incomes and is predicting increasing reductions with the open EEC market in 1992.

Some farmers have already taken advantage of set-aside schemes but many are still concerned and this concern has been exacerbated through a general reduction in underlying land values which has, in many cases, created financial pressure as borrowings begin to outstrip the banks' lending criteria.

Throughout this period the game of golf, in particular, has increased in popularity, aided in part by the incursion of Japanese businessmen who, realising that the UK is under-provided by Japanese standards, are avidly seeking what they perceive as bargain-priced UK investments in line with their commercial commitment to the UK as a manufacturing base ideally placed for European expansion.

These factors have had an effect on planning authorities who are finding leisure proposals for land which, officially, is over-productive, hard to resist.

It is known that there is a considerable catchment within the Provincialshire area for golf club membership and that there is underlying demand for more facilities as existing clubs become over-subscribed and subscriptions rise at several times the rate of inflation.

Not surprisingly, many farmers and landowners nationally – with the trend apparently stronger than the national average in Provincialshire -are beginning to investigate the possibilities of achieving substantial life-time capital gains and moving out of farming by selling their land to leisure developers.

There has already been a small number of recent planning approvals for golf course development in the area and these appears to be fuelling the demand from landowners who wish to jump on the bandwagon before it disappears.

What does the market need?

The market contains need for a number of basic products. These are:

site consultancy for landowners
site finding for developers
site and scheme valuation for financiers
planning consultancy

Some of this work should also spin off into other areas both in the leisure industry (hotels and licensed trade valuations and consultancy) and in the general commercial area (from improved national contacts with major surveying firms, developers and institutions).

In addition, once established as a specialist in this area, there should be ongoing business available as a consultant in adjoining regions.

Market volumes

Number of developable sites in the county
A report issued by the Department of Golf Course Development suggests that, on the basis of local population, approximately 50 golf course complexes could be accommodated within the county. There are, at present, three of championship standard and 15 of varying qualities. Underlying market demand should therefore support development of 30–35 new complexes over the next 5–10 years (the timescale envisaged within the report).

It is hard to see the present local authority being easily persuaded to this kind of density but a realistic level of 20–25 could be projected.

Each course requires between 300 and 500 acres (120–200 ha) of land for a viable development to take place. At agricultural values locally this suggests an average sale price of £600 000 to £1 000 000 and this can be expected to increase as planning permission is granted and developers compete.

Commission rates on sale should remain solid at around 1.75 per cent–2 per cent. There is little evidence of major players in this market showing any keenness to reduce prices, particulary considering the amount of work potentially involved.

Over 10 years this gives a total commission market of, say, 25

25 × £16 000 available – £400 000. A similar commission is available when acting for a purchaser in this market – £400 000. Valuation fees for lenders at this level are based at around 0.5 per cent on valuation, i.e. – £40 000. Planning fees would base at around 0.5 per cent i.e. – £40 000. Giving a total market over 10 years in the region of £880 000 i.e. – £88 000 per annum. Valuation and planning fees annually are – £8 000 per annum with significant growth potential.

Market share

It is estimated that a market share of approximately 20 per cent of sales and purchases could be achieved, i.e. ± £16 000 per annum. Valuations and planning should be more productive at around 40 per cent i.e., £3 200 per annum. (Note that detailed reasoning for these conclusions is not included in the illustration but should, obviously, be included in a 'live' plan.)

Competitive position

Mr Surveyor

Mr Surveyor has practised in Newtown, the county town (but not the largest town) in Provincialshire for over 20 years and has a wide contact network both within the professional community and with local farmers. He has regularly participated in the local cattle market and approximately 15 per cent of his existing business consists of agricultural compensation work. He also has established track record as a valuer of both commercial and residential property and is a panel valuer for most of the leading lending institutions (although business from many of these sources has reduced since the financial institutions bought into estate agency).

Although he has regularly earned a reasonable income and has approximately £500 000 equity in freehold investments for his retirement his liquid capital is limited and annual capital expenditure is normally budgeted from income.

He is well liked and trusted within the county and many people use his services in preference to those provided by larger institutions as they respect his independence of mind and spirit.

He sees the possible diversification into leisure as a way of both expanding his income potential and protecting his practice against further inroads by the 'Majors' against his residential valuation work.

Major surveying firms

The emergence of leisure as a potentially profitable sector in the property market has long been recognised by the major surveying firms most of whom have either a partner specialising in the area or, in some, a full-scale department.

It is known that several of these firms are actively seeking sites for retained clients at the present time and that a number of local landowners have already been approached.

These firms are able to offer professional breadth to their clients and attract retaining developers through their London and international operations.

At a local level, while their professionalism is readily acknowledged, there is a certain reticence, particularly among the agricultural community, at the idea of dealing with 'foreigners'.

The leisure partner of one of the leading firms actually lives in the adjoining county 'Oldshire' where his family plays a leading role in the 'county set'. These connections have already given him some penetration into the county set of Provincialshire.

Mr Flashman

A year ago Mr Flashman left one of the major surveying firms to practise on his own account in Provincialshire. He has a residential office in Newtown and is attracting an admiring young clientele, impressed by his modern office and liberal spending habits.

While with the major company he spent two of his three post-qualification years working in their leisure department and is actively involved in nursing a new golf course development some 5 miles (8 km) from Newtown which, it appears, he inherited from his time with the major company (at the cost of some internal bad feeling).

Mr Flashman is actually from Newtown originally and, having attended Newtown School, has a useful range of contacts amongst the younger members of the professional community. He is, however, viewed with some suspicion by older members who are wary of risking too much upon his early success, particularly in view of the alleged circumstances surrounding his, rather precipitous, departure from the major firm.

Other competitors. There are 15 other surveying firms in the county, most of them now institutionally owned and bereft of their original well-connected partners. None of them are known to be actively targeting the leisure market although all of them 'dabble on the fringes' from time to time.

SWOT analysis

The market place
  Strengths
    Food surplus creating redundant land
    Growth in leisure activity
    Japanese market pressure
    Mid-term growth predicted
    High value operation needs professional advice

  Weaknesses
    Developers need considerable expertise so relatively few in number
    Capital intensive
    Developers quickly form 'institutionalised' supplier links
    Food balance may change

Green pressure reduces land output potential thereby increasing
attractiveness for food production

Farmers may prefer farming (albeit on lower income) to retirement

Opportunities

No local 'expert'

Penetration would assist business survival

Attractive synergy potential

Threats

Economic decline may reduce long term demand

Japanese may move to mainland Europe

Leisure market could reduce

External experts may monopolise market

Mr Surveyor

Strengths

Local reputation

Basic entrepreneurial and surveying skills

Established core business

Good local contact network

Low inherent cost structure – minimal outgoings

Weaknesses

Little or no developer contact or reputation

No specific track record

Limited financial resources for market development

Limited institutional or financial contact

Opportunities

Early entry could develop strong local position

'Professional' synergy would augment existing business areas

Early successes would attract developer contacts thus reinforcing
competitive advantage

Threats

Failure to attack could rebound on existing business

Mr Flashman could position Mr Surveyor as 'old fashioned' to his
business detriment

Majors could freeze out through penetration pricing to key developers

Developers may not find Mr Surveyor credible as an advisor through
lack of track record

Majors

Strengths

National contact network

National breadth and reputation
High quality young staff motivated to achieve
Industry specialisation and visibility
Extensive cash resources for market development
Access to Developers and funding institutions
'County' contacts
Planning expertise
Track record

Weaknesses
Local contacts
Local suspicion

Opportunities
Develop local contacts
Act as purchasing agents for retained clients and build local track record and reputation
Use monopolistic developer contacts to squeeze local competition out

Threats
High profile achievers can be perceived as 'yuppies' thus increasing suspicion and damaging local contacts
Staff are 'short termist' in outlook and will not develop ongoing relationships
Institutionalised developer contacts can dissolve
Developers want results not promises
Outmanoeuvring the 'local man' may be perceived as 'dirty tricks' by other locals and damage prospects

Mr Flashman
Strengths
Sparky local achievement and track record
Youthful contact network
Perceived energy and aggression
Demonstrable track record with local development
Post-qualification London experience
Low level London contact network (may not be workable)

Weaknesses
Element of mistrust in professional community
Unproven staying power
Relative youth restricts credibility as an advisor
Town background may be a disadvantage with farmers
Little established capital for development
Core business is still on growth path and probably has cash flow problems

Little 'establishment' credibility yet

Opportunities
Leisure success would enhance reputation for achievement
Established track record enhances credibility
Perceived expertise should generate professional instructions and open synergy to attack Mr Surveyor and other professional surveyors' instruction bases

Threats
Youthful impetuosity could damage reputation
Senior professionals might divert clients
Perceived youth discredits professional advice

Strategic summary

The market place has some attraction to Mr Surveyor. Faced, as he is, with diminishing potential for professional work a new market opening up is certainly worth further investigation. The market itself is not wholly secure as it depends upon a number of imponderables which are outside his ability to control. Many factors, particularly in combination, could render the market out of existence. For Mr Surveyor, however, as opposed to his competition, the risk factor is relatively low as it applies to a support product area for his core business rather than to the core business itself. The risks – and rewards – are potentially greater for his main competitors.

There are some key factors which need to be addressed to achieve success in the market. These are:

local contacts who trust the advisor
contacts with developers which can be expanded to profitability.

Mr Surveyor scores high on the first key factor, although he could certainly improve his credibility through some successful results. The second factor, given the London orientation of key developers, may be more difficult to attain.

The key long term benefit available to Mr Surveyor within this market is more likely to be in the development of a new professional market as a valuer. He may achieve limited success in the sale/purchase market but is always vulnerable to price competition and 'client locking' from large competitors.

He must also be wary of his potential vulnerability to Mr Flashman in his core business. Many influential professional introducers of business change jobs relatively quickly (building society manager, conveyancing solicitors, bank managers) and young replacements tend to respond to demonstrable success amongst their own age groups.

Options available

Stay out of the business altogether and concentrate on maintaining market share in his core business;

Develop the market place on an individual basis by reinforcing links with farmers and persuading both them and developers of his potential as an 'honest broker';

Join forces with Mr Flashman to make best use of his youth and aggression to maximise local contact, at the same time expanding the core business.

Negotiate a merger or sell-out with a major player.

Option 1

Aged 46, Mr Surveyor still has 10–15 working years ahead of him. He faces growing competition to his core business and a direct threat from Mr Flashman. If he does not take advantage of market opportunities he is vulnerable to an 'old fashioned' label and may find that his core business is increasingly eroded. The option is, therefore, a relatively high risk strategy for his continued business.

Option 2

There is little risk involved in increasing links with the local community – as long as he can deliver the goods when required. There is the rub; he has minimal links with developers and is competing against possible institution-alised links with developers from a London connection. He may be fortunate and generate a specific localised link but may, in doing so, forfeit some independence (or perception of independence) in the eyes of the local community.

Option 3

Major players are locally short of direct knowledge. They may, therefore, welcome initial involvement with one who can 'smooth their way' through his contacts. They will, nevertheless, wish to generate their own links as part of their own long term strategy and Mr Surveyor may be viewed as an expendable short term stepping stone. This is, therefore, a relatively high risk strategy. In addition, a major player is unlikely to recommend Mr Surveyor as an advisor or valuer if they can use their own resources. A very careful hand will need to be played if long term benefits are to result.

Option 4

Mr Flashman is gaining some credibility and is a medium term threat to the core business. Unfortunately he is a hothead and an alliance may prove very uncomfortable as his powers increase and Mr Surveyor's powers decline. There is an additional risk in that the benefits of an alliance to Mr

Flashman, in the short term, may be greater than the benefits to Mr Surveyor. Mr Flashman may be tempted to rush in, earn the benefits of Mr Surveyor's reputation, then rush out again once his own name is adequately made.

Option 5
Provincialshire is a useful market place but Mr Surveyor's breadth of experience and his age are somewhat against the idea of a joint venture with a major, most of whom will feel that they can probably achieve their objectives without him. If, on the other hand, a willing collaborator could be found, there are significant potential advantages to Mr Surveyor. Against these advantages are a number of disadvantages, in particular a potential loss of autonomy and lack of control over his personal destiny.

Conclusion

Weighing these options, Mr Surveyor proposes to opt for option 3. The other options have considerable potential risk, in particular the potential for threats to his autonomy and long term loss of his core business. Option 3 carries with it the risk that a major or majors may wish to use him as a stepping stone but he believes that, in the timescale envisaged, his personal reputation will maintain his existing links and that, whilst he may not achieve a significant personal market share as a broker, he will, nevertheless be able to develop significant and valuable ongoing professional relationships which will enhance and maintain his core business.

Tactical constraints

Option 3 has two principal tactical strands. Mr Surveyor must develop relationships with a major company with interests in the leisure industry and, at the same time, cultivate those elements of his contact network that are likely to generate future leisure business.
The first of these strands can be approached through:

Existing personal contacts
Existing professional contacts
Direct personal approach

Direct mail, telephone selling and advertising are too impersonal for such a delicate assignment and are therefore discounted.
Of more immediate tactical significance is market intelligence and this means research. Appropriate research into this area involves answering the following questions:

Which major companies are interested in the leisure industry with specific reference to golf course development?
Which of these have no local representation?
Of these, which have the strongest credentials in terms of public profile track record and links with developers?
From the short list which is likely to welcome a local approach?
What track record does a chosen target company have in ongoing dealings with local contributors?

Research will need to be undertaken with a low profile and will need to be handled in a sensitive manner. It involves no large scale fact finding and Mr Surveyor proposes to undertake it himself.

On the basis of research contact negotiations can be opened. These will be best handled directly by Mr Surveyor but, to maintain an element of control, early soundings will be taken by a firm of solicitors acting on Mr Surveyor's behalf.

The second tactical stand is again most suited to personal initiatives from Mr Surveyor. The objective is to develop his personal contact network and this means personal contact.

Mr Surveyor is well positioned to exploit a grapevine system. He meets many farmers at the weekly cattle market and can sow seeds amongst his closer colleagues with a high probability that his message will be passed on by word of mouth.

Once development links are forged a personalised mailing to selected target clients will reinforce the message.

There is a third area of research required. That is the identification of prime and secondary candidate sites for development. Much of this research is already feasible from Mr Surveyor's knowledge and experience of the area. Some will involve desk research from Ordnance Survey maps and census reports. The objective of this research area is to generate a 'prospect profile' database which can then become the basis for sales and acquisition activity where it may be used to identify site opportunities, either to their owners or to potential developers.

Timescales

	Start	Finish
1 Develop local contacts	Immediate	Ongoing
2 Research development database	Immediate	6 months
Develop major contact		
3 Initial search	Immediate	3 months
4 Shortlisting	3+ months	6 months
Negotiations	6+ months	9 months

		Target mailing network
	Develop client Research database	
		Negotiate
Initial search	Shortlist	

There are no known external constraints to be applied.

COSTS		Capital £	Annual £
Develop local contacts	Hospitality		
	Mailing 50 @ £5	250	1500
Research database	40 hours @ £60	2400	
Secretarial assistance	50 hours @ £10	500	
Major contact	20 hours £60	1200	
Shortlist	15 hours	900	
Negotiations	30 hours @ £60	1800	
Professional assistance	20 hours @ £80	1600	
Secretarial assistance	30 hours @ £10	300	
Consumables, say		500	
		————	————
		9450	1500
		————	————

Note: Mr Surveyor's time is charged at £60/hr. Much of this time, however, is an opportunity cost and would involve working out of normal office hours. Direct costs are considerably lower.

	£
Costs excluding Mr Surveyor	
Mailing	250
Secretarial assistance	800
Professional assistance	1600
Consumables	500
	3150
	————

Ongoing servicing costs for Mr Surveyor are estimated at 6 hours per week.

15 000
————

Index